The No-Prep Bible Study Series

Jesus' Most Challenging Parables

What People Are Saying

I was recently introduced to Kenny Beck's "little" Bible study books, and I soon realized there's nothing "little" about them! They are "big" on usability, relevance, and personal impact. Kenny's unique format is biblical, well-organized, and with a focused Q&A that is very useful in creating a context for personal introspection and group discussion. These lessons are perfect for anyone wanting to jump-start a small group Bible study. Recommended!

—Daniel M. Wright, author of *The Redemption Corridor*, Oconee County, SC

Jesus' *Most Challenging Parables* is a quick read loaded with interesting facts, humor and anecdotes, and modern-day applications. All five lessons shed new light and highlight each parable's full intended meaning. I highly recommend it to anyone wanting to more fully understand Jesus' parables.

—Ken Barker, Retired Senior Music Editor: Word Music & Lifeway Publishing, Nashville, TN

Kenny Beck's *Jesus' Most Challenging Parables* opens the parables up in a way I had not envisioned. Simply a delightful read! Perfect for a group Bible study or for deepening one's own understanding of the Gospel message.

—John Appleton, West Chicago, IL

Jesus' Most Challenging Parables is an easy-to-use Bible study that will deeply challenge the reader. Each study has on-point examples from a current perspective that are enhanced by interesting historical information. First-rate!

— Karen Belcher, Adult Bible Teacher, Houston, TX

Jesus' Most Challenging Parables brings five of our Lord's many parables to life. Using a combination of exegetical teaching along with historical perspective, Kenny helps us understand these parables the way Jesus originally intended them. Plus, Kenny's insightful questions help us apply those truths to our lives so we can shine brighter for our Lord Jesus Christ.

—Frank Figueroa, *Reasons For Hope* Evangelist, Mililani, HI

Jesus' Most Challenging Parables provides five delightful study guides on some of Christ's most familiar parables. Kenny's upbeat conversational writing style coupled with deep insights and probing questions makes this book an excellent tool for both personal and small group Bible study. Kenny's passion for the Gospel and love of Bible teaching shines through on every page!

—Tim Long, St. Augustine, FL

The No-Prep
Bible Study Series

Jesus' Most
Challenging
Parables

Kenny Beck

Dedication

To the Heart, Soul & Mind Community Group

Contents

Acknowledgements

Special thanks have to go first to my wife, Melissa, and daughter, Mallory. These two highly talented ladies have handled all the editing, layout, and artwork for this book. What you hold in your hands exists because of their ideas and handiwork.

Additionally, I'd like to give a quick nod to one Bible teacher in particular: Mark Lanier. I've absorbed a certain biblical perspective and viewpoint from listening online to Mark's world-renowned teaching in his long-running Biblical Literacy class at Champion Forest Baptist Church of Houston.

Finally, I must mention three pastors who have had a major impact on my spiritual life: the late Dr. John R. Bisagno, Ryan Rush, and Roy Meadows. All three of these men have inspired my spirit, enlightened my mind, and been a shining personal example to me.

The No-Prep Bible Study Series

The *No-Prep Bible Study Series* is designed to meet the needs of the untold thousands of small groups engaged in Bible study. They are known in the church world as Community Groups, Life Groups, Small Groups, Adult Bible Fellowships, and even by the old-fashioned name of, yes, Sunday School Classes.

By "no prep," we mean no preparation on the part of the **leader or the participants**. You can simply read the short text, answer the questions, and bring a **focused and meaningful** Bible study to conclusion in 45 minutes.

These studies are geared for Christians across denominational lines. Indeed, every study has been trial tested on real small groups from different denominations. Participants have invariably found these unique studies to be engaging and thought provoking.

Group Tips

- Your group should designate a leader to be in charge of three things:
    - Starting on time
    - Keeping it moving
    - Finishing on time
- Always check the given answers to make sure you stay on track.
- Be kind and don't let one person dominate.
- Budget 45 minutes and stick to it!

We pray that God blesses you and speaks to you as you study *Jesus' Most Challenging Parables*.

Other No-Prep Series Books

Available on Amazon.com:

- *Jesus' Most Popular Parables*
- *The Most Glorious Psalms Ever*
- *Happiness vs. Purpose*
- *Telling Others the Story of Jesus*
- *Your Most Valuable Stuff*

Coming in 2023:

- *Lessons from the Life of David*

Interpreting Parables

Jesus told a lot of parables during his earthly ministry. No less than 30 are recorded in the Gospels. Christ seemed to enjoy creating illustrative little stories to help us understand and remember important spiritual truths. In fact, it may have been his favorite teaching technique!

But before jumping into the five parables in this book, let's quickly run through four important interpretive guidelines.

Guideline #1

Look for the one main point. Jesus created each little story almost always to illustrate but one point. Looking for lots of little truths will inevitably obscure the main truth.

Guideline #2

Don't over analogize. Not every element in a parable is representative of something. Find the main metaphors and stick with those. Bad theology tends to emerge when Christians over analogize Jesus' parables.

Guideline #3

Don't spend too much time ascribing motives and emotions to parable people. Remember, the characters exist to drive the story line and get us to Jesus' main point. They are not real people! Dwelling too much on their supposed motives and emotions can dilute the main thrust of the parable.

Guideline #4

Be on the lookout for sets of parables. Occasionally, Jesus would tell a set of parables all illustrating the same point. When this happens, it is best to look at the set of sister parables together to see what they have in common. That's where the meaning ultimately resides.

Hopefully, with these four guidelines under your belt, you'll be better prepared to explore these five parables that will likely challenge your thinking in unexpected ways.

1

The Pharisee &
The Tax Collector

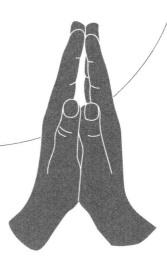

Focal Verses

Luke 18:10-14 (ESV)

[10] "Two men went up into the temple to pray, one a Pharisee and the other a tax collector. [11] The Pharisee, standing by himself, prayed thus: 'God, I thank you that I am not like other men, extortioners, unjust, adulterers, or even like this tax collector. [12] I fast twice a week; I give tithes of all that I get.' [13] But the tax collector, standing far off, would not even lift up his eyes to heaven, but beat his breast, saying, 'God, be merciful to me, a sinner!' [14] I tell you, this man went down to his house justified, rather than the other. For everyone who exalts himself will be humbled, but the one who humbles himself will be exalted."

The Study

Understanding The Context

Many of Jesus' parables come with a twist or turn meant to intentionally surprise us. That's the case with "The Pharisee & The Tax Collector." This parable is supposed to deliver a theological shocker.

But Jesus' parables rarely shock us anymore. That's mainly because we've heard them over and over. Familiarity kills surprise. For instance, my family has watched the super popular movie *A Christmas Story* so many times that we aren't surprised when Flick gets his tongue stuck on that frozen pole on the elementary school playground.

Another reason Jesus' parables don't surprise us is that we lack the cultural understanding of his first-century Jewish listeners. To understand the context of this parable, we need a quick tutorial on Pharisees and tax collectors back in Jesus' time.

Modern Americans tend to think of the Pharisees as "the bad guys." That is the wrong perspective! The Pharisees were the good guys trying to keep Judaism from disappearing under the cultural onslaught of Hellenization. And the law-keeping and righteousness of the Pharisees was very impressive to the average Jew.

According to theologian Arthur W. Pink, "The Pharisees had the reputation of being the most exemplary models of Judaism. They were looked up to as having attained the very pinnacle of personal piety, and the common people supposed that such heights of spirituality were beyond their reach."

1. Which people in modern churches are usually considered to be examples of righteousness that regular members tend to admire?

Most study Bibles fill you in on tax collectors in first-century Palestine. They were Jews who worked for the Roman Empire and basically swindled each and every person in their district by collecting way more tax than was actually owed. Nobody was more loathed in Palestine than the extortionist tax collectors.

2. Name a specific person (or two) who is famously known as a dishonest swindler that the public reviles today.

So here's the cultural context:

- Pharisees = righteous and admired
- Tax collectors = dishonest and reviled

With that understanding, you are now ready to read about the fictitious Pharisee and tax collector that Jesus created to show us two different ways that people approach God.

Two Approaches to God

Besides alerting you to the important context, let's do one more thing to try to bring the surprise factor back into this parable. Let's ignore the initial verse in the passage—verse 9. Luke kind of spills the beans with an introductory sentence describing the whole point of the parable. **Trust me, read verse 9 later if you wish, but not now!**

Read Luke 18:10-14 inserting the word "righteous" in front of "Pharisee" and the word "dishonest" in front of "tax collector." (This will help keep you in the mindset of Jesus' original listeners.)

3. What was the approach the righteous Pharisee took towards God?

4. What was the approach the dishonest tax collector took towards God?

Those two approaches could not be more different. The Pharisee approached God with pride in his good deeds and a big dollop of comparison to less righteous people. In contrast, the tax collector approached God with penitence and contrition for his sins.

Interestingly, we find a real tax collector right around the corner in Luke's Gospel.

5.   What was the name of the real tax collector in Luke 19 (starts with the letter "Z")?

6.   What actions did that tax collector take?

Theological Shocker

The shocking twist in this parable happens in verse 14. Jesus surprised his Jewish listeners by saying that it was the dishonest and reviled tax collector who went home forgiven. Oops! Jesus' listeners were expecting the righteous Pharisee to be the one who was pleasing to God, not the loathed tax collector.

That leads us to this challenging takeaway:

Good people don't go to heaven.

Forgiven people go to heaven.

7.   Pause and evaluate those two contrasting phrases.

Most people just assume their good deeds will be what gets them into heaven, or maybe their good deeds will be weighed against their bad deeds. Those are dangerous assumptions to base your eternal destiny on!

The radical concept of "good people don't go to heaven, forgiven people do" was the theological shocker that Jesus was emphasizing to his listeners that day.

The Two Systems

Here are the two drastically different systems underpinning the two phrases of our main takeaway:

Good / Bad   =   *The Merit System*

Forgiven / Unforgiven   =   *The Grace System*

Basically, our fictitious Pharisee thought that God operated on the merit system and that he could gain God's favor through good works.

8.   Do people today try to earn God's approval via good deeds?

9.   What is another possible name for the merit system?

My junior high boys PE teacher (Coach Green) warned us on the first day of class that he would be operating on the merit system. Boys doing good things would be rewarded, and boys doing bad things would be made to run laps till they dropped. That's a good way to control a bunch of unruly junior high boys. But it isn't how God operates.

God operates on the grace system. Salvation isn't given to those who earn it. Salvation is given to those who repent and have their sins forgiven at the foot of the cross.

Shouldn't I Be Good?

All this emphasis on forgiveness might leave you asking, "Well, shouldn't I be good?"

The answer is: "Of course you should be good . . . **after** you've been forgiven!"

About ten years ago, my church gave out jillions of little white gym towels for every member to take to their fitness place. I still use mine today! These towels had the church name and logo embossed on them along with a two-word biblical quote: "Do good. – Galatians 6:10."

That's a good short message for a gym towel.

But "doing good" is not the salvation formula!

It is so important to note that this exhortation to "do good" is at the very end of Galatians. The Apostle Paul spends the first 4½ chapters of Galatians explaining that salvation is by faith and faith alone. Then, in Galatians 5:13, he shifts gears and starts talking about what we should do **after** being saved by faith.

That was so typical of Paul. First, he'd teach theology, then he'd talk ethics. And that's where doing good things for the Lord comes in—after receiving forgiveness.

A Modern Pharisee

Prominent women's speaker, Lori Joiner, spent her teenage years in Houston. She tells her life story in chapter one of her instructive book, *Raising Children unto The Lord* [1]. By Lori's own admission, she was a very rebellious teenager getting into tons of trouble but not quite bad enough to get thrown in jail.

She also lived somewhat of a double life by faithfully attending church with some neighbors who cared about her. Interestingly, Lori had an attitude very similar to our fictitious Pharisee.

Here's how Lori says it in her own words: "Funny enough, I thought of myself as a Christian. When I compared myself to others doing drugs, going to jail, smoking, etc., I figured I was better than them. I based my salvation at that point in me being just slightly better than others."

Isn't that the way most people figure? I'm better than so-and-so, therefore God must be smiling on me.

In October of her senior year, Lori's youth minister held her back one night after the service and told Lori that she was a sinner and needed forgiveness based on Christ's dying in her place. Lori placed her faith in Christ that evening and left behind her sliding scale of good works where she ranked herself just barely ahead of jailed teenagers.

Make doubly sure that you are approaching God through His grace and forgiveness system based upon Christ's sacrifice on the cross for you. Good people don't go to heaven, forgiven people do.

My Answers

Question 1

In most churches today, the pastors, teachers, elders, and deacons are the folks that tend to be examples of righteousness that regular people look up to.

Question 2

In modern America, two well-known swindlers are: 1) Ponzi-scheme artist Bernie Madoff, and 2) Sam Bankman-Fried, the mastermind of the FTX crypto debacle. These two guys are today's poster boys for dishonest swindlers.

Question 3

The fictitious Pharisee emphasized his good deeds. He also played the "I'm-better-than-so-and-so" card. That's the way almost all of humanity tends to approach God—emphasize our goodness, minimize our badness, and tell God "At least I'm not as bad as Susie Q."

Question 4

The fictitious tax collector emphasized his sinfulness and begged God for mercy. If you dig into the Greek underlying the phrase "be merciful to me," you find the verb form of the word "propitiation" which is a fancy theological word for "atoning sacrifice." In other words, **the atoning blood of Christ is lurking closer in this verse than you probably realized!**

Question 5

Zaccheus was the famous real-life tax collector who was saved and changed when Jesus' visited him in Luke 19.

Question 6

Zaccheus tells the Lord he is going to give half of his wealth to the poor and restore all those whom he has defrauded. Something seems to have happened inside little ole Zaccheus.

Question 7

Those two phrases challenge our thinking big time. Most people just naturally suppose that being good is the way to impress God and get into heaven. But, according to the Scriptures, that is not the case. **Our goodness is not impressive to God** (Isaiah 64:6). What the Scriptures do state over and over is that the route to heaven goes through repentance and forgiveness of sins at the foot of the cross.

Question 8

Yes, people today try to earn God's favor with their good works. If you are at all tempted to think this way, the best book on the subject is *What's So Amazing About Grace?* [2] by Philip Yancey. This book drives home the fact that nothing you can do will ever earn you God's favor. The grace system really is so amazing that we have trouble comprehending it. Hence, we need a good tutorial book like W*hat's So Amazing About Grace?*

Question 9

Another good name for the merit system is "the reward system." But I prefer calling it "the merit system," which instantly implies **merits** for good behavior and **demerits** for bad behavior. The merit system is still used at some schools even today—like at Hogwarts, "That'll be 5 points from Gryffindor, Miss Grainger!"

2

The Sower

Focal Verses

Luke 8:11-15 (NLT)

[11] "This is the meaning of the parable: The seed is God's word. [12] The seeds that fell on the footpath represent those who hear the message, only to have the devil come and take it away from their hearts and prevent them from believing and being saved. [13] The seeds on the rocky soil represent those who hear the message and receive it with joy. But since they don't have deep roots, they believe for a while, then they fall away when they face temptation. [14] The seeds that fell among the thorns represent those who hear the message, but all too quickly the message is crowded out by the cares and riches and pleasures of this life. And so they never grow into maturity. [15] And the seeds that fell on the good soil represent honest, good-hearted people who hear God's word, cling to it, and patiently produce a huge harvest.

The Study

Jesus' Very First Parable

To say that Jesus taught in parables would be a big understatement. Jesus not only taught in parables but is truly associated with the word parable itself.

My NIV Study Bible lists some 40 different parables that Jesus told. The fast-moving gospel of Mark has 9, while Matthew has 23. The winner is Luke with 28 parables, including biggies like "The Prodigal Son" and "The Good Samaritan."

Interestingly however, the gospel of John has exactly zero parables. Why is that? How could John write a gospel about Jesus, the parable-machine, and not include even one parable? Most scholars believe John wrote his gospel last. Hence, John probably had already read the other gospels and noticed that Jesus' parables had been well covered. So he chose instead to record some of Jesus' lengthy discourses—like the Upper Room Discourse which occupies a full five chapters!

Only a handful of Jesus' parables are recorded in all three synoptic gospels. "The Sower" is one of them. That already is a clue as to maybe this one is important.

But the bigger clue is that "The Sower" is the first significant parable to show up in both Matthew and Mark. Scholars generally feel that "The Sower" was indeed the very first parable Jesus ever taught.

1. Do you think "The Sower" being the first parable somehow makes it more important?

2. On the other end of the spectrum, would you speculate that Jesus' last parable might hold special importance?

Focusing on the Main Topic

Absolutely bedrock to understanding any parable of Jesus is to first figure out what that parable is mainly dealing with. "The Parable of The Sower" is about fruitfulness. Everything in this parable points towards whether or not we bear fruit for the Lord.

The main error I see folks make in this parable (and many others!) is they get sidetracked onto salvation status. Instead of us focusing on the main thing Christ was trying to teach, the focus gets shifted into figuring out who in the parable is saved and who isn't. While that is definitely an important issue, **it usually leads to missing the main point of what Jesus was teaching.**

I've created a list of Jesus' ten most popular parables along with their main topics and put it on page 55. Consulting this list before studying a parable will alert you as to its main topic and help you avoid being drawn down needless rabbit trails.

The First Two Soils

Read Luke 8:11-15.

3.   What does the seed represent?

We are so quickly drawn into the four soils that we almost always overlook what the seed is. **The seed is the Word of God!** We will see how this fact should impact us at the very end of this study. But let's dive straight into those four different soils. See which one you fit into.

The first soil is "the footpath." It is a **hard soil** that the seed can't even penetrate. These folks are not receptive to the message found in God's Word. They harden their hearts and even the devil is brought into the picture.

4.   Which do you think is more of the cause of someone's rejection of the Gospel—the hardening of their heart or the wiles of the devil?

5.   What is the obvious takeaway here?

The second soil is "the rocky soil." It is a **shallow soil** that prevents a new little plant from developing decent roots.

6.   How do these people receive the Gospel?

7.   What is specifically mentioned as the cause for them to wilt?

8.   What is the obvious takeaway here?

The Last Two Soils

If you are reading this book, you probably aren't like those first two soils. You probably have accepted Christ, and hopefully you won't fizzle out quickly for Christ like a short-lived New Year's Eve sparkler.

It's the third soil that often challenges the average American Christian.

The third soil is described as a "thorny" soil. It is a **weedy soil** in which the weeds simply crowd out the desirable fruit-bearing plant.

9.   What does Jesus say keeps believers in this category from producing fruit?

Over in Matthew's account of "The Sower," Jesus is recorded as explaining the weeds more fully as "the worries of this life, the lure of wealth, and the desire for nice things."

10. Which of those three things might trip you up the most?

One super loose paraphrase has Jesus saying, "worrying about tomorrow, making money, and having fun." That is probably too loose, but it hits very close to home.

It's not that you aren't supposed to have any fun in life. The point is that **focusing exclusively** on the pleasures of this life doesn't leave you much time or energy to focus on producing fruit for the Lord.

Hence our main takeaway:

A life of pleasure

crowds out

a life of fruitfulness

Re-read that and let it sink in.

11. Is that a fair statement regarding the thrust of the weedy soil?

Here's a more challenging way of stating our main takeaway:

God is more concerned

with your fruitfulness

than your comfort level

12. Is that more challenging wording too aggressive?

Obviously, you don't want to be like that third soil which bears no fruit for the kingdom. You want to be like the fourth soil. It is described as **good soil.** I love every scrap of the NLT's rendering of these "good soil" people: "honest, good-hearted people who hear God's word, cling to it, and patiently produce a huge harvest."

13. Which of those four characteristics of the "good soil" people stands out to you?

Be A Sower!

The main thrust of this parable is to challenge us to bear fruit for the Lord by not fizzling out and not chasing after a life full of pleasure.

But one thing gets overlooked when we think only about those four soils: **You and I need to be sowers! We need to sow the Word of God!**

That happens when we:

- Get our friends to read God's Word
- Invite and take our friends to church (or small group) where they will hear God's Word

Being a friend to a non-Christian is a good start. But it is not actively sowing the Word of God. In most of the recent testimonies I've read, the person came to salvation by reading and pondering the New Testament. Here are four specific people:

- Walker Hayes – Nashville, TN (2018)
- Micah Wilder – Orlando, FL (2005)
- Rosaria Butterfield – Syracuse, NY (1999)
- Masami Kerby – The Azores (1984)
- Denis Lamoureux – Cyprus (1979)

14. How can you get the Word of God into your friends' hands?

As to inviting someone to church, you've probably never heard of Albert McMakim, but you have undoubtedly heard of Billy Graham. Albert McMakim was a young worker on the Graham dairy farm who persuaded a 16-year-old Billy Graham to go with him to a revival meeting in Charlotte. Billy came to Christ that evening and went on to become the most prolific evangelist of our age.

15. Who could you try to persuade to visit your church (or small group) with you?

Albert took the initiative and got Billy exposed to the powerful Word of God. You and I can do what Albert did. We can invite people to church!

Wrapping Up

I want to wrap up by giving you a quick visual on bearing fruit for the Lord.

My wife and I always buy some pumpkins for Halloween. We get several micro pumpkins for indoor decorations and one regular-sized pumpkin for the front porch.

Last summer, we spent a week with our good friends up in Anchorage, Alaska. On our final day there, we all went to the Alaska state fair and saw Alaska's award-winning pumpkin. I guarantee you Cinderella could fit inside and ride it to the ball!

You get the point. We need to be busy working and bringing all sizes of pumpkins to the Lord—small, regular, Alaskan-winners. Let's be that good fourth soil that produces a huge harvest for the Lord!

My Answers

Question 1

I'm not sure "The Sower" being the first parable makes it any more important than the others. But some people believe otherwise and consider it some sort of anchor parable.

Question 2

In my opinion, Jesus' last three parables do have a special importance. A few days before His death, burial, and resurrection, Jesus told three parables—"The Wise Servant," "The Ten Bridesmaids," and "The Talents" in Matthew 24:45-25:30. Jesus was explicitly prepping his followers for his future second coming. Those last three parables strongly encourage us not only to live expecting His imminent return, but to be working, producing, and doing things for Him. Sounds like important last words to me!

Question 3

The seed is God's Word which means the Bible. In fact, most Christians use the terms "God's Word" and "Bible" interchangeably.

Question 4

On the whole, I find that the Scriptures place more responsibility for rejecting the Gospel on the person who does so rather than on the devil. That doesn't mean the devil isn't involved. He is. The devil is a deceiver and blinds people's minds to the Gospel according to 2 Cor 4:3-4. But there are also verses like Eph. 4:18 describing people who decide for themselves that the Gospel is bogus and harden their hearts against it.

Question 5

Don't be like this hard soil! Don't reject the Gospel!

Question 6

These people receive the Gospel with joy. Joy is good! Emotions are good! But just accepting Jesus emotionally doesn't prepare a person for the long haul. A person needs to grow some sustaining roots so that they don't fizzle out like a little sparkler on New Year's Eve.

Question 7

"Temptation" is the cause cited here in Luke's Gospel. But if you look at the Matthew and Mark accounts of this parable, you'd find something a little different. In those accounts, Jesus is more specific and says **"persecution and suffering"** are what causes these people to wilt. I've personally noticed that those two things, especially suffering, are the main causes of Christians fizzling out. A couple of prominent Christians who've "fizzled out for Jesus" due to suffering and evil are super-skeptic Bart Erhman and former Houston pastor Tim Sledge.

Question 8

Don't be like the shallow soil! Don't fizzle out on Jesus! Endure until Jesus calls you home!

Question 9

"The cares, riches, and pleasures of this life"

Question 10

The older I get, the mellower I become. I'm less and less tempted by the lure of wealth and the desire for nice things. Do I still worry? Yes. But I'm gradually learning: "Don't sweat the small stuff; and it's all small stuff!"

Question 11

Yes, that is the sentiment expressed in that third soil. It challenges us because it causes us to **evaluate our lives through a different lens**—the lens of fruitfulness instead of earthly pleasures.

Question 12

The more challenging wording is aggressive, but it is also fair. The Scriptures constantly exhort us to spiritual growth, giving and helping others, and proclaiming Him. Those are the fruit-bearing things. Conversely, the Scriptures are awfully thin when it comes to encouraging us to seek loads of pleasure in this life.

Question 13

Boy, I love them all: *honest, good-hearted, cling, patient.* I guess I like "patient" the most. I've always kind of related to the tortoise in the tortoise and the hare story. The race doesn't go to the swift. It goes to the slow and steady. Ditto for a life of bearing fruit for the Lord. It simply doesn't occur overnight.

Question 14

There are lots of ways to get the Word of God into your friends' hands. All sorts of interesting books and films are chocked full of God's Word. Christian autobiographies are great for this! (A fabulous new one is *Glad You're Here* [3] by Walker Hayes and Craig Cooper.) You could even give them this parable booklet! The list is endless. Use your imagination.

Question 15

Undoubtedly, you and I will run into people that the Lord will whisper to us "invite them to church this Sunday," or "try to get them to come to small group next week."

3

The Lost Sheep

Focal Verses

Luke 15:3-7 (NLT)

[3]So Jesus told them this story: [4]"If a man has a hundred sheep and one of them gets lost, what will he do? Won't he leave the ninety-nine others in the wilderness and go to search for the one that is lost until he finds it? [5]And when he has found it, he will joyfully carry it home on his shoulders. [6] When he arrives, he will call together his friends and neighbors, saying, 'Rejoice with me because I have found my lost sheep.' [7] In the same way, there is more joy in heaven over one lost sinner who repents and returns to God than over ninety-nine others who are righteous and haven't strayed away!"

The Study

A Little Breather

After two challenging lessons, this study should give you a breather. In fact, our main takeaway today might even leave you feeling warm and fuzzy on the inside.

The parable of "The Lost Sheep" is the first in a set of three that Jesus told in Luke 15—"The Lost Sheep," "The Lost Coin," and "The Lost Son." You can already see the connection across the three parables—something is lost!

"The Lost Son" is typically called "The Prodigal Son." That's fine. Just realize it is easy to miss the connective tissue of "something being lost" by going with the title "The Prodigal Son."

Today's study will indeed focus on the theological concept of being lost. But we will also look at two heart-warming things that are almost always overlooked.

The Overlooked First Element

Read Luke 15:3-7.

"The Lost Sheep" has five things that happen. Let's call those things elements and put them in sequential order.

The last four elements are so obvious that I've gone ahead and written them in for you. I am leaving the first element blank for now:

-
- Lost
- Search
- Found
- Rejoice

It's a pretty straightforward story. A sheep gets lost. A search is made. The sheep is found. The shepherd rejoices.

But people rarely notice that there is an element that comes before "lost." This element is much easier to see if you read the sister parable "The Lost Coin."

Here's the first sentence of "The Lost Coin" from my first edition NLT: "Suppose a woman has ten valuable silver coins and loses one."

1.   What seems to be that missing first element before "lost"?

I'm guessing you noticed that the lost coin was both "**valuable**" and "**silver**."

I'm told that archaeologists rarely find silver coins from the time of Christ. They find jillions of bronze coins, but very few silver ones. Why? Because silver coins were so rare back then. Nowadays, you and I don't think much about the quarters and dimes in our pockets. But a silver coin back in Jesus' time, that was a valuable item!

Go back and write the word "valuable" in the first space on our list of parable elements.

The missing silver coin was very valuable to the woman. And the little sheep that wandered away was very valuable to the shepherd.

That leads to our main takeaway:

You are very valuable to God!

2.   Without getting puffed up, how does that make you feel?

Here's another way of putting it. You matter! You matter to God!

You matter so much that God is going to come searching for you if you get lost.

You Are So Lost!

Go back and circle the word "lost" every time it occurs in "The Lost Sheep."

3.   How many times does the word "lost" occur?

That's quite a bit. And it is a clue.

Most study Bibles point out that the lostness of man is a big emphasis across the three parables in Luke 15. The word "lost" occurs four times in "The Lost Sheep" and twice in "The Lost Coin." "The Prodigal Son" uses the word "lost" twice at its climax points of v. 24 and v. 32.

By my count, that's eight times "being lost" is mentioned in Luke 15. Yes, the lostness of man is a **huge common element** across these three parables.

Of course, each "lost" story is different.

4. How does a sheep usually get lost?

5. How do coins get lost?

6. How do rebellious sons and daughters get lost?

The concept of "lostness" comes at us in several distinctive ways in these parables. A sheep wanders off. A coin is misplaced. A rebellious teenager runs away.

7. Which parable best reflects our spiritual state of lostness?

Clearly God doesn't lose us like a silver coin. And while we could be said to wander away from God like little sheep, that doesn't quite capture the gravity of the sin nature that we are born with. "The Prodigal Son" is the illustration that hits closest to home. We are most like the prodigal son who rebelled against his father, demanded his inheritance, and then ran away and blew it on riotous living.

Many times, we are highly reluctant to admit our lost rebellious status. We'd prefer to view ourselves as one of those 99 good sheep in the parable that did not go astray.

Allow me to introduce one other sheep verse into this study. The very first verse that our four-year-old son learned came from the *ABC Memory Book* by Scripture Memory Fellowship. As you might imagine, it started with the letter "A:" "All we like sheep have gone astray, we have turned every one to his own way" (Isaiah 53:6). Later on, we found out our son was more than a little confused with the theology behind this verse when he asked, "Mom, why do we like sheep so much?"

But all humor aside, the universality of sin and lostness of man is clearly taught across both the Old and New Testaments. Romans 3:10 puts us on notice, "There is none righteous, no not one."

God Wants You Back!

That's enough about the bad news.

You are valuable to God and He wants you back!

We tend to talk in terms of **us searching for God.** That is indeed true. But it is also true that **God came searching for us first.** According to 1 John 4:19, "We love Him because He first loved us."

In my mind's eye, I see the shepherd in the parable lovingly calling out the name of his little lost sheep while searching the countryside. "Fluffy! Oh Fluuuffy!"

8. Is it fair to say God searches and calls for us by name?

Recently my church hosted an evangelist named Yankee Arnold. Towards the end of his incredible sermon, he said something I will never forget, "God loves you so much that He'd rather die than live without you."

Yes, God came out of heaven to get you back!

The Overlooked Last Element

Most study Bibles say that God's rejoicing when He gets us back really is the main point of "The Lost Sheep," "The Lost Coin," and "The Prodigal Son." Nevertheless, we have a tendency to overlook (or at least downplay) God's rejoicing at the end of these parables.

9.   Do you have celebrations when you find your lost things?

10. Why is that?

We rarely throw celebratory parties when we find our missing smart phones, glasses, car keys, or credit cards. We usually just feel relieved and quickly resume our busy lives.

But the more valuable the item that you lose, the more likely you'd be to stop and celebrate when you find it.

Years ago, our 18-year-old son was working at the local Walmart for the summer. One day he came out of Walmart to find our family's Chevy Astro Van had been stolen from the parking lot. We weren't overly wealthy and the loss of that van was a significant blow. You could say that van was very valuable to us. After a few days, we were pretty sure that our van was gone forever.

However, a week later, my son handed me the phone and said the sheriff was on the line. The sheriff told me that our Chevy Astro Van had been found locally with only minor damage done to it. My son could tell from my side of the conversation that our van had been found. Happiness was starting to bubble up inside both of us.

When I hung up the phone, we literally danced around in circles with our hands on each other's shoulders yelling "The van is found! The van is found! The van is found!"

According to the parable of The Lost Sheep, God's reaction is similar.

Heres' the bottom line. **You are immensely valuable to God.** And when you repent and return to God, the Scripture says He is overjoyed to get you back!

My Answers

Question 1

The first element in both parables is that someone had something that was **valuable**.

Question 2

Understanding that you are valuable to God probably makes you feel a little more esteemed, wanted, and loved. One man in my Sunday School class recently told us that his brother was a broken down man in prison who finally trusted Christ when he came to the realization that he was still valuable to God. No matter what you've done, you are still valuable to God.

Question 3

It depends on your translation. The word "lost" occurs four times in the NLT and three times in most other translations.

Question 4

Sheep usually get lost by **wandering away**. I'm no shepherd, but supposedly they nibble on grass further and further away until they are out of sight.

Question 5

Our little lost coins usually show up in the washing machine, under couch cushions, and in every nook and cranny of our cars. Honestly, our coins have very little value to us nowadays. Perhaps a better modern example might be your smart phone. It typically gets lost when it **falls out of your pocket** or **you misplace it.** When that happens, you notice almost immediately and start retracing your steps until you find that very valuable phone.

Question 6

Rebellious sons and daughters get lost mostly by **running away** from home. "The Prodigal Son" is entitled *The Boy Who Ran Away* [4] in the Arch Book Children Series. I heartily recommend these old booklets from the '60s and '70s. My favorite is *The Good Samaritan* [5], which is written in absolutely stunning rhyme. Start with that one!

Question 7

The parable of "The Prodigal Son" comes closest to depicting our spiritual state of lostness. According to the Scriptures, all of us are born with a sin nature. That is a nice way of saying that we rebel against God and do our own thing for our own pleasure much like that fictitious prodigal son.

Question 8

Yes, God knows and cares about every person by name. He doesn't love humanity in just a general sense. He loves and searches for individuals!

Question 9

We tend not to have celebrations when we find things like our misplaced smart phones. We usually just scoop it up and go on our merry way.

Question 10

There are several possible reasons: 1) You probably found your missing item fairly quickly. 2) The lost item was probably not one of the most valuable things in your life. 3) All the **physical things** you have on this earth **are not eternal things**.

4

The Ten Bridesmaids

Focal Verses

Matthew 25:1-13 (NLT)

[1] "Then the Kingdom of Heaven will be like ten bridesmaids who took their lamps and went to meet the bridegroom. [2] Five of them were foolish, and five were wise. [3] The five who were foolish didn't take enough olive oil for their lamps, [4] but the other five were wise enough to take along extra oil. [5] When the bridegroom was delayed, they all became drowsy and fell asleep.

[6] "At midnight they were roused by the shout, 'Look, the bridegroom is coming! Come out and meet him!' [7] All the bridesmaids got up and prepared their lamps. [8] Then the five foolish ones asked the others, 'Please give us some of your oil because our lamps are going out.' [9] But the others replied, 'We don't have enough for all of us. Go to a shop and buy some for yourselves.'

[10] "But while they were gone to buy oil, the bridegroom came. Then those who were ready went in with him to the marriage feast, and the door was locked. [11] Later, when the other five bridesmaids returned, they stood outside, calling, 'Lord! Lord! Open the door for us!' [12] But he called back, 'Believe me, I don't know you!' [13] So you, too, must keep watch! For you do not know the day or hour of my return."

The Study

A Three Part Gospel

The Gospel has three parts to it.

- Christ has died
- Christ is risen
- Christ will come again

Many churches in mainline denominations have their congregation recite those exact ten words every Sunday. Go ahead, live dangerously and **say those three phrases out loud right now.**

What you just said is called "The Memorial Acclamation." If someone forced you to boil the Gospel down into just 10 words, those would get the job done.

1. What verb tenses are used in The Memorial Acclamation?

Yes, those three tenses cover it all—past, present, and future.

The future return of Christ is no small element in your New Testament. Here are eight of the more prominent passages:

- Matt 24:30
- John 14:3
- Acts 1:11
- Phil 3:20

- 1 Thess 4:16
- James 5:7-8
- Revelation 19:11-16
- Revelation 22:7, 12, 20

There are more, but those are the biggies. If you find time later, you might want to check out all eight passages. But for now, let me point out the three times where Jesus specifically says He's coming back: Matt. 24:30, John 14:3, and the triple "I'm coming back" to end your Bible in Revelation 22.

2. Do you think your church spends the right amount of time teaching on the return of Christ?

3. On a percentage basis, what amount of time do you think churches should spend teaching about the return of Christ?

4. Do you think your church spends the right amount of time singing about the return of Christ?

The Advice Interlude

Jesus spoke at length about end time events and his future return in Matthew 24-25, a passage which we call "The Olivet Discourse."

I have studied this passage countless times over the years. But it wasn't until one Saturday afternoon in 2016 that I finally grasped the outline which had been staring me in the face in my ESV Study Bible.

In Matthew 24-25, Jesus tells us **what will happen** during the end times in a strong chronological sequence. The only thing is, Jesus stopped right in the middle (24:32 – 25:30) to give us advice about **what to do** in light of His future return.

Once you understand that outline, you can successfully process what you are reading. Some of "The Olivet Discourse" is telling you what will happen, and some of it is telling you what to do!

Jesus used seven illustrations during his advice interlude. The first four illustrations are very short—the fig tree, the days of Noah, two in the field, the thief at night. They are so short I call them parablets.

The last three illustrations are full-blown parables. That is where we find "The Ten Bridesmaids." Now you have a good working context for this parable. **Jesus is telling us what to do in view of his imminent future return.**

The Main Point

Read Mathew 25:1-13.

This parable mimics a typical Jewish wedding of the era.

The late arriving bridegroom clearly represents a delaying but certain-to-return Jesus Christ. It is hotly debated, however, as to who the ten bridesmaids represent. They either represent humanity in general or perhaps only the expectant Christian community. I favor the ten bridesmaids representing humanity in general. Nevertheless, whenever I teach this parable, I carefully explain the **very strong pros and cons of each position.**

Let's forego that contentious discussion and go straight to the heart of the parable.

5.   What is the main point of this parable? (Verse 10 has a strong clue.)

According to respected commentator D.A. Carson, the main point of "The Ten Bridesmaids" is **preparedness**. A similar word we could use here is **readiness**. Put a box around the words "those who were ready" in verse 10. That's essentially what differentiates the five wise bridesmaids from the five foolish ones. The wise ones were ready! We need to be ready for the return of Christ whether He is coming back in a two-stage return that includes a rapture event or in a one-stage return that has no rapture event.

Christians disagree mightily on end-times viewpoints and have proffered many different timelines. We won't touch those disagreements today with a 29-foot pole! Basically, the parable of "The Ten Bridesmaids" tells us to be **prepared and ready** for Christ's return, no matter how it goes down!

In fact, that is our main takeaway:

Don't let Jesus' return catch you unprepared!

Here's how to be ready for Christ's return:

- Believe in Him
- Be doing whatever He tells you to do

This parable plainly states some people will not be ready at the return of Christ. Don't be one of them!

That Important Final Verse

Read Matt. 25:13 one more time.

Circle that important last sentence: **"For you do not know the day or the hour of my return."** Jesus said this exact same sentence three more times back in those earlier parablets in the Olivet Discourse—24:36, 42, 44.

It seems like Jesus really wanted to drill into us that we won't know when He is going to return! Here's the tale of the tape from all four warning verses:

- No one knows
- The angels don't know
- Jesus himself doesn't know
- Only God the Father knows
- Jesus is going to return **when we do NOT expect it!**

So Jesus plainly tells us over and over that we don't know and won't be able to predict when He is returning.

And yet . . . . we still have plenty of date-setters telling us they've figured out exactly when Jesus will return! How can that be?

6. Why do some Christians go against Scripture and predict a day for Christ's return?

Here's what I've dubbed "The Date-Setter Tango."

- Predict a day two to three years into the future for Christ to return
- Give lots of unbelievably complex reasons
- Totally diss Matthew 24:36, 42, 44; 25:13
- Watch the movement build as unsuspecting Christians buy into it
- See the date come and go without the return of Christ
- Rinse and repeat

7. Can you recall any recent dates that were predicted for Christ to return?

Scholars have noted at least 35 major date-setting hullabaloos throughout the history of the church. They seem to be coming faster now because eight of them have occurred during my lifetime. Here's the three biggest hullabaloos in my memory.

- 1988 – "88 Reasons" – Edgar C. Wisenant
- 2015 – "The Four Blood Moons" – Mark Biltz & John Hagee
- 2017 – "Rev. 12:1-2" – Scott Clarke & Steve Cioccolanti

8. What kind of damage is done by date-setters?

9. What should be our response to the next date-setter?

Yes, date-setters, as well-meaning as some of them are, do extreme damage to the cause of Christ. They **discredit** themselves, **disillusion** many Christians, and **depreciate** the return of Christ. Our main response should be to vigorously repeat Jesus' four-fold statement here in the Olivet Discourse where He clearly states that nobody will know!

Maranatha!

Back in 2012, the Lord prompted me to start ending my prayers with the word "Maranatha." I've done so ever since.

"Maranatha" is an old Aramaic word that means "Our Lord, come!" That excitable exclamation point really is part of the meaning. Another acceptable translation is: "Come, Lord Jesus!" I'm told that "Maranatha" is frequently said in an excitable fashion in some churches in Africa. Christ's future return is definitely part and parcel of the Gospel for these African Christians.

The word "Maranatha" occurs one time in your Bible. Paul used it as some sort of sign-off at the end of 1 Corinthians. Plus, "Come, Lord Jesus!" is how your Bible virtually ends in Rev. 22:20.

I find that ending all my prayers, both private and public, with "Maranatha" keeps the imminent return of Christ near the front of my mind. You might want to try using it before saying "Amen" and see what it does for you.

Maranatha! Come, Lord Jesus!

My Answers

Question 1

I'm pretty sure my English major wife would call those three verbs some complicated type of past, present, and future tenses.

Question 2

At one church that I attended for a very long time, it took me about five years before I started to speculate that the preacher was steering clear of any and all Bible passages dealing with the return of Christ. After a couple of more years, I was sure. Probably too many of our contemporary churches are like this. They simply avoid the subject for various reasons—some good, some not so good.

Question 3

There are many very important topics that churches ought to cover. The return of Christ is just one of them. So a very small percentage of teaching time, like maybe 2-3% might make sense. I try to teach my Sunday School class a short set of lessons on the return of Christ once every 5 to 7 years. That works out to around 3%. That seems sufficient to me.

Question 4

Many of our old hymns have a final verse focusing on the return of Christ. One quick example is "How Great Thou Art." There were even a few old hymns that focused **exclusively** on Christ's return—like John W. Peterson's "Jesus is Coming Again." But most modern contemporary Christian music is devoid of references to the return of Christ. So almost definitionally, we probably aren't singing about Christ's future return enough—certainly not as much as we used to!

Question 5

The main point is being ready for Christ when He does return. **Preparedness** is what differentiates the wise bridesmaids from the foolish ones. The wise bridesmaids brought along plenty of additional oil for their lamps. Hence, **they were ready** when the groom finally did arrive.

Question 6

Most date-setters are very smart and biblically astute. Many are well-meaning individuals. But all of them are dead wrong to spend their precious time and effort trying to figure out when Christ will return. There also seems to be a certain amount of self-aggrandizement in play for at least some of these date-setters. Here's one extra thought to ponder. Will God allow some date-setter to get glory by successfully predicting the return of Christ? I don't think so. This will be the Lord's special day and He will not be sharing His glory with some really smart date-setter.

Question 7

Here's some notable date-setter hullabaloo years: 155, 970, 1284, 1504, 1524, 1648, 1666, 1792, 1844. The Jehovah's Witnesses went on a roll predicting the return of Christ in 1878, 1881, 1914, 1918, and 1925 before setting down their crystal balls. Hullabaloos occurring during my life-time include 1988, 1994, 1997, 2000, 2008, 2012, 2015, and 2017. Over the years, I've collected quite a few books authored by date-setter guys. It's interesting to read all the goofy ways—11 by my count—that date-setters diss Jesus' warnings that nobody can know the day of His return. Unbelievably, many of them not only diss Jesus' warnings, but flip it and say that the Lord expects us to figure out when He's coming back. Nothing could be further from the truth!

Question 8

Date-setters **discredit** themselves, **disillusion** many Christians, and **depreciate** the future return of Christ. The damage is real and it is substantial. The Lord is not pleased with date-setters and He will hold them accountable.

Question 9

The last major date-setting hullabaloo was on Sept 23, 2017. Six days before that, I calmly explained to my adult Bible class the crazy interpretation of Revelation 12:1-2 concocted by date-setter Scott Clarke. Scott's terrible interpretation was what started this hullabaloo and it spread like wildfire across the internet. I also reviewed my class on Jesus' four-fold warning against date-setting (Matt 24:36, 42, 44, 25:13.) Most of my class members (but not all!) were thereby inoculated from that 2017 hullabaloo. I think that should be our approach—use any and all predictions for the return of Christ as an opportunity to go through, yet again, Jesus' words that "no one knows the day or the hour!"

5

The House
Upon The Rock

Focal Verses

Matthew 7:24-27 (ESV)

[24] "Everyone then who hears these words of mine and does them will be like a wise man who built his house on the rock. [25] And the rain fell, and the floods came, and the winds blew and beat on that house, but it did not fall, because it had been founded on the rock. [26] And everyone who hears these words of mine and does not do them will be like a foolish man who built his house on the sand. [27] And the rain fell, and the floods came, and the winds blew and beat against that house, and it fell, and great was the fall of it."

The Study

A Bold Savior

Jesus made many bold claims about exactly who He was. Here are a fast three:

- Jesus claimed to be one with the Father (John 10:30)
- Jesus claimed to be end times judge (John 5:22, 27)
- Jesus claimed to be end times raiser of the dead (John 6:40, 44, 54)

The first is a direct claim to deity on a par with "If you have seen me, you have seen the Father" (John 14:9). The last two are indirect in that Jesus is claiming to do things in the future that only God can do.

If you or I made such bold claims, I'm afraid we'd be correctly laughed out of the room. Unlike you or I, however, Jesus did plenty of miracles to back up His claim to deity. In fact, Jesus pointed to His many miracles as testimony to His deity (John 14:11).

Today's challenging parable comes from Jesus' famous "Sermon on the Mount" which occupies Matthew 5-7. Jesus starts off this long discourse with "The Beatitudes" and then proceeds to elaborate on the high ethical standards He expects from His followers.

Even while Jesus is essentially teaching us Christian ethics, He slips into bold-claim mode four times by my count. In Matthew 5:11, Jesus claims that His followers will be persecuted on account of Him. In 5:17, He claims that He Himself will perfectly fulfill the old Mosaic Law. In 7:21-23, Jesus claims that He will be judging people at the end of time.

Jesus' fourth bold claim comes in the parable of "The House Upon the Rock" which is the capstone finish to the "Sermon on the Mount." In fact, "The House Upon the Rock" may contain the boldest claim Jesus ever made. See what you think as we dig in.

Understanding The Elements

Read Matt 7:24-27.

This parable is so familiar there's even a children's Sunday School song about it. You probably remember it: "Ohhh, the rains came down and the floods came up." And of course, there were hand motions!

But let's get out of children song mode and do our due diligence with this challenging parable. "The House Upon the Rock" has three elements. Let's go through them.

1.   What does a house represent?

2.   What does a house's foundation represent?

3.   What do the rains, floods, and winds represent?

Jesus is talking about big issues here. The house represents **your whole life.** The house's foundation represents **what you are building your life on.** And the rains, floods, and winds represent **the inevitable storms of life.**

When you quickly pull that all together, Jesus is saying, "If you build your life on Me and My words, when the storms of life hit you, your life won't collapse into a pile of rubble."

4.   What are some of life's biggest storms?

5.   What does Jesus say you are if you build your life on Him?

6.   What does Jesus say you are if you don't build your life on Him?

Absorbing The Claim

Notice that Jesus did not say there are lots of different foundations you can build your life on. According to Him, **there are only two foundations!** You can either build your life on the firm foundation of Jesus or you can build on sand.

That implies that people following other religions will get flattened when the storms of life hit, especially life's biggest storm of all—death.

7. Name some people who've founded religions and the religion they founded.

According to Jesus, building your life on any other religion is like building your house directly on the sand at the beach. That house will not stand up when Hurricane Betty comes barreling through.

Today's parable is not only challenging, it is sobering. Christ is boldly claiming that anyone's life that is not tethered to Him will ultimately end up in shambles.

8. Where do we find Jesus' best known claim to being **the only way** to God?

Laying That Firm Foundation

Making Christ the firm foundation of your life is encapsulated in one word—**believe**. Don't try to work for your salvation. First comes the believing, then comes the doing. Ephesians 2:8-10 gives us that basic outline for salvation—faith first, then better behavior follows as a result. **But exactly what do you need to believe?**

The answer to that question is at the climax of the emotional new double autobiography entitled *Glad You're Here*. The authors are country music artist Walker Hayes and Nashville pastor Craig Cooper. These two men and their families both moved to Nashville around 2013 and eventually became as close as two families can possibly be. Incidentally, Walker Hayes' biggest country hit was "Fancy Like." If you are young, you probably heard "Fancy Like" many times when it went viral on TikTok in 2021.

For many years, Walker was a heavy beer-drinking atheist who wanted nothing to do with Jesus. Eventually, he hit alcoholic rock bottom. At that low point, Walker began voraciously reading the Gospels. Belief in Christ began bubbling up in his heart.

A week or so later, at a Sushi restaurant in Nashville, Walker described to Craig how he'd been reading the Gospels and finished by saying, "Craig, I believe. I believe all of it."

Taken by surprise and looking for a bit more clarity, Craig asked, "Walker, are you telling me that you believe that Jesus Christ is the Son of God and that you want to live your life for His glory?"

Walker responded, "Yes, that's what I'm saying!"

It's that basic. Believe that Jesus Christ is the risen Son of God and begin living your life for His glory. You will then have Jesus Christ as the firm foundation for your life.

Wrapping Up

Let's wrap up this study with a song a little older (and sturdier) than "Fancy Like."

"The Solid Rock" was written back in 1834 by Baptist pastor Edward Mote. Its connections to "The House Upon the Rock" are unmistakable. Here's the first verse and chorus of "The Solid Rock" found on page #283 in my old maroon hymnal:

> *My hope is built on nothing less*
>
> *Than Jesus' blood and righteousness;*
>
> *I dare not trust the sweetest frame,*
>
> *But wholly lean on Jesus' name.*
>
> *On Christ the solid rock I stand;*
>
> *All other ground is sinking sand,*
>
> *All other ground is sinking sand.*

Is your hope built on nothing less than Jesus' blood and righteousness? If not, I encourage you to make Jesus Christ the sure foundation of your life—today!

My Answers

Question 1

A house represents a person's life.

Question 2

A house's foundation represents what a person is building their life upon. Here are some other ways of expressing it: What is the **anchor** to your life? What is your life **tethered** to? What is at **the core** of your life?

Question 3

The rains, floods, and winds represent the big storms of life.

Question 4

Some of life's big storms include: chronic illness, hospitalization, dementia, isolation during a pandemic, death of a spouse or child, losing your job, divorce. Some of life's storms involve your real house—it could be destroyed by a tornado, flooded by a swollen river, or made uninhabitable by mold. Ultimately however, the biggest storm you will face in life is your own death. You will be out of control and at the mercy of God at that point.

Question 5

Jesus calls it like he sees it. He says you would be **wise** to build your life on Him.

Question 6

Jesus says that you would be **foolish** to anchor your life around anything other than Him. That is a very bold and exclusive claim. But that's what Jesus said.

Question 7

Confucius, Buddha, and Muhammad quickly come to mind as founders some of the world's oldest religions. In 1828, Joseph Smith said he dug up some golden plates in western New York, translated the "reformed Egyptian" hieroglyphics on them, and then gave those golden plates away to an angel never to be seen again. Thus the *Book of Mormon* was born and Mormonism was started. More recently Mary Baker Eddy founded

Christian Science, and L. Ron Hubbard invented Scientology. Building your life on any of these religions, according to Jesus, would be foolish.

Question 8

In John 14:6, Jesus point blank said, "I am the way, the truth, and the life. No man comes unto the Father but by me." Note that Jesus didn't say he was "a way" or "one of many ways" to the Father. He said he was **the** way, **the** truth, and **the** life—a triple whammy of exclusivity.

Notes

1) Lori Joiner, *Raising Children unto the Lord: Helping Children Build a Strong Foundation in Christ* (Lori Joiner, 2022).

2) Philip Yancey, *What's So Amazing About Grace*, Grand Rapids, Michigan: Zondervan, 2006).

3) Walker Hayes & Craig Allen Cooper, *Glad You're Here: Two Unlikely Friends Breaking Bread and Fences* (Chicago: Moody Publishers, 2022).

4) Irene Elmer, *The Boy Who Ran Away* (St. Louis: Concordia: 1964).

5) Janice Kramer, *The Good Samaritan* (St. Louis: Concordia: 1964).

Jesus' Top Ten Parables

When you are studying a parable of Christ, it is crucial to know what the parable is mainly about. Remember, Jesus almost always created each parable to illustrate just one big point.

We get into trouble when we try to make every element of a parable represent something in the real world. That simply is not how parables work.

Below is a handy list of Jesus' top ten parables along with their main topics. The first five come from *Jesus' Most Popular Parables,* which was the very first book in the "No-Prep Bible Study Series." The last five come from this book.

Parable	Main Topic
The Prodigal Son	Grace
The Good Samaritan	Loving Your Neighbor
The Rich Fool	Greed
The Talents	Working for the Lord
The Unforgiving Servant	Forgiveness
The Pharisee & The Tax Collector	Two Approaches to God
The Sower	Fruitfulness
The Lost Sheep	Your Value to God
The Ten Bridesmaids	The Return of Christ
The House Upon the Rock	Building Your Life on Christ

Quick Tips for Group Leaders

- Start on time
- Finish on time
- Smile and be friendly
- Shoot for participation, not open discussions
- Listen to group members when they speak
- Keep the study moving
- Learn new people's names
- Don't let one person dominate
- Finish strong with a quick summary
- Always promote the next study

For more specific ideas to help you get these things done, visit our "Group Leader Tips" page on our NoPrepBibleStudies.com website.

Statement of Faith

The following Statement of Faith is proffered as an interdenominational bedrock basis for this book. It is extremely brief and without Scripture references, but certainly represents Christianity at its core.

The Nature of God

- God is creator
- God is holy

The Nature of Man

- Man is created
- Man is born with a sin nature

Man's Situation

- Sin separates man from God
- Man can't extricate himself from his sinful predicament

God' Solution

- God provides a solution for man's sin by the atoning sacrifice of His Son, Jesus Christ on the cross
- Man needs to accept the atoning sacrifice of Christ and believe in His resurrection from the dead

About the Author

Kenny Beck has enjoyed teaching adult Bible classes for over 35 years. His current Bible class typically runs over forty people ranging from age 20 to 85.

A typical Kenny lesson features a colorful handout or two, a huge white dry erase board, a good dollop of class participation, and plenty of enthusiasm. All the studies in this booklet are drawn from real live Sunday Bible lessons.

Vocationally, Kenny was a CPA in Houston for three years before finding happiness as a piano teacher. He has been a full time private piano teacher in far west Houston since 1984.

Kenny has co-written a couple of contemporary Christian songs with his Nashville pal Jeff Nelson entitled "Forever His Blood" and "Take My Life." Both have been published by LIFEWAY. Additionally "Forever His Blood" was released on You-Tube in 2015.

Feel free to contact Kenny at kennybeck99@gmail.com

He would love your feedback!

ACCID ENTAL MAGIC

ACCID ENTAL MAGIC

For Rebecca,
A fellow Potterhead,
from

Keshava ~~Guha~~

K[signature]

22.11.22

HarperCollins *Publishers* India

First published in India by
HarperCollins *Publishers* in 2019
A-75, Sector 57, Noida, Uttar Pradesh 201301, India
www.harpercollins.co.in

2 4 6 8 10 9 7 5 3 1

P-ISBN: 978-93-5357-396-6
E-ISBN: 978-93-5357-397-3

Typeset in 11.5/16. Minion Pro at
Manipal Technology Ltd, Manipal

Printed and bound at
Thomson Press (India) Ltd

MIX
Paper
FSC FSC® C010615

For my parents
and
for my sister

Some Argentines without means do it;
People say in Boston even beans do it.
Let's do it—let's fall in love.

COLE PORTER

1

Back in Bangalore, in the last year at engineering college, it had been Kannan's habit of a Friday to bunk class with his friends Vinay and Ashok in favour of a morning show at the cinema, Tamil or Hindi if they had to, but ideally Hollywood, and to lunch at the Tao Fu Bar and Restaurant, consisting of Chicken Manchurian and rum or whisky with Pepsi, at retail price. On his arrival in Boston in August 1996, he had found waiting for him in his postbox a letter from his brother, who had been C. Santhanam in Bangalore but was now Santa C. Nam, and lately insisted on Kannan calling him Santa, pronounced the American way, and not anna. Santhanam had been in the US five years, first for an MS at Carnegie Mellon, and now as an engineer with Dell, in Austin.

Kannan was on a knock-off version of the same path, the imitation as pitiful as a low-budget Tamil remake of a Hollywood action film. He had only been admitted—miraculously, with a scholarship—to one master's programme, at Northeastern. Their mother had spent years bragging to the extended family about Santhanam's achievements. Now they paid her back with malicious questions. 'We hear that Kannan is off to study in the Northeast. Is the university in Nagaland or in Manipur?'

Santhanam had said that he ought to be happy that he had got in anywhere, given his attitude and track record. His letter began: 'You have been lucky enough to be given a chance. Even at a place like Northeastern, it is not too late to make something of yourself.' What followed was a list of instructions organized by underlined subheadings. This wasn't advice: any hope of redeeming himself, and of making a life beyond Northeastern in the US, depended upon his meticulous compliance. The orders concerned three broad themes: conserving money, achieving good grades, and positioning oneself for employment and an H-1B visa. He arrived at the final item:

18. ALCOHOL

I have heard that you have taken to drinking. I hope this is not the case. Now that you are in the US you must cease this habit. Otherwise you will drink away your scholarship and start sending me begging letters which I will ignore. Alcohol here is very expensive. For the price of a rum and Coke at a bar you can eat three filling meals at Taco Bell or three days' worth of frozen food. Fortunately (so far as I know) you don't smoke. Think of your scholarship as a loan that has to be paid back with discipline and hard work. If you get a job, and at that point you want to piss away your income, go ahead. It will be your money.

Kannan had done as he was told without, as far as he could, admitting as much to Santhanam. He had taken the courses Santhanam had listed, had always sat in the second row, had earned the free room and board that came with working as a Resident Assistant, and had never stepped into a bar or liquor store, even through two years of tailgate. com and his money.

In his first weeks in the US, in the late summer of 1996, Kannan had not been lonely—Santhanam's letter had assured him that if he followed those instructions, he would be too busy to afford the luxury of loneliness—but he had experienced the utterly new and blissful sensation of aloneness, in this country that was so wonderfully empty. In Boston, a city that would be described to him as dense, even cramped, he could step out on to the main street in the middle of the day and be so far away from the next person that he could sing at the top of his voice without attracting attention. Other than those few minutes every day spent bathing or on the toilet, he had never really been alone at home, and even that time was penetrated by his mother, mindful of the rising price of water, yelling at him to hurry up.

The year that Santhanam went off to college at IIT Madras, their grandmother moved into the boys' room. He often found himself of an evening saying those most alien words, 'I have to study,' seeking the only respite possible from the twin hectoring voices. He began to understand his father's daily habit, on his return from work at a nationalized bank at exactly 5.30 p.m., of hiding himself behind first the newspaper and then a religious book—one that he surely must by now know by heart—and ignoring all remarks directed at him, until dinner was served. What he had seen as his father's hatred of his wife and mother was merely the quest for aloneness, in a two-bedroom flat and city and country where it could not be found. But this was a perverse form of aloneness, based on rejecting the world rather than claiming a clear space. And where his father was forced into society, and even into conversation, by meals, Kannan could now eat alone. Besides, 'turning meals, which are a simple matter of nutrition, and need take no more than seven minutes at the most, into social occasions' was number six on his brother's list of 'Common and Unnecessary Ways to Waste Precious Time'.

He had marvelled, in that first year at Northeastern, at how little he missed Vinay or Ashok or his other college friends. The other Indian in his MS course, a Bengali from Hyderabad, was keen to be both friend and study partner, but Kannan rebuffed his advances with an unaccountable firmness. But they shared a meal every two months or so, and once they ventured out to Arlington to watch a Hindi film shown, as at home, with an intermission. In the men's room, filthier than any he had seen in a Bangalore cinema, Kannan waited for him to finish using the only urinal. After two minutes or so, he turned to see why it was taking so long, and saw that his classmate was masturbating. He walked out of the cinema and took the next bus back to Fenway.

On 7 July 2000, as he waited in line with three dozen strangers outside WordsWorth Books & Co. to pick up their midnight copies of *Harry Potter and the Goblet of Fire*, Kannan was patted lightly from behind on the left triceps. He turned to see a large, near-bald man, in his fifties or older, his eyes beaming rays of warmth and curiosity at Kannan. He couldn't remember having inspired a gaze like that before, in anyone.

'I just wanted to see where you were in the book.' *Prisoner of Azkaban*. 'You must be rereading a favourite passage. I wish I'd remembered to bring my copy.' The excuse was transparent; not waiting for a reply, he introduced himself as Curtis Grimmett, the host of a weekly public radio show. Occasionally another member of the queue would wave or otherwise solicit Grimmett's attention. Each time he briefly acknowledged them and turned wordlessly back to Kannan.

In the years to come Kannan would remember nothing of what they had spoken of that night. Of course they must have talked about the first three books, but back then he had known so little, had been so shamefully ignorant and inarticulate even as he had read those books twelve times each. Still, Grimmett had left with his email and cellphone number, had emailed in the morning and called a few hours later to invite him out to 'drinks and dinner.' The drinks were not presented as optional.

In this way, near the end of his fourth year in Boston, for the first time he defied Santhanam.

At Grendel's Den in Harvard Square, sitting with Grimmett at a fat U-shaped bar in a yellow-brown basement suffocated by frantic, unceasing talk and laughter so loud it sounded recorded, he had remembered Tao Fu and its open rooftop, grimy plastic chairs and flat wooden benches topped by happy, spreadeagled afternoon nappers and thought, this is no way to drink. In this country of personal space and abundant silence, drinking was nighttime and raucous, and driven by the pressures of social and sexual fulfilment. At home, where no one had ever known privacy or quiet, you could drink to relax, and submit yourself to a soothing haze of pleasant thoughts. Only months later did he say that this had been his first American bar.

He ordered a rum and Coke. Back in college, Vinay and Ashok had preferred whisky, which got you there quicker, but he'd only been able to manage rum, usually Old Monk, which was both sweet and pungent, like gutter-water flavoured with apple and butterscotch. This rum, Captain Morgan, was so mild and inconspicuous that he didn't really feel as if he was drinking. Grimmett paid for the drinks. Kannan didn't offer; he had no idea whether he was supposed to. The next time, he offered, but Grimmett held up a hand that brooked no disagreement. The march of their friendship proceeded under Grimmett's sole direction. Grimmett always paid, and in those early encounters where he did almost all the talking, Kannan wondered if he was buying an audience. But by their fifth meeting Grimmett changed, began indeed to question Kannan about every detail of his life in India and in Boston. No one had ever subjected him to this sort of curiosity. And to every answer Grimmett supplied a fact or anecdote about himself, tangentially related, for which the original question sometimes seemed like an excuse. But it never took more than ten or twelve minutes for the conversation, as it now was, to return to Harry Potter, the key their friendship was played in.

Grimmett had very little neck, and a head whose shape Kannan had taken first for a watermelon laid on its side but that was in fact, he realized with great satisfaction on a nighttime walk in late October, a Halloween pumpkin. This was a fruit he knew well, the Great Hall at Hogwarts being filled with the stuff every year, most vividly on the night when Harry and Ron saved Hermione from the troll, the night on which the Trio was forged. Grimmett had been born in June 1946, five years after Kannan's father, and he too could be called overweight, but while his father's thin arms and chest drooped down into a convex belly, Grimmett had the full, egalitarian heaviness that came with a lifetime of beef and turkey, as opposed to rice, milk and sugar. He had never married, was the only child of two only children, 'We were a Chinese family, demographically speaking,' he said. He had lived always in Cambridge, except for eight years in England, initially as a student to avoid the Vietnam draft. His mother's sudden death in 1976 had forced him back. His father had died in 1983, leaving his son the house in North Cambridge near what used to be Radcliffe College, and enough money to leave him with little need to work.

'But I have worked, in all kinds of jobs. To pass the time, for company, to really get to know my city and my society. Anything that didn't involve a corporation or working with my hands. I've taught sixth grade at a private school, been a Freedom Trail tour guide, manager of a used bookstore, warden at a girls' summer camp, only childless member of a school board, artistic director of a literary festival that had to be cancelled because we couldn't raise the money, assistant building supervisor at both Harvard and Tufts, cashier at an old Art Deco cinema in Brookline, and then in 1987 a friend needed someone to fill the unwanted stepchild, the 10 p.m. Friday night slot, and my radio show was born. No one believes my list of jobs, you know. They think I'm just trying to add colour to a dull life spent reading and talking and living off my inheritance. But I did them all.'

Kannan had never had any talent for judging character. With the exception of his brother, he had never felt that he truly understood any human being other than himself. He certainly didn't understand Grimmett, but he knew instinctively that he was in the company of a man who had never learned how to lie, that most basic quality that separates children from grown-ups and humans from beasts. These were the facts of Curtis Grimmett's life, all relayed to Kannan in those first monological meetings.

In his letter of 1996, and in the faxes and emails that followed, Santhanam had warned against the chimerical temptation of friendship with Americans. It won't work, he said; it won't end well for you. And I won't be there to clean up your mess.

Whatever sort of American friend Santhanam had in mind with these warnings, it couldn't be someone like Grimmett. Still, for once the thought of his brother consoled Kannan. If Santhanam took such a view of friendship with Americans, it must be because he'd never succeeded in making one.

Her skin was white but her heart was black. That, at any rate, was the verdict of Laurent Kameni, graduate student and teaching fellow in Francophone literature. One Tuesday afternoon after class in the fall of her senior year at Harvard, he had asked her to meet in his office in Boylston Hall to discuss her final paper on Senghor. The small talk that invariably opened these encounters did not, on this occasion, yield to business.

'You don't know, Rebecca, that I came to see your play.' The previous week she had played the lead in a student-written stage adaptation of *Pretty Woman*, five shows in the renovated Adams Pool Theater, formerly the venue of Harvard's wildest parties. 'I'm sure you didn't notice me, actors tend to blank out faces in the audience, even familiar ones. But I was impressed. You are a very sensual performer. Not like the others. Your skin is white, but your heart is black.' It sounded even more ridiculous in the French in which it was spoken: '*Votre peau est blanche, mais votre cœur est noir*' (why on earth was he using the vous form?)

Laurent wore flamboyant used clothes whose theatrical origins Rebecca alone recognized, and he spoke in a deliberately hushed baritone prone to sudden bursts of acceleration. He made frequent reference in class to his Cameroonian bush roots, often in preface to an attack on the complacency with which whites regarded their privilege. Most students thought him charismatic, many sexy. To be flirted with by Laurent was exciting enough; to have him tell you that you were an African at heart was a tribute to be cherished.

Rebecca laughed off the compliment, and made the appropriate excuse—she had to meet her boyfriend. But later that day she saw Laurent's remark as both undeserved and vaguely unsettling. She could not deny that her performance as Vivian Ward, the hooker who wins the heart of a corporate raider, was sensual. She was amused and even proud at the judgement of the *Harvard Crimson*'s otherwise contemptuous reviewer: 'Rebecca Nicholls '00 plays Vivian with an airy, careening sexuality reminiscent of the Pool Theater's Dionysian past.' But the idea that this made her in any way African seemed almost racist. Later, she looked Laurent up on the Romance Languages department's new website. The political attitude to literature that he brought to the classroom was rooted in his work. His doctoral dissertation dealt with the influence of Frantz Fanon on the literatures of Cameroon and Senegal.

Fanon, she discovered, was the author of a book called *Black Skin, White Masks*, an account of the psychological torture inflicted on the African soul by European colonisation. And this, by a student of Fanon, was an act of misappropriation not merely brazen but profane. It was the pick-up-line equivalent of the Bible speech that Samuel L. Jackson delivered before each hit job in *Pulp Fiction*. It wasn't sexual harassment, even if Connor, the first person she told, had promised to beat the crap out of Laurent, and then, softening, had suggested she report the incident. Was it reverse racism, as her roommates—five white, one Asian-American, one mixed-race—insisted?

Her mother, annoyed at being interrupted in the midst of an account of an ad campaign she had recently created for Concordia University, told her to stop obsessing over a mere compliment, and an insipid one at that. Rebecca decided to concede this. For the rest of the semester, her relations with Laurent were silently transactional; over time, graduate teaching fellows tended to fade into each other in her memory.

On Columbus Day, 2000, the eight former roommates were to have their first reunion since graduation, at the Cape Cod house of Lydia Tilbrook, now an editorial assistant at a New York publishing house. Annabel Chung, like Rebecca, had stayed on in Cambridge after graduating, and with Connor away in England for a year, there was never any question of Rebecca living with anyone else. This Friday evening, the cars on the I-495 moved as if ploughing a rice paddy, and Rebecca wondered at how thoughtlessly her decision to room with Annabel—don't call me Anna, never anything other than Annabel— had been made.

Annabel had studied biochemistry, premed, at Harvard, and was now one month into her job at a Boston-based consulting firm that specialized in medical and pharmaceutical clients. Rebecca was already accustomed to her particular manner of talking about work. 'You wouldn't believe the kind of idiot that populates corporate America,' Annabel said, but Rebecca had better believe it, given how often she said it. 'You have no idea—*no idea*—how narrow and slow and just boneheaded some of these MDs are. There's not a chance I'm wasting my time at med school after this.'

The Cape Cod long weekend came after a week in which Annabel had been stuck in western Massachusetts at a client hospital that, she assured Rebecca, took incompetence to previously unimagined heights. She was drained and burned out and in no way looking forward to a weekend of long drinks and idle chit-chat.

'*The last fucking thing* I need now is Lydia and Christine and their endless boy talk.'

'Maybe they'll have other things to talk about now, like work.'

'That would be perfect, just perfect—a hell week at work followed by listening to Lydia tell us how arduous it is to work in *publishing*.'

The silence that followed held the illusory promise of release, but Rebecca knew that Annabel would soon find a new subject. So she switched on the radio, turning at random to a classic rock channel. This had its desired effect. Annabel's right hand shot out by reflex, and she changed stations rapidly, settling finally upon WBST, which, she later informed Rebecca, was the youngest, most intellectual and by some distance the least popular of Boston's NPR affiliates. Bizarrely, for a

Friday night, there was a call-in talk show on. A man from Malden was talking about life as the single father of twin girls. 'Not *this* shit,' said Annabel, and then, brightening, 'no, wait, I know this. It's not the show with the sex therapist. I used to listen to this in high school on Friday nights. It's called *The Lonely Hour*; it's hosted by Curtis Grimmett, an old liberal white guy who just talks about whatever interests him each weekend. I haven't heard this in years! You might like it, actually; he's obsessed with England.'

The single father from Malden was describing a set of four English children's books about a boy wizard. He had read the first three Harry Potter books aloud to his daughters, but on reading the fourth alone—having heard that the themes might be less suitable for eight-year olds—he found himself compelled as by no book since *A Separate Peace* in high school. He had gone online and discovered a small but growing community of adults who were Harry Potter obsessives.

CALLER: As you can imagine, Curtis, a father in my position doesn't really have a social life, or any kind of life outside of work and parenting at all. But this incredible woman over in Scotland has given me a community of new friends, and an interest that I can share with my daughters but also call uniquely my own.
GRIMMETT: That was Matt Pennington of Malden, who says that J.K. Rowling's magical Harry Potter books—magical in every sense—have truly changed his life. He's not the only one. With me in the studio to discuss Harry Potter as an Internet phenomenon are Jenny Springer, founder of an all-adult fan group called Harry Potter for Big Kids, and a pioneer of the online Harry Potter community; and Ezra Miller, who might just be the youngest-ever guest on *The Lonely Hour*. Ezra is thirteen years old and already a dotcom entrepreneur; he runs potterworld.com, a Harry Potter fansite visited by over fifty thousand people each month.

'Have you heard of these *Harry Potter* books?' asked Annabel.

'Vaguely.'

'I'm impressed that there's a book series you don't know all about!'

'Well, they're children's books, right? After our time.'

'Not just children's books, by the sounds of it.' Ezra Miller, whose precocity had decided to express itself as hucksterism, was arguing, in a voice far too uncracked for this time of night, that they were the most important books of our time. The *New York Times Book Review*, by creating a separate children's books bestseller list to force Harry Potter off the regular fiction list, where it had occupied the first four places, had revealed itself as hopelessly behind the times.

> MILLER: Do you know what the print run for *Harry Potter and the Goblet of Fire* was, Curtis? You know, I don't need to tell you, it was four million copies. Four million! That's four times as many copies as the *New York Times* sells. They've shown that they're a twentieth-century company. They still want to be the gatekeepers. We're living in a new world where they can't do that. Imagine that you drove a horse-carriage in 1900 and someone told you carriages would disappear in ten years. *The New York Times*, newspapers, they're the horse-carriages of today. In ten years, I'll be twenty-three, and Harry Potter would still be on the *New York Times* bestseller list, except that the *New York Times* won't exist.

'I wish they'd tell us *why* these books are taking over the world,' Rebecca said. 'All three of them just seem to take that fact for granted.'

'They've really drunk the Kool-Aid, haven't they? They sound like members of a cult. And what a group! A Jewish eighth-grader from Brooklyn, a thirty-something realtor, isn't that what she said she was? And Curtis Grimmett.'

'Four million copies though. And that's just so far. Pretty large cult.'

Grimmett was still talking as they pulled into Lydia's driveway. The girls came out two by two, their hugs were clench-tight, they had evidently left their drinks inside. The eight of them together again, but this was no reunion, Lydia said. 'This is a return to the proper state of things.'

The Alladi Lending Library was, on most days, only an eight-minute walk from home. Ten minutes for some people, but in a city of amblers Malathi made up for her small steps with determination and practical footwear. Eight minutes was enough for optimism and curiosity to soften to nostalgia, and then be brutally displaced by anxiety.

Alladi was just off Radhakrishnan Salai or, as everybody she knew still called it, Edward Elliot's Road. The 1920s bungalow, once rented, entire, by the library, had been knocked down and replaced by a three-storey commercial building. Two storeys were occupied by a diagnostic clinic that did a thriving business in ultrasounds. Alladi, she had been told, had been relegated to the basement. What else might have changed? The rules, she was sure, were the same: you borrowed each book at ten per cent of its MRP, five per cent if it was a children's book (this was determined by the book, not the age of the borrower), and you got to keep it for two weeks, after which you were charged a further ten per cent per day. No renewals, not even for *A Suitable Boy*. You had to wait two months before you could borrow the same book again. All that mattered was this: was Vimala aunty still in charge? And how would she react to the sight of Malathi before her, twenty, and asking for *Harry Potter and the Prisoner of Azkaban*?

On the first count, she had total certainty. Vimala aunty *was* Alladi. There had been a series of assistants, but no other librarian. And she fancied she knew what Vimala aunty would say. Not for her the admission of surprise, or marvelling at how Malathi had grown. For one thing, she hadn't grown more than two inches. There would be the initial reproach for Malathi having stayed away seven years; then there would be joy.

Malathi was six the first time her mother took her to Alladi. By eight she had read all the books in the primary section of her school library at least twice. She knew this said as much about the school than it did her. But it meant that every Saturday morning at 9 a.m., she was to be found waiting for Vimala aunty to open the library. She was allowed one book a week; in the summer, depending on her exam results, she could stretch this to three or, in one glorious year, four. That summer she went on all days of the week that began with a T or an S.

In those first years—those were still the 1980s—she could never think of *owning* books. Even Alladi, at an average of three rupees per book, was a luxury. Each time her mother would say: choose the book carefully, think about whether it is worth it. She knew that this meant worth the money, not the time. But as her father's business grew, he, knowing the route to his younger daughter's affection, began first to buy her books, and then to dispatch her to Landmark in Nungambakkam High Street with two hundred rupees. Buy whatever you like. Keep the change, but there never was any. Alladi couldn't compete with being able to claim possession of a book, *for all time*, as if it were part of one's own body, or rearranging one's books every day just for the sake of it, or choosing which friend to lend which book to: was she worth it? Once a week at Alladi became once a fortnight. After her mother's sudden illness and death her father was thrusting more Landmark-money at her, more often. She thought it must be his way of consolation through distraction, and wasn't sure whether to be a little guilty as she shopped; until, after about a year of this, she realized that this was no strategy. In her mother they had lost the only check on his natural liberality. When did she notice that she had stopped going to Alladi? Perhaps she never had.

She was going there now only in desperation. Landmark, where she had bought the first two books, hadn't received *Prisoner of Azkaban* yet; nor did they know when it would arrive. When she protested that the book had been out in the UK for two whole months, one sales assistant after another offered only uncomprehending silence. Drawing on a reserve of consumer indignation she didn't know she had, she demanded to see a manager. 'You know how these things are, ma'am,' he said. 'Hollywood movies take a few months to come to India. It must be the same with books. Actually it probably takes longer, movie prints don't have to come by ship.' Must be! Probably! It is your business to know these things, sir! And it takes less than a month by cargo ship from the UK to Madras. But if Landmark didn't have it, no bookshop would.

That left the memory, disinterred at this time of great need, of Vimala aunty's magic. Malathi could construct no rational account of how Alladi would possess already a book that didn't seem to have arrived in India at all. The children's section of the library had held books she had never seen anywhere else in India: *The Owl Service, A Tree Grows in Brooklyn.* Vimala aunty had kept up correspondence with children's librarians in Britain and the US. But those were older books, classics. Perhaps all she could hope for was that Vimala aunty would know how these things were done; how to order a book from abroad when even Landmark wasn't stocking it yet.

Malathi would recognize Vimala aunty anywhere, but she couldn't conjure a vision of her, only a few component parts: always a salwar-kameez, pink or red, never a sari, a tight bun of undyed hair, a Parker fountain pen, which might have been thought an indulgence except that in all the years Malathi had known her, there was only the one. What she remembered best was how Vimala aunty had loved her; what a favourite she had been. Not that the librarian ever declared affection, verbally or physically; but it is always more pleasurable to discover that one is loved by implication. She knew by the way that Vimala aunty would stop whatever else she was doing to watch Malathi as she browsed—by the questions she asked as Malathi returned the old book each Sunday ('How did you like it?' if it was something she had recommended; 'Was it any good?' if she hadn't read it herself), and by the exceptions she made to the famously inflexible rules. Malathi could borrow Agatha Christie and Georgette Heyer at the children's rate; she could borrow the books she loved best as often as she liked; when pressing *The Lord of the Rings* upon her, Vimala aunty said, 'I haven't ever read this, but it's my son's favourite book. You can have it for three weeks. Just this once.' Malathi knew that it was for her alone that Vimala aunty transgressed. Alladi, for all the wonders of its collection, attracted few children, and none of those read as Malathi did. Only Malathi enabled Vimala aunty to follow the librarian's highest calling of taking a child and building a person with books.

But as the plot where the bungalow had once stood came into view, the memories yielded, the illusion broke. The new building was a heartlessly unliterary thing, three stories of glass and grey Alucobond. Alladi hadn't even been allocated all of the basement. The new library stood opposite the open door of the men's toilet. As she entered she was appalled by something that ought to have been obvious. There were no windows. But then she heard what Vimala aunty would have said to a child Malathi: in this room are windows to every place on God's Earth, and to countless worlds beyond this one.

She couldn't know what Vimala aunty would say now. There was a single librarian's desk, at which sat a young man, no older than twenty-five, but already in possession of a lota-shaped belly that spread uncomfortably over the desk as he slept. A notebook in front of him bore the crest of Pachaiyappa's College. It was a Saturday; this might be a weekend job for a student.

'Excuse me?' She was deliberately soft. Fortunately, he wasn't a deep sleeper.

'How may I assist?'

'I'm looking for a book. *Harry Potter and the Prisoner of Azkaban* by J.K. Rowling.'

He registered nothing at this. It was scarcely better than at Landmark.

'Are you a member?'

'Yes, Malathi Venkatraman, you can look it up. It might be under S.V. Malathi.'

He opened a blue thing that looked from outside and inside to be an oversized address book. Malathi didn't remember having seen it before. Vimala aunty stamped the books as she issued them, but the directory of members and what they had borrowed, plus the catalogue of books themselves, had always appeared to exist in her head.

'No name like that here. Are you a member?'

'Yes, but I haven't come for some time. I think not since 1992. Maybe there is an older directory.'

'Oho, then you are not a member. Membership is per year only.'

'How much do I have to pay to renew my membership?'

'Nothing like renew, you have to become a member again. Three hundred rupees.'

More than the cost of buying the book, whenever it came out. How much had her mother paid, in 1985?

'Okay. But first can you let me know if you have the book I want?'

'I cannot able to do that, madam. Only for members.'

After she had paid and been given her cardboard membership card and receipt, she browsed the shelves and then the catalogue; it turned out there was one. *Philosopher's Stone* and *Chamber of Secrets* had been borrowed out; there was no mention of *Prisoner of Azkaban*. The new librarian directed her to a notebook which listed requests. If more than one person had requested a title, there was a waiting list. John Grisham's *The Testament* had been requested sixteen times. Malathi added hers.

'Does Vimala aunty still come here?'

'Who?'

'Vimala madam, I mean?' She must have initials or a surname, unknown to Malathi.

'I don't know such a person, madam. Dr Seshadri is president of the Trust. I am the librarian.'

Her father was home for lunch, waiting for her.

'How was your expedition? Did you manage to find the Henry Potter?' She had spoken of no other books for months, but he always said Henry Potter. It wasn't his little joke; he was a man who liked to say and do things properly. He always referred to the leaders of the Anglo-Saxon world as William Clinton and Anthony Blair. After all, he didn't know them personally. Malathi had said, his name is Harry, that's all he is ever called. That may be, he said, but Harry is short for Henry.

'No, they didn't have it. No one in town does. Vimala aunty wasn't even there.'

'Mrs Jagannathan? She moved to America, years ago. Her son is in the Valley, she is looking after the grandkids. Poor woman, must be bored out of her mind.'

No one had ever bothered to tell Malathi.

'What should I do about the book?'

'We will have to call your cousin in Atlanta. He can bring it with him in December. It will make a nice change from his usual stationery.' Her cousin in Atlanta was under the impression that India remained a land without pencil sharpeners or ball-point pens.

'No, chhi, I don't want the American version. All the spellings will be wrong. They even change the titles. I'll just have to wait, and pray that the wait is short.'

She only had to wait three days. The manager from Landmark called to say, who knew how fast ships travelled these days? She would be the first person in Madras with a copy.

2

By Election Day 2000 Kannan had established a daily schedule. The mornings were for debate, the evenings and most nights for fan fiction. That fall his responsibilities at work had receded almost to the point of non-existence. When work was thrust his way, he had become an expert at passing it on to someone else, either on the grounds that it wasn't his technical area or, more commonly, that he was working on a 'special project' for Eric or Brendan, the website's co-founders. No one at tailgate.com had seen Eric or Brendan in weeks. Brendan was running a quixotic campaign to rename Logan Airport after Ted Williams. Eric was rumoured to be in California, trying to sell the company or a stake in it to Yahoo!.

Kannan had been tailgate.com's third employee and first programmer. He had built the site more or less on his own; Eric always said that he and Brendan had a deep spiritual understanding of the Web, but were happy to leave the technical understanding to others. They'd never had much to do with their Indian lead programmer— after all, you couldn't talk to him about sports—but, two years and a dozen programming hires later, he continued to project the illusion of a private link to the co-founders. The 'special projects' lie never met with any scepticism.

On most days he could get away with only two or three hours of actual 'work', usually right after lunch. But he had never felt busier, or more alive. He always reached the office by eight, and spent the first hour reading and digesting the new messages on the Yahoo! group Harry Potter for Big Kids. HP4BK represented the fandom intelligentsia. It was a chatty, erudite, insular club, and at this stage it was impossible for Kannan to be more than a lurker. The active members addressed each other by nicknames, not always Harry Potter-related, made in-jokes that he rarely understood, and seemed without exception to be American and British. The British members were treated with absolute reverence. He found it impossible to tell from screen names whether a poster was male or female and, especially when the banter rose to flirtation, this discomfited him. But HP4BK was so much more elevated and sophisticated than the rest of fandom that he felt privileged even to be able to read the messages.

After catching up on HP4BK, he spent the rest of the morning in the groups and forums where he felt confident enough to post; where, indeed, he was beginning to be taken seriously, even to be respected. The Boston Gobstones Club had been founded by the radio show host Curtis Grimmett, and had offline aspirations too. Grimmett had been suggesting for some time that they meet weekly, in the 'pit' outside the Harvard T-stop.

Then there were the various Harry/Hermione groups. This was, Kannan sensed, where the real future of fandom lay: in debating 'ships', or romantic pairings. The most intense and fractious debate on HP4BK dealt with the relative merits and likelihood of Ron/Hermione and Harry/Hermione as couples. This debate had the potential to tear Harry Potter fandom apart. He had thrown his lot in with Harry/Hermione. He wasn't even sure any more why he had done so, other than perhaps out of a sense that Ron was simply too unintelligent to go with a girl like Hermione. But choosing a ship was like supporting a sports team: once you joined the tribe, leaving was not an option and loyalty was absolute. In time, you forgot why you had joined in the first place.

In his first year at tailgate.com, Kannan had stayed at the office as late as he possibly could, and gone straight home to bed. These days he left work by five, and caught the bus into Central Square to have coffee with Grimmett. He always thought of him as Grimmett, even as his friend asked to be called Curtis.

'For a long time,' Grimmett had said, 'I was deeply uncomfortable with my first name. When I was a student in England, during Vietnam, my friends noted my year of birth and, putting two and two together to make five, concluded that I had been named for Curtis LeMay.' He didn't appear to register Kannan's blank incomprehension at this name. 'They loved the irony of a leftie draft dodger being named after a trigger-happy, probably racist wingnut. The more times I told them that Curtis was my mother's maiden name, an Americanization of Kertesz, the more they insisted on addressing me as "Bombs Away!" So for many years I asked to be called Grimmett, my surname, which is the way teachers address their students at those English boys' schools. When I came back to the US, I had a new problem. I was stunned by the crass informality that had taken over our culture of addressing people. Maybe it was always there, but I didn't notice it when I was a kid. Anyway, in the late '70s, whenever I introduced myself to someone as "Curtis Grimmett", they would reply, "Nice to meet you, Curt!" The presumption of it! And the idea that in America, everyone has to be known by an amputated version of their actual name, in the quest to immediately establish intimacy. Whereas anyone who actually knew me would know how it horrified me to be addressed as Curt. But the tyranny of Curt had the wonderful effect of restoring my faith in my real name, which isn't an evocative or musical name—a Rubeus or a Severus—but contains within it the history of my mother's family and their path to America. Oh, and isn't it so fascinating that Rowling, with her wonderful gift for names—is there a finer name in all literature than Albus Dumbledore?—reserved for her hero the plainest, commonest name one could think of?' Occasionally Kannan would add a 'Curtis' at the end of a sentence, out of a slight deference, but most of the time he avoided addressing Grimmett by any name.

Kannan had never given any thought to his own name, other than a vague notion that, by comparison with his Bangalore contemporaries, he had been saddled with something too traditional. Grimmett was the first American who had insisted on saying it right. Three weeks' practice and he had perfected even the subtly interruptive double N. And he was fascinated by the south Indian naming system it exemplified, the system that rooted Kannan to Chidambaram, a town that he had never visited but that made up the first half of his name. Kannan couldn't answer any of his questions (Why does your name contain only the name of your ancestral home, and not also your father's name? How did your family make their way from Chidambaram to Bangalore?), so Grimmett read everything he could on the subject, online and in the Boston Public Library. He had come to the conclusion, he said, that Kannan was descended from a family of priests at the great Shiva temple in Chidambaram, 'where you must take me one day, or perhaps I'll be the one taking you.' Grimmett used Kannan's full name to construct for him a Harry Potter screen name: chudcannon26. 'Chud is one key away from Chid, short for Chidambaram, and "cannon", obviously, is an Americanized Kannan. You won't always be twenty-six, of course, but it's the age at which you enter Harry Potter fandom, and it's more intriguing than using your birthday or birth year. And it all adds up to you, like Ron Weasley, being a devoted fan of the Chudley Cannons.'

Today he was to visit Grimmett at home for the first time, to watch the results come in. He couldn't deny that Grimmett was a friend, as close a friend as he had known. Did this mean he'd finally made the sad journey from aloneness to loneliness? Grimmett himself was lonely, or had been before he'd met Kannan, there was no doubt. Almost fifty years in this city and his only guest for an election viewing party was someone he'd met just four months ago. He often asked about Kannan's

time at Northeastern, naturally he was curious about the experience
of the young immigrant student. At first Kannan had said only this:
his studies had kept him busy, he had no natural talent for computer
science and had to work twice as hard to make up, he had taken the
RA gig to save money. But last week he had felt an urge, not one that
he had ever consciously known, to confess. To tell his friend that the
dominating memory of the two years of his MS was the pure joy of
aloneness. He didn't expect Grimmett to understand.

Grimmett had asked Kannan with great, almost mournful,
sensitivity, 'Were you lonely? What did you miss most about home?'
Kannan had said, I was too busy to be lonely, my brother always told
me loneliness was a luxury we couldn't afford in the US. But when he
spoke at last of aloneness, Grimmett thought he understood. India
was, after all, an unceasing, manic crowd and now, with an expanding
economy, three hundred million young people driven by Darwinian
hunger, life there must be a mad contest for resources and opportunity.
He saw Kannan aged twelve in a classroom with sixty furious scribblers,
Kannan aged eighteen, buffeted by the waves of tougher people trying
to board a bus, admitting defeat. But Kannan said, no, I never really
minded crowds, or at least not consciously. I took them for granted.
Home was where I longed most to be alone.

Sometimes Kannan reminded himself that it was too early to be sure
about Curtis Grimmett. Too early to know exactly where they stood,
or how resilient the foundations. In early October they had had their
first disagreement.

Athena Alice—even they didn't know her real name—was the most
popular author in fandom. If J.K. Rowling was the most popular author
on Earth, Grimmett once said, then Athena Alice probably meant
more to more people than, say, Don DeLillo ever would (Kannan
didn't bother asking, 'Who is Don DeLillo?'). Each new instalment of
her Malfoy Chronicles—a trilogy comprising *Malfoy Manor*, *Malfoy
in Love* and *Malfoy Rex*—effectively shut down parts of fandom for

several hours as everyone stopped whatever else they were doing to read simultaneously. The latest chapter of *Malfoy Rex* had been downloaded 350,000 times on fandoms.net.

Kannan thought he liked the Malfoy Chronicles, but he wondered if he was able to separate his authentic reaction to the stories from his awareness that they were loved all the way from HP4BK down to Ezra Miller's Potterworld, and must therefore be special. And he usually failed to access the jokes that were, he was told, their chief appeal.

But with the latest chapter he had real progress to measure. He hadn't just understood the jokes; he had actually laughed at three. This allowed him to feel in genuine communion with the rest of fandom; it gave him something to look forward to discussing with Grimmett.

Kannan was at work when the scandal broke. A school librarian in Minnesota had accused Athena Alice of plagiarism. Kannan knew the gravity of that word all too well. International students, they'd been told at Northeastern, especially those from countries like India, didn't understand the concept of intellectual property. One instance of plagiarism and you'd be expelled and on the next flight back to Bangalore in disgrace. The librarian had documented twelve separate instances. Athena Alice had stolen plot lines, pilfered jokes, copied entire passages from Terry Pratchett and Tamorah Pierce.

Kannan's first thought had been of Professor McGonagall's words in *Chamber of Secrets*: 'This is the end of Hogwarts'. This was the end of fandom. He needed Grimmett to tell him it wasn't so.

But Grimmett was exultant. 'There is justice in this world,' he said. 'A great fraud is found out at last. That brave woman in Saint Paul! I wonder whether we'll remember this as Malfoygate or Athenagate or Alicegate?' He went on in this way for over a minute before he noticed Kannan's discomfort.

'But Kannan, I didn't think you were much of a fan of hers, either?'

How could Grimmett take *pleasure* in something like this? In an event that might tear fandom apart?

'All I have is a vision of life without fandom. How can there be fandom without Athena Alice? Think of the hundreds of thousands of people who love her.'

Later Grimmett would apologize, three times by email, every other day in person. But Kannan could not easily forget what he had said in the café, what must, after all, be the expression of his authentic self: 'Fandom would be *better off* without her, Kannan. No individual is indispensable to fandom other than J.K. Rowling. A fact we would all do well to remember.'

Grimmett was right—there was only one JKR, only one reason why they or anybody else was here. But the vision of a broken fandom that terrorized Kannan hadn't troubled Grimmett; and in that lay the gulf between them.

More than anything, Curtis Grimmett was surprised at the success and extent of his own dishonesty, if you could call withholding—profound and calculated withholding—an act of dishonesty. He'd thought he had no talent for it. Maybe he'd been wrong. Grimmett always preferred to avoid lying, even white lies, and especially at home. It didn't matter if it was on the phone, or in an email; the stench of it hung around for days afterward, as if from a carcass that, for religious reasons, had to be kept rotting inside the house. He hoped that withholding might fall in a separate category, morally, from lying. And these were exceptional circumstances.

The withholding, he had concluded, was unavoidable, if he was to preserve the regard Kannan obviously had for him. Who knew how the kid would react to the truth? Kannan said, repeatedly, that he had no interest in politics or history, and you couldn't find a more ignorant fellow, for his level of intellect and formal education. Kannan had even said that the Harry Potter novels were the *only* books he'd ever read, if you excluded textbooks that were written and read to be memorized, four pages at a time. He had made it through school, college and graduate school without books ever being more than an unwelcome distraction from his studies, or a duller form of entertainment than the alternatives. Grimmett hadn't known what to do with this information. I thought Brahmins were the custodians of culture, he had said: not just the educated class, but the class that hoarded knowledge. I thought reading books wasn't optional, it was life itself. Well, said Grimmett dolefully, I suppose yours is the first generation of the Indian middle class to grow up with television.

He had wondered, fleetingly, if Kannan's ignorance was representative of Indians, but this couldn't possibly be so. It must, rather, be representative of young people anywhere. They seemed to have no sense of the world having an existence and a history that preceded their own. Kannan had been born in, what, 1974? You couldn't expect him to know a thing about the world before that.

Even so, he shouldn't take this for granted. After all, Kannan had said very little about his family. What if he had grown up on stories of how they suffered under the British? What if he had a grandfather who went to jail with Gandhi? Or maybe that grandfather had fought in the jungles of Burma in the Indian National Army, with the Japanese. It could well be that Kannan knew no history except that the British were the racist colonial oppressor. His country hadn't been around even as long as Grimmett—as historical wounds went, these were orchard-fresh. They must still be brought up to it, in school, taught to hate the British like the Armenians hated the Turks, or the Eritreans the Ethiopians.

How, then, to explain to Kannan that, while he did genuinely love Harry Potter, the propulsive force behind his commitment to the cause, behind his total immersion in a community of people who looked and thought nothing like him, was his Anglophilia? *Not* the Anglophilia that surrounded him in Boston, of young women in search of their own Mr Darcy, and their parents with the trips to England to 'take in Stratford' and the Changing of the Guard, and especially not their grandparents simpering over *Upstairs, Downstairs* or *Brideshead*. Not

the New England affinity for 'the old country', with its erotic fixation
with those features of English society that had led to the creation of
the United States: royalty, land-holding patterns that had scarcely
moved on from feudalism, and, above all, 'manners', that unspeakable
euphemism for class snobbery. Grimmett despised patriotism over all
other vulgar follies, but unlike the New England Anglophiles, he did
approve of the American Revolution. In his first years back he had
said 'lift' and 'pavement' and had used British spellings at all times.
But he had come to accept that he was American, and that Anglophilia
shouldn't mean pretending otherwise.

His love was for contemporary Britain, the country that he had
known for eight indelible years, with its pulsating multiculture and
active tradition of social criticism, a simultaneously ancient and new
country in which the public institutions that were cherished national
icons were the health service and the BBC, rather than the army or
empire. Five years in Birmingham as a student and researcher, three
years in London as a publisher's reader. He had never quite come to
terms, on his return, with the thinness of contemporary life in the US;
the vast swaggering ignorance of the rest of the world; with his father,
who claimed to be a liberal and did not know a single black person, or
with patriotism, the national disease that they suffocate you with even
if you resist it, never more so than in that bicentennial year.

At first, the question of empire had hung over his Anglophilia, in the
way that he had been tormented, as a nine-year-old, by the knowledge
of Thomas Jefferson's slave-owning. But the way in which the Britain he
knew had disowned empire, without the 'moving on' that really meant
airbrushing, only deepened his love. While still recovering from war,
she had opened her doors to immigrants from all over the Empire, the
Caribbean and East African and South Asian families that would shape
the emerging multiculture that he found in Birmingham. In January
1968, eight months before he arrived in Birmingham, Harold Wilson
announced the withdrawal of British forces east of Suez, drawing a line

under his country's centuries-old pursuit of global hegemony. This, only two months before My Lai.

Grimmett had been aware, of course, of the poems of Philip Larkin, the slow funerary laments for national greatness. And of Enoch Powell, to his admirers a man who combined Cato and Cassandra in a single body; his rejection of the modern world was disguised as prophetic fire. But they were the enemy, and more importantly, they were on the wrong side of history. He had gone to Birmingham to study sociology, and soon attached himself to the Centre for Contemporary Cultural Studies. Its director, Stuart Hall, had come to Oxford as a Rhodes Scholar from the West Indies, a contemporary of V.S. Naipaul. Unlike Naipaul, he had held on to both his integrity and his accent, a rum-and-honey-soaked Jamaican baritone that made no concessions to Englishness, and added music to his hypnotic oratory. In America, this man who eviscerated the traditional, class-bound boundaries of 'culture', who laid bare the intermarriage between culture and power, would have been ostracized for his Marxism, and narrowly categorized as a black thinker, speaking to and for only the others of his race. In Birmingham and in London, he attracted admirers of all races and backgrounds, even if Grimmett himself was never close to admission into the inner circle.

The Lonely Hour had recently broadcast its 700th episode, and Grimmett had never yet forsaken an opportunity to turn his show into a celebration of Britain. But he held no illusions about his audience. Britain as it was, rather than as it had been, barely ever registered, even in Boston.

And then came Harry Potter. He bought the first two books in December 1998, on a tip from a long-time listener. They were funny, well-plotted, sometimes moving, and the products of a mind so recklessly, uninhibitedly inventive that the books themselves seemed unable to contain it. And while this J.K. Rowling had borrowed the trappings of the traditional boarding-school novel, her books were unmistakably the products of his Britain. He regretted only that he knew no children, for he would have bought copies for every child that he did. *Prisoner of Azkaban*, which he bought on release, he could recognize immediately as far more than a children's book. It was time to dedicate a show to these books. In the course of his research, he encountered Harry Potter for Big Kids.

He and Kannan must have spent—no, this sort of calculation was beyond him—well, then, *countless* hours talking Harry Potter, and yet he had no means of conceiving Kannan's relationship to the book's Britishness. Kannan might simply never think in those terms or, who knew, he might even be drawn to Britain through the books. Anglophilia of the right sort could be something they might grow to share ... but the impulse behind the withholding was too strong for Grimmett to take this chance.

Was the withholding mere selfishness, a desire to protect a friendship that gave him pleasure, and a regard, Kannan's regard, that gave him something greater than that? If it was, then in the process of protection the friendship lost, through inauthenticity, much of what it could have been. No, that wasn't right; that *could have been* was meaningless. Kannan might have been repelled by an early declaration of his Anglophilia, repelled through bemusement rather than revulsion. There was another narrative available to Grimmett, one that was obviously self-serving, but the fact of its being so didn't mean it wasn't or, rather, couldn't be true. By his withholding Grimmett had enabled and preserved a friendship, but he might also have allowed Kannan's private love for Harry Potter to deepen without the impediment of politics. Whether or not this was true, the withholding only need be temporary. In a few months—he could be sure it wouldn't take more than that—he could confess everything with no risk to their friendship.

On Election Day morning, the Harry Potter groups were as quiet as the near-empty office that had never felt less like a tailgate. Kannan was used to the theatre of elections. At home, counting day held all the hushed nervousness of a World Cup final. In May 1996, his parents had sat slack-jawed and less than a foot apart for four hours as the BJP was slowly, miraculously, revealed to have won a plurality of seats. Atal Bihari Vajpayee, the only statesman in a country of politicians, the only man capable of restoring India's self-respect, was to be prime minister. They were a hundred seats short of a majority, but the smaller parties were bound to fall in line. Kannan knew nothing of politics, except that Vajpayee was a force capable of silencing his mother, uniting his parents and invigorating his father all at once. He was prime minister for thirteen days.

Eight hours to Grimmett's. Until then, he had no choice but to invert the usual order and spend the day reading fanfic. He calculated that he had spent more hours talking to this white, fifty-four-year-old radio talk-show host than anyone else he had ever known, other than Santhanam perhaps. Longer by far than with his mother or grandmother, who had never offered conversation.

Five-thirty and Kannan rang the doorbell. Evidently Grimmett had tenants who occupied the first floor. In India, they would have called it the ground floor. He had started to think of these things the American way; Santhanam would be proud. He realized now that apart from giving him the address, Grimmett had never said anything about his house. Like all the others on this street, it had two storeys, and a porch too small for sitting in, a feature he had noted all over this city, and one that always made him think of his maternal thatha's house in Salem. Those broad, canopied verandas in front and back were spaces of both welcome and refuge. But even if these American porches had been large enough, he couldn't see anyone sitting in them: here, houses were for living inside, not outside.

From the outside, the house bore no imprint of its owner. Upstairs was another matter. It was less like an apartment than like a used bookstore that also dabbled in records. It had been a decade or more since Kannan had seen an LP outside of a shop. His mother would have called it cluttered, the home of a vague, careless man, but it was anything but. She measured objects in a house by number and utility, not by organization or coherence. Knowing Grimmett, these books and records must be rearranged often, each time the subject of fierce attention. Then there was a wall of labelled cassette tapes. Grimmett would describe these as recordings of radio shows, most of them from BBC Radio 4, formerly known as the Home Service and, by either name, the Platonic ideal of talk radio.

In the week since Grimmett had proposed this meeting, and in all the quiet hours of today, the apartment had resisted Kannan's attempts at visualization. Kannan had no truck with expectations, they were only the preconditions for disappointment. But when looking forward to an event, he would place himself there, a few days in advance. When this worked, it meant that he had scoped out the place. Everything was easier when done for the second time. This was a very different business from expectations, which are always some combination of our hopes and fears, and, for most of us, tend inexorably towards the former. But while Kannan could visualize the conversation, the food and drink, even the way Grimmett sat when at home, he couldn't see inside the apartment itself.

So it was that the onrush of familiarity was as unexpected as it was comforting. At first he thought, this is a self-serving illusion, I am trying to deny that I could not visualize. And next: maybe I could not see it, because there are some things I can't see, but I knew it because I know Grimmett. Third came what must be the truth: it is partly that I know Grimmett, and partly it is the lack of usable furniture. This was what removed Grimmett's apartment from America and placed it in Bangalore or Madras. There was a kitchen table that sat, at best, three, a single coffee table that served as a magazine rack, and two armchairs at forty-five degrees to the fireplace, the frayed ottoman between them piled with books, the first three *Harry Potters* heading each pile. That was all, so he didn't have to ask Grimmett where to sit. And as he had seen himself doing, he chose a Sam Adams, the likeliest match between his own tastes and Grimmett's silent approval.

With hours left until polling stations closed, the TV networks had nothing to do except interview voters as they left the booth. Grimmett was supposed to spend this time bringing Kannan up to speed on the election and its stakes. He began to explain how the results in most states were a foregone conclusion, which was why the networks were focusing exclusively on those up for grabs, the swing states. Kannan had to rescue him; having used the election as a pretext for the meeting, there was no way Grimmett would voluntarily shirk his duty. 'We've got plenty of time for you to tell me about that later. Was there something else? You look like you have news.' This was only half-untrue. Grimmett always had news, after all. And Kannan knew that his own news, the delivery of which he had spent a week visualizing, would be more compelling to Grimmett than any Muggle election.

'Well, since you insist ... Actually, before that, I have a shameful confession to make. I don't think I'd be a very enlightening or insightful election guide. I've grown detached from politics, meaning the sport of electoral party politics, rather than political issues. The way we do it in this country, in particular, the unending, unedifying television spectacle ...' Kannan knew that Grimmett could have gone on for hours about the election. He tended to know more about the things that he claimed ignorance of than most people did while claiming expertise. But in rescuing his friend he felt an advance. It must have happened gradually, but he recognized it only now. He couldn't have done it a month ago.

'My news is fandom-related. It has to do with the ongoing fallout from the Athena Alice thing.' To Kannan's shock and relief, the scandal had only grown Athena's legend. Her friends succeeded in constructing her as a victim. The plagiarism was only the unfortunate consequence of her rushing each chapter in an attempt to placate her fans. Some people, they implied, just resented her fame, or the fact that they were not in some imagined Inner Circle of her friends.

Now Grimmett began to speak of the opportunity the scandal presented. fandoms.net had suspended Athena Alice and taken her fics down. HP4BK could take advantage of the fics' temporary unavailability to set up their own website. With exclusive access to the Malfoy Chronicles, they would have an immediate audience. Theirs would be the first site in fandom to publish only the best, to curate and edit every fic until it was worthy of Harry Potter. Then he paused for dramatic effect. This wasn't like Grimmett, whose conversation generally went like an express train on a curved path: digressive, but no stops.

He had paused now because he had hoped to excite Kannan: this new site was to be a home for Kannan, a place where Kannan could, in time, be a star. He wanted to confirm that he had succeeded. But Kannan wanted only to carry out the conversation that he had visualized.

'Curtis'—by opening with his name, in the requested but still unnatural form, he was sure to redirect Grimmett's attention—'do you remember last week, when we were talking about Hermione, about the dynamics of the Trio?'

Last week Kannan had proposed that Harry and Hermione, not Harry and Ron, was the deepest and most essential friendship within the Trio. He suspected his friend would approve: the subject of Hermione, 'her unfathomable depths of wisdom and generosity,' was prone to send Grimmett into deep reverie, his eyes glazed and wrists cocked, fists rhythmically knocking together as he contemplated the ultimate reality of the universe. Kannan was not quite ready to propose things that Grimmett was likely to disagree with. But Grimmett didn't look softly moved in the way that he should; he looked sharp, and critical in a way Kannan didn't recognize, and he took much longer than usual to speak, and when he did he said that not only was that quite right, but there was a post in it, a post that shouldn't be left unwritten. And Kannan had posted to Gobstones, but he had known that Grimmett had meant something else, he had meant that Kannan was ready. Over the week that followed, Kannan had come to agree.

The interruption seemed to delight Grimmett. 'I'm not likely to forget a thing like that. Were you unhappy with the replies?'

'No, they were as you'd expect, with Gobstones. But I've been thinking that I should have sent that to HP4BK instead.' He paused, to watch Grimmett as much as to let him respond, but Grimmett said nothing, he only switched the position of his feet, which he always crossed at the ankles.

'But it might have been a good thing, actually, that I didn't. I wanted to ask you about another idea I have for a first post on HP4BK.' And he paused again, not knowing why he kept doing it when he had visualized this conversation so many times. But visualizing wasn't scripting, and it might be, he saw, that he simply wasn't used to issuing so many uninterrupted sentences.

'Are you waiting for me to say something, Kannan? If not, please keep going; can't you see I'm on tenterhooks?'

And the sentences came out of Kannan uncatchable, like breaths rather than words: each time he was conscious of not knowing quite what he had just said, as if he couldn't hear himself. This meant that later he would remember not what he had actually said but only what he had intended to say. His first post on HP4BK would posit a theory of Harry Potter in which J.K. Rowling was not the last word but merely the first, the prime mover, the originating genius, the only possible creator. And the wonder of fandom, and of fan fiction in particular, was of a universe in rapid, later gradual, but perpetual expansion, its developing boundaries well beyond even the creator's conception. He would lay out, as no one had ever done that he had seen, what it was they might all be doing.

He had visualized all this as a conversation, Grimmett driving as ever, Grimmett saying at least two words for every one of his. Not as the first, hopefully only, monologue of his life.

At first Grimmett said only, 'That's a remarkably beautiful way of putting it, Kannan.' And then another unfamiliar silence, one that, later, Kannan saw as Grimmett's way of saying, right now I don't want to help or teach you, I simply admire what you've said. Briefly, Kannan felt like Harry to Grimmett's Dumbledore, his awe at the older man's omniscience suspended, in that glorious moment, by his knowledge that he had genuinely moved Grimmett. But as he saw Grimmett's left eye twinkle with a solitary tear, he had to look away, to the TV. The sound had been on throughout but it was only now that he registered that, in the eastern states, the polls had closed. He looked back to his friend, and saw that they were ready to begin the work of drafting the post.

3

Rebecca had arrived at the spring of her senior year with no career plans whatsoever. Her conception of life as inevitably non-linear, indeed sinuous, was inherited from parents for whom, both individually and as a couple, peripateticism was a source of identity.

Philip Nicholls was now a professor of political philosophy in Toronto, but not before brief careers in law and the Peace Corps and an abandoned PhD in economics. His only fixed instinct being a distaste for the intellectual life of his native country, he took up teaching appointments in three continents. While living in Beirut, forty and already seven years divorced, he met and married Liz, ten years younger and teaching high-school English. She had gone to college pre-med but ended up majoring in French and Spanish—she knew only that she wanted to travel—and had worked as an au pair in France and as a language tutor in New York before landing her job in Beirut through an uncle at the American embassy. It was only in Toronto, in an unexpected new job as an advertising copywriter, that she had put down roots. 'What other people call drifting is what I call living,' she had told Rebecca on her first day of college.

'They confuse plans with life. As always, Dylan said it best: *life* is what happens when you're busy making other plans.'

A twelve-year-old Rebecca might have said: Liz, that was John Lennon. At eighteen she knew to let it pass. For Liz Nicholls, Bob Dylan was assumed to be the source of all real wisdom.

They had conceived Rebecca in Beirut, but she was born in London. Annabel accused her of introducing this second fact into conversation rather more than was necessary. 'Every time someone mentions the word London, you don't *have* to say you were born there.' When she started at Harvard in the fall of 1996, the Nicholls' move to Toronto, when she was nine, divided her life neatly into two. She didn't feel especially English or Canadian, but her background was precisely exotic enough. As her friend Lydia put it: 'An American who's never known America—you're straight out of Henry James or Edith Wharton!' Of course, Rebecca did know America, in the way a child at boarding school knows her family. Every summer and winter was spent between grandparents' houses in the Baltimore and Philadelphia suburbs, places that, given how much time she had spent there, she knew with a strange vagueness. Each year at college brought the death of another grandparent, moments at which she was struck by the lack of detail, visual or otherwise, in her memories of the American parts of her childhood. The summers, in particular, seemed shapelessly dull. As a child she must have thought them a form of penance before real life resumed each September.

But on one decisive occasion, Rebecca chose to opportunistically play up her dual identity as simultaneously American and not-American. In the fall of her sophomore year, she had applied to work for the Admissions Office as a tour guide. Competition, even by Harvard standards, was intense: few campus jobs paid better, and none was considered more pleasant. At the interview, when asked what qualities separated her from her fellow undergraduates, she remembered Lydia and, almost choking on the sheer humbug of the thought, said, 'I'm an American, but I grew up outside the US, on two continents. So I can understand where both American and international applicants are coming from.'

For almost three years, Rebecca led families—generally a high-school junior or senior with their parents—on a walking tour of Harvard Yard and Harvard Square.

She liked best the applicants who were willing to linger wide-eyed with her at the Yard's Quincy Street gate, standing halfway between modernist masterpieces by Corbusier and Henry Moore, without showing any recognition of either name. Moving up Quincy, pointing briefly at Sever Hall, the desiccated work of Henry Hobson Richardson, she stopped them again on the sidewalk between Memorial Hall, its lonely Gothic presence like a vestige of another, abandoned future for Harvard, and the unloved brutalism of the Graduate School of Design.

One afternoon in the fall of her senior year, Rebecca paused on the sidewalk in front of the Graduate School of Design and was about to deliver her spiel when she decided that the pair in front of her were not in fact mother and son, or indeed related at all. For one thing, the boy, whose silence throughout the walk she had taken, perhaps unjustly, for Asian deference, looked Korean; the woman, who had asked a series of questions that could not all be of personal interest, was Chinese. Evidently, Rebecca was not expected to tell the difference. 'I'm Connie and this is Richard,' was all the woman had said by way of introduction. Concluding that this woman would, in time, reveal her secret, she carried on with the tour.

Back at the admissions office, Connie asked Rebecca if she had any definite plans for life after graduation. 'If you don't, you should come work with us. If you do, change those plans; you're too good a fit for this business.' The left half of her business card was a logo: *IvyEdge*. The right half: *Connie Zhou, Founder and CEO*, with a phone number and an address on Commonwealth Avenue in Back Bay. Rebecca didn't have to ask what sort of business this was. On 14 August 2000, less than a year after serving as Connie's tour guide, she started work as a college admissions consultant at IvyEdge.

For four years she had been physically present in New England without ever relinquishing her status as an American abroad. Yet now, at twenty-three, she was about to settle into American life itself, for Britain would not have her. Harvard offered, in the form of a number of one-year fellowships for graduate study in the UK, the glorious prospect of postponing real life in favour of a year of drinking that somehow ended with the conferring of a degree. These fellowships seemed like nothing else she had ever encountered to have been designed especially for her. She applied to over a dozen, including ones for Celtic studies and international human rights. Connor agreed to defer his management consulting job in Boston for a year. They could spend the breaks between terms travelling Europe. These British terms seemed so short, it was almost as if the terms were the breaks.

She was rejected by every fellowship. Celtic studies and human rights didn't even interview her; she could understand that, those applications had been transparently opportunistic. She had never been rejected before, not even by something or someone she didn't want. With her more-than-decent grades and recommendation letters, she was a victim of the judges' weakness for cynical resume-padders and their perverse construction of the principle that fellowships ought to go to the most 'deserving', understood to mean disadvantaged or even just non-white. Only this explanation survived a thorough analysis of the names of the fellowship winners, which included the founder of an anti-AIDS NGO in Kenya and the American, of Han Chinese parents, president of Harvard Students for a Free Tibet. Connor didn't bother with fellowship applications: his parents were happy to pay for his masters' in international political economy at the LSE.

This was, she later decided, the first of only two times that Connor ever surprised her. He, who had never thought of going to England before she suggested it, now refused to even consider giving up his year in London. His prep school had had an exchange programme with Eton that his parents had refused to send him on—having heard his classmates drone on about Lord's and the Wall Game, he was not going to turn down another chance to experience England. This story had the translucent quality of hastily constructed myth, but Connor stuck to it. If she couldn't find a way to join him in London, she was best off finding a job in Boston, where he would visit her over Christmas and Easter, and join her for good the following July.

A long weekend with Connor's family in Belmont was all civility, sometimes warmth, even if she could never quite read his mother, a champion rower in her youth and now a proficiently unrevealing talker. She gave Rebecca a pearl necklace, a goodbye present, since 'I guess we won't see you for a while with Connor in London.' And then the traditional trips with their roommates: Connor to China and Japan, Rebecca and the girls to Italy, staying in cheap hotels or the better class of hostel. Lydia, whose senior thesis in History and Literature had dealt with English literary representations of the Grand Tour, insisted on referring to their drab Florentine hostel as the 'Pensione Bertolini', but she was disappointed in her vigilant lookout for serious-looking young Englishmen.

Annabel started work two days after they had moved into their new apartment. Rebecca's late start date at IvyEdge gave her four weeks with no duties bar decorating. They occupied the second floor of a triple-decker on Columbia Street, their neighbours upstairs and downstairs all graduate students at MIT. The place was large, by Cambridge standards, although this characterless patch of mid-century Cambridge, only a mile east of Harvard Square, known as Area 4 for statistical purposes and claimed by hopeful but inaccurate realtors for either Central or Inman Squares, was no Cambridge that she knew. Actually, it wasn't quite characterless: it had the wan character of no man's land, in between Central, Inman and MIT, no longer semi-industrial but also not on the way to being anything else. The apartment itself was shabby, not quite derelict, because dereliction implied a superior previous state, and she imagined that it had already looked thirty years old when first built. But it had plenty of light, and could—with her mother's advice—be rapidly uplifted.

And now the days stretched forward before her as long and thin as reeds. If, in thinking of her life, she had consciously organized time at all, it had been in academic years and their components: fifth grade, sophomore year, senior spring. For the first time since early childhood, she could live in days. She could read for pleasure, for the first time in years, although sadly not in the park across the street, which looked as if it had once been fit for that purpose, but by steady utilitarian encroachment—a basketball court, a running track, a softball diamond—was no longer.

Initially in search of books, she set forth into Boston. She had always been aware of how slightly she knew the city. The 'Harvard bubble' excluded almost totally the city beyond. The cities she had lived in, London and Toronto, she could never fully know—indeed, to be condemned to fall just short of knowing a place was what it meant to live in a great city. Boston's sheer intimacy seemed at first to disqualify it from any claim to greatness. In two weeks of walking, she felt not only that she knew Boston but that she could hold a model of it in her hand. It wasn't a mere matter of size, even though she could walk to anywhere in the city in an hour—unlike Paris, where she had spent a summer in high school, Boston did not make up in intensity what it lacked in scale. The Paris of the arrondissements was tiny, but it resisted knowledge just as fiercely as London.

The offices of IvyEdge were the converted third floor of a townhouse. Connie Zhou, her husband—a partner at a white shoe law firm—and their twin daughters, aged eleven, lived below.

Connor, quoting his father, liked to describe Boston as 'the most European city in the United States', and Rebecca saw Back Bay first as an ersatz version of Kensington or a particularly Haussmanized Parisian neighbourhood. On closer inspection, it was rescued by the incompleteness of its imitation; it lacked the self-confident uniformity of those places. The houses were brownstone or red-brick in roughly equal proportions, but they bore the imprint of the urge to distinctiveness. Each facade was marked by flights of fancy—stucco work or an unusably small balcony—details that made no attempt at consistency. And no one could deny the watercolour-prettiness of this stretch of Commonwealth Avenue, the road divided into two by parkland lined with statuary, leading all the way to the Public Garden. In the office, though, only Connie's room was park-facing.

Rebecca was one of three new recruits, all women. Their arrival doubled IvyEdge in size; Connie had used a network of freelancers in the past, but with demand for college consulting exploding, she had decided to aggressively expand the firm, in particular by seeking clients outside its Boston catchment area, in New York City and the better prep schools of the Northeast. On that first day, Connie addressed the team in a tone simultaneously confessional and conspiratorial. Rebecca felt like an intelligence agent being briefed for a field mission.

'I'm guessing that you may have worried, or perhaps your friends or families have asked you, about the moral implications of admissions consulting. That we're exacerbating the inequality of opportunity. That we're impeding the meritocratic process of college admissions. That we're counteracting noble initiatives like need-blind admissions and inner-city outreach programmes by giving the children of the rich an unfair advantage. Let me tell you, you have nothing to worry about, because it's hard to tell which of these arguments is the biggest pile of horseshit. There is nothing meritocratic about elite college admissions policies. They're not even trying to be meritocratic. Take Harvard, for instance. Oh yes, Rebecca, I know you all want to think everyone earns their way in through ability and hard work, but let's get real. They could institute a rigorous admissions test, or even just use the SAT, and meritocratically admit students that way, based on pure academic ability—no racial or ethnic or class selection involved. Instead they reserve just a part of their class for meritocracy and select the rest through quotas—people from Massachusetts, legacies, athletes, Hispanics, African-Americans. It's the same at Princeton or Columbia or Amherst or Stanford. Your qualities as an individual applicant are less important than your membership of the ethnic group you were born into—nothing could have less to do with merit. And our clients—some of them white, often Jewish, or Chinese or Korean or South Asian—were born into the wrong groups. These colleges have undisclosed quotas to limit the number of Asians—it's just like the Jewish quotas of eighty years ago, except there's no public outcry since these are Asians we're talking about. And it's not just the quotas. They ask applicants to write essays about their background and personal experiences. And they lap up those sob stories about growing up with a Dominican single mother—uneducated but full of inner strength—and six elder siblings, one of them addicted to crack, and seeing gang violence on the streets and dreaming about Harvard. They don't even care if they're true! If anything, we're making things *more* meritocratic by helping our clients best express their talents. Unlike some other firms, we don't take on every student who comes to us. I'm not interested in some rich lacrosse player who wants us to write his essays. We take on kids who have demonstrated excellence but need help to gain an edge in the admissions process. That's a term from finance, by the way—we provide that edge through better knowledge, better preparation, and a deeper understanding of admissions offices.'

Rebecca had heard variants of these claims before from Asian-American friends. Annabel was especially exercised by the fact that a prep school–educated child of black Harvard alums benefited just as much from the quotas as the disadvantaged inner-city students they were designed to encourage. By restricting the number of Asians, she said, Harvard was trying to pretend that the population of the best and the brightest looked, at least in ethnic terms, more or less like American society in general. This was a versatile fantasy; it assuaged liberal white guilt while simultaneously reproducing the white elite by unfair means.

Rebecca watched Connie, without looking away, for any sign that her declaration of moral fervour was ungenuine. At five foot two you could keep most of her in close vision, her bright, puffy, unlined face and her sturdy, straight, pant-suited figure. She was like a cathedral whose stone walls left you confused as to whether they were acid-aged imitation Gothic, or the flawlessly preserved real thing.

The work began.

Through the end of October and the early application deadlines to the best schools, Rebecca had been busy, busier than she had thought possible at such a job, and too busy to dwell much on Connor and his life in London. They had bought international calling cards and spoke at least every other day. Speaking so often, especially when their days were repetitive, meant that conversations tended to lapse into dull particulars that didn't sum to any mutual understanding of their new lives. She thought of those couples in earlier times, writing letters every week or two weeks, letters that often crossed paths, each one a narrative, slowly and deliberately constructed—or not so, if the writer was like Connor. And in the weeks spent waiting for a new letter, the last one would be reread and reread, each line committed to memory like a poem. Sure, she and Connor had it easier. But she wasn't sure phone calls were any better than letters at bridging distance.

And then, at the start of November, there was an email from Connor as long and detailed as any letter. Its subject line was blank, and it began with several paragraphs about his studies and life in London, written with an enthusiasm never so evident over the phone. Perhaps emails were the answer, then—doing the job of letters without the waiting. She wondered what had finally prompted this one. And then she came to the final, longest paragraph:

> So, as you can see it's been a really eventful first term in London and I've learned a lot about myself. And I've been thinking a lot about us, and I've come to the conclusion that it's best we break up. We had two great years together and I'll always feel so privileged just to have known such a beautiful and funny and intelligent woman,

let alone to have been with her. But our lives are clearly pulling in different directions now. I'm looking at whether I can stay on here after this year. BCG have a London office, with a lot of opportunities for European travel. Also, I met someone here and we really clicked. It's so hard for anyone to compare with you but I think she and I have more in common, especially the way my life seems to be going. Anyway, I really want to stay friends. This is what's best for both of us. In the days ahead I'm more than willing to talk about all of this. Just give me a call.

love
C

For the first time in her conscious life, Rebecca confronted the world with a plea for sympathy. She had long seen herself, with quiet pride, as being in this respect quite unlike everyone else. The problem with seeking sympathy was not only the appearance of weakness but, even more abhorrent, the inevitable loss of control. And she knew that by not debasing her currency of emotional need, she had ensured that if she ever did need consolation, she would get it.

She reached out first to the two people whose sympathy was hardest-won. Her father said only, 'If you allow this to affect you in any serious way, you'll be setting feminism back half a century,' and hung up the phone. She knew there would be an email later. Professor Nicholls relied upon email attachments, as he once had on post, to convey his feelings to his daughter without having to say anything himself. When, as a freshman, she had threatened to concentrate in social anthropology, he sent her a paper by Martha Nussbaum denouncing cultural relativism. The news that she was dating a final-club jock was met with a selection from Heloise's letters to Abelard, and her decision to join IvyEdge by Marx's *Economic and Philosophical Manuscripts of 1844* and *On the Jewish Question*. This time, there was to be no email. Four days later, a package arrived with her father's annotated first edition of *The Feminine Mystique*, accompanied by a handwritten note: *Don't tell me nothing has changed.*

Annabel was away on work, in Cleveland, and by the time she got through to her, Rebecca had been single for twelve unconsoled hours. For once, Annabel was genuinely shocked. But shock soon gave way, not to sympathy, but to a perverse fascination. 'Wow,' she said. 'I always said Connor had zero personality. And it turns out he's a cold-hearted asshole.'

There was sympathy later, great treacly masses of it, from her other roommates and from her mother. Connor had surprised everyone. Liz Nicholls, remembering the gift of the necklace, speculated that his mother had put him up to it. 'And if those milquetoast suburbanites think that you're not good enough for their son, darling, then good riddance to him and to them.' Rebecca remembered why she hadn't gone in for sympathy before.

But had she ever needed to? Certainly not since the age of sixteen, her Paris summer, when she had her braces taken out and dyed her hair red for the first time. She had never been broken up with before, had never gone more than a few days single without seeing a queue of suitors spring up before her. She'd often wondered whether, if Connor ever did break up with her—a purely academic exercise, since it could never happen—she'd be wounded more by a first, unexpected rejection than by losing him. And now she had her answer. The shock of rejection, even in this ruthless way, wounded much less than losing Connor. Connor, whose steadfast reliability Annabel had taken for dullness. Who would get absolutely hammered at parties and then solemnly declare to his final club brothers that having Rebecca made him, without question, the luckiest man alive. Who, inspired by one silent disapproving look from her, worked himself up to being a more than decent dancer. The way he applied himself to everything, to her most of all. The two of them every night, his taut, flexible diver's body with its Corinthian columns of lean muscle contorted towards the sole purpose of giving her pleasure. And the sexual quality that made him most unlike any other man she had known: his freakish recovery, the way his climaxes were followed not by lethargy but, only minutes later, by the desire and ability to go at it again. Connor, who was more likely to change genders than to break up with her. And she had built her life around him. She was in a ridiculous job, a petty and contemptible job, all so that she could be in Boston waiting to receive her man on his return. Her father was right: it was disgustingly pre-feminist. But she had done it, had been happy to do it. Or at least had thought little of doing it.

Then there was the matter of the word 'love', and of the phrase 'I love you'. She remembered the time he had first said it: after sex, about a month after they had started dating. She had said 'I love you too,' of course. What else did you say in that situation? Say nothing, or say 'you're very sweet', and you needlessly filled the air with awkwardness. Taken seriously, it was ludicrously premature, and could not possibly be meant. But it was really just a thing couples said; no more than the socially required form of 'I like you', a way to end phone calls and punctuate sex. Over time she didn't come to grant it any greater weight, even as she saw that Connor really did think that he loved her. And now she felt the full cumulative force of all those weightless I love yous.

She didn't even know whether or not to call. On one level it was absurd to not talk about it, not seek a proper explanation. But that was all she could hope for, an explanation, a defence. Not a conversation— his email made that much clear. Two years together, ended by his decision and his announcement of that decision. How long had he been thinking of this? Probably since he met this girl whom he had more in common with, whom he couldn't even bother to name. He hadn't given her a chance to decide with him, or even let on that he had any doubts or concerns about their relationship. She had fancied herself the impenetrable one. Connor was an open book, but he was always denied access to her deepest thoughts, such as the insincerity of her I love yous. But she had planned her future around him without knowing anything of what he now felt.

She wouldn't call. She was not going to demean herself by pleading pathetically that he give it a chance, that he sublimate his decision into a conversation. And if she didn't plead, but asked for an explanation, she would end up hearing all about the new girl. There would be plenty of time for that later, for an obsessive curiosity towards the girl who had usurped her place. But now she wanted to hear nothing about her. She summoned what she hoped was a very considerable amount of dignity, and replied to the email. She didn't pretend to be anything other than heartbroken. But since he thought he had the right to simply decide, and that he owed her nothing, there was nothing to talk about. She wished him and his new love well.

The day Betty Friedan arrived in the mail, Annabel returned from Cleveland with two hardcover sets of the four Harry Potter books. 'These are the books Curtis Grimmett was talking about on *The Lonely Hour* that time,' she said. 'I hear they're really addictive. I don't have any work this weekend, and I thought this might be more fun for us than going out.' In the weeks between the Cape Cod retreat and Connor's email, Rebecca couldn't recall having ever thought about Harry Potter or Curtis Grimmett's show. Lydia and Christine had sent flowers, accompanied by a card demanding that she visit them in New York before Thanksgiving. She spent two hours rereading Connor's email and her reply, wondering if she had been too quick to think it definitive, whether there was any phrase that suggested an opening. But no, there was nothing. Annabel told her to get off the computer and, when she did not, forcibly switched off the CPU. Embracing defeat, Rebecca got into bed with *Harry Potter and the Sorcerer's Stone*.

4

It had taken Kannan eleven months to draft that first post to Harry Potter for Big Kids, taken him all that time even if he typed the thing itself in fifteen minutes. That evening, as they waited, separately, for the replies to come in, Grimmett typed several emails of his own, addressed not to the group as a whole but to the half-dozen members he had come to know best. The members whose humanity and intellect he had most regard for, and whose regard for him was unmistakable, as tacky as it was to acknowledge it.

He saved each one as a draft, for now. They were lightly individualized, but they all made the same claims and appeal. chudcannon26, I know him IRL, he is in fact a friend. He's not used to doing this sort of thing. That's putting it too mildly: he's never been in any sort of community, never felt that the broadcast of his thoughts was a possibility, much less a right. Some of us can settle into a group like this as easily as if we were passing between different rooms of our homes. He is not of a background that allows for such comfort. I can only guess at how much this post has required of him. Up until now, he has looked on HP4BK through a one-way mirror. But he has felt this exclusion not as envy but as reverence. Now he has entered, and what happens immediately after is crucial. If he is ignored, he may retreat behind the one-way mirror, I fear forever. And I want to impress upon you how much will be lost if we allow that to happen. All of us love Harry Potter beyond measure, but even in this company he stands out for the visceral force of his love (he didn't expand on this, didn't talk about how perhaps one could best understand Kannan's love for Harry Potter through the bhakti tradition of his ancestors—that would be meaningless to them), for his knowledge, for his insight. And that insight, that vision, would deepen exponentially if he were properly admitted and given encouragement. Beyond even the magic on the pages of Harry Potter is its emancipatory power. For the first time in all human history we have a cultural object of real aesthetic value from which no one, whatever their background, need be excluded. If we do what we must, and it asks little of us, then Kannan, and soon others like him, will feel the wind of Harry Potter at his back, pushing him beyond the one-way mirror, irrevocably into the warm heart of our social and cultural life. He'll never be an outsider again.

Kannan had sent his post at 10.15 p.m., which was fandom prime time. The member-parents had put their children to bed, and even early sleepers were around for one last look at HP4BK. Grimmett gave himself two hours. If by then Kannan had made no impression, he would send the emails.

For the first half-hour he stepped away from his desk, so as to avoid refreshing his inbox obsessively. In the meantime he turned to an old favourite, one of a handful of radio recordings he could count on to divert his attention at a time like this: Paul McCartney's 1982 appearance on *Desert Island Discs*. Halfway through John Lennon's 'Beautiful Boy'—it was meant to be the emotional centrepiece of the episode, but this time he wasn't as moved as usual—he allowed himself a look at his watch, and then he walked back to the desk. In twenty-eight minutes there were eleven new messages on HP4BK. Nine of them were responses to Kannan. This on a group in which there were usually at least six discussions going on at once.

The early replies all began with welcomes, some of them cautious: 'If I'm not mistaken, I haven't seen you post here before.' Chudcannon26 wasn't a distinctive name, but nothing new escaped this lot. It was truly a club. And then:

> I hesitate to ever say that somebody is speaking for JKR herself, but suffice it to say that, for the first time, I feel like someone is speaking for all of fandom. This at a time when we're becoming so divided.
>
> Before I try to add your point, which was so beautifully expressed that maybe there's no point trying to add anything, I just wanted to say thank you.
>
> I feel like your post really speaks to what we're all doing here, why this isn't just a writer and her fans, this is so much more.
>
> I struggle every day to explain to people what I'm, no, what we're, doing here. What fandom is, what it's for, why it's important, why it's beautiful. I rarely even try because I fail to explain to myself first. Now I have the words.

Even the three replies that offered disagreement did so in a tone of genuine respect, a tone so rare on HP4BK that it felt imported from some other fandom or earlier time. They admired the force of his point, they were moved by it, but they wanted to remind everyone that we shouldn't get above our station. JKR has the last word; we're just waiting on it.

The twelfth reply came from Perdita, an author of Harry/Hermione fan fiction that Grimmett knew to be among Kannan's favourites. For the first time since Grimmett started reading he was nervous. For most of her post she looked to be on the side of the critics. Why her, of all people? Then he came to the end:

> But I don't think you ever meant to say that we in fandom are taking over from JKR. Would you allow me to tweak your metaphor?

Let's say JKR is the first *and* the last word, but we're here to fill
up so much of the space in between and as you said, to expand in
all directions. In the end it's not a question of ownership, but of
belonging, and you've helped us all see that.

Before writing those unsent emails, as he'd waited, at home, for Kannan
to post, Grimmett had allowed himself to wonder how they might
celebrate a success. He wouldn't explicitly propose a celebration, of
course, but he wanted Kannan to see that he understood the moment's
significance. Best to do something both different from their usual
routine and on Kannan's terms.

Hadn't Kannan played basketball in India? They could go see the
Celtics. Grimmett had only done that once, in high school, for a friend's
birthday. All seven of them were going for the first time, and all with
the same prayer: to see 'Red' Auerbach light the cigar that signalled his
certainty that the game was won. All Grimmett remembered of that
day was that the Celtics lost. But the others with him, he was sure, had
told sons and maybe now grandsons of the first time they saw Coach
Auerbach light his victory cigar. If he had descendants, he thought, he'd
have a better story for them. He would say that he was at the old Garden
the one time that Red lit too soon. Red lit up, the Boston thousands
leered at the opposing coach with their reflected contempt, and the
Celtics went on to lose.

Or they could go to an Indian restaurant. Up until now Grimmett
had avoided the sad predictability that this would surely represent. Now
it would feel different, and even if Kannan scorned the food, it would
be his judgements that shaped the tone of the evening. But best of all
would be some way of getting Kannan himself to choose the manner
of the celebration. Grimmett longed to change the pattern of their
friendship, to yield control, to achieve a balance in which he gained
nothing by his own age and race. It was easier when one person made
the decisions. Easier for Kannan too. But easy wasn't right, and in the
long run, he knew that their present arrangement would circumscribe
the friendship.

Now they had something to celebrate, something beyond any of his own fantasies. He could remember few, if any, posts on HP4BK that had elicited such appreciation. By a first-time poster? Unthinkable. Kannan was sensible enough to know that not every post would be received similarly. But he had been admitted, and need never leave again.

Grimmett had thought he would be happier even than Kannan at this, his jubilation unmixed with shock. And he was happy, he must be happy, but he was unable to fix his mind to that happiness, as horror at himself arrived and spread itself everywhere happiness ought to have been. Those emails contained all anybody ever needed to know of his arrogance, his narcissism, his patronizing disloyalty. How could he have ever thought that Kannan needed any help from him, let alone backchannel machinations that took the form of begging letters? Two explanations offered themselves, and he couldn't measure the more unpalatable. Either he was truly guilty of placing himself above Kannan by virtue—although in this case he meant by sin—of his age, his Americanness, his cultural capital and, yes, his race. Or he was unable to allow Kannan autonomous life, and wanted to consider himself responsible for Kannan's success. It must be both. The only consolation was that the scale of the horror suggested the possibility, however remote, of improvement. And that having seen himself for something like what he was, he could still be happy for Kannan.

He would keep those unsent emails in his drafts folder as reminders of what he was capable of, of what he could descend to. The next day, rereading them in advance of meeting Kannan, he noticed that in every case he had referred to his friend as he. A number of the replies to Kannan's post had assumed that chudcannon26 was a woman.

'CITY SEES FIRST POTTER QUIZ' was the headline in the *New Indian Express*. That one was poorly done: anyone would think it was a quiz about pottery, and skip over to the next article. But *The Hindu* invited its readers to 'COME TEST YOUR WIZARDING METTLE', and while that sounded too much like an advertisement, it was sufficiently intriguing. Besides, the people Malathi knew tended, especially of a Sunday, to read every word in *The Hindu*. You couldn't say that of the *Express*.

This was, she was certain, the first time she had ever appeared in the newspaper. When she came first in the English BA at Stella Maris, she noticed with disappointment that the annual toppers' lists consisted only of students of engineering and medicine. Her sister reminded her that they had been both been mentioned in their mother's obituary notice. That doesn't count, she said; Appa paid for that, it's an ad, not an article. This time actually counted. You couldn't buy your way onto the city news page of a newspaper. To be featured as the subject of an article in *The Hindu* felt like a second birth: she had been recognized as an authentic participant in the cultural life of Madras.

The quiz was to be held on 14 November, Children's Day, as part of a promotional campaign for the new Bharathi Book Mall, and Malathi had come upon the commission through pure luck. Her fruitless visit to Alladi had awakened, or perhaps fabricated, a powerful interest in Vimala aunty, and guilt for having neglected her. She managed to acquire an email address for Vimala aunty's son in Cupertino, California, but she waited to write. She wanted something more interesting to say for herself than a CV of her past seven years.

That was how she came to think of Dog-Ears. Even her desperation for a copy of *Prisoner of Azkaban* hadn't brought to mind the legendary bookshop that was said to occupy a room in an outhouse of a hospital on the southern bank of the Adyar river. Even Vimala aunty, who saw no need for anybody to buy books when they could come to Alladi, had spoken of Dog-Ears, and of its owner, Mrs Chari, with reverence. Going to Dog-Ears for the first time would be reason enough to write to Cupertino.

Dog-Ears occupied a room so small that it ought not to be fit for anything larger than an STD/ISD/Xerox shop. The walls must have held bookshelves, but these could scarcely be seen through the books that rose from the floor. Some piles stood safely vertical, some at Pisa-tower angles; the overall effect was of a freeze-frame of trees in a storm. The shortest pile was a foot taller than Malathi. Eventually—in a room twelve feet by eight at most—she saw through the piles the woman in a cotton sari that must be Mrs Chari, reading a paperback that appeared to have a blank cover and spine. Before she could speak, two customers walked in. They had entered simultaneously, but looked unconnected.

One walked up to Mrs Chari, carrying a book, and asked, 'Do you have any self-help books? Something like this?'

'Self-help books? Wouldn't that defeat the purpose?'

He said nothing, but didn't move either.

'In other words, you've come to the wrong place. Good day.' As he left Malathi was able to make out the title of the book he had walked in with: *Swami Dayananda Saraswati's Winning Formulas to Become Successful Managers.*

The other customer, a slight man in his thirties, had adopted the latrine position so as to scan the books nearest the floor, which gave Malathi her chance.

'Excuse me, ma'am? I was wondering if you could recommend me any new novels.'

'Well, that depends on what old novels you like.'

'It's hard to pick just a few ... but my favourites are the Harry Potter books.'

'I'm afraid this isn't a Harry Potter kind of shop.'

Malathi was not about to retreat like the man in search of self-help.

'If you don't mind my asking, what's the book you're reading now? I noticed it doesn't have a cover.'

'Ah, clearly you haven't seen one of these before. It's a galley; a pre-publication copy. The publisher sent it to me in the hope that I'd order it and recommend it to readers. It's the hot new novel of this winter, by a young man called Pankaj Mishra. *The Romantics.* You can take a look, if you'd like.'

Malathi took the galley in hand, but while she pretended to flip through it she did so with glazed eyes; she had never been able to tell anything about a book by glancing at it. She needed to begin at the beginning, ideally with some information about what she was embarking upon.

'I think I like it so far,' said Mrs Chari. 'But I'm only on page 73. Far too early to make up one's mind. He certainly writes well.'

But now the remark about Harry Potter came back to Malathi, and she saw that she could not continue this conversation, not at any rate if she had to be civil. Vimala aunty may have revered this woman, but there were higher loyalties at stake.

'I'll leave you now,' she said. 'Thanks for showing me the galley.' And she took advantage of the room's size to leave so quickly that Mrs Chari could make no audible reply. As she walked towards the main road to catch an auto, the man from the shop chased her down. She had misjudged him; he looked twenty-five at most, and bursting with an awkward vitality.

'You left so quickly,' he said. 'I meant to give you our card.' *Bharathi Book Mall: Chennai's First and Only Book Mall.* 'If Harry Potter is your favourite, then we're a Harry Potter kind of shop.'

When Malathi first visited Bharathi, she saw what they meant by book mall. The section for actual books was vastly outstripped, in square footage and tradable value, by CD-ROMS, stationery, stuffed toys and GRE crammers. But they were so glad to see her that they offered within minutes to have her host a Harry Potter event. She suggested an essay contest; they insisted on a quiz. That was what would draw the children in. Ten thousand rupees' worth of gift vouchers for the winners, and twenty thousand rupees for her. She could stretch that to a hundred books, even in these times when a paperback cost five trips to the cinema. Or forty of those Modern Library hardbacks that, until now, she could only allow herself once a year as a birthday treat. Bharathi didn't stock Modern Library books, or many others that appealed to Malathi. No matter, the young man said; here are the publishers' catalogues. Take them home and browse, and come back and order whatever you like. She would reserve fifteen thousand rupees for herself, and spend the rest on GRE and GMAT books for America-aspiring cousins. She didn't want to be thought greedy. She would tell her father, and anyone else who asked, that her voucher had been for ten thousand rupees, and that she had only kept half.

5

On that Saturday when she and Annabel lay down to read side by side, Rebecca turned left after an hour to see how her friend was getting on. If you were going to read this way, that is, socially, surely you ought to take breaks together: take stock as you would after each act of a play.

'This is good,' she said.

Annabel didn't look away from her book: the only sign she gave of having heard Rebecca was a slight frown, an intensification of purpose: don't interrupt me again.

Fifty pages later, Harry was about to play his first Quidditch match, against Slytherin.

'Come on. We have to talk about this.'

Annabel was a slow reader. Rebecca, grateful for her mother's yoga tutoring, contorted herself quickly enough to see where Annabel was before she could slam her book shut. She was three chapters behind.

'If you say one more word I'm going to read in the living room. Can't you control yourself? I'm not going to let you tell me what happens.'

Rebecca finished *Prisoner of Azkaban* shortly after 5 p.m. the next day. Annabel had only just started it. It looked like she might have to wait a whole week to go over it all together. But she was sure, already, of two things: she wanted to be able to talk about this with more than just Annabel. And if she were to look beyond her own circles, and seek out strangers, she would have little difficulty finding the right people. And then the memory came to her: the Yahoo! group Harry Potter for Big Kids. The founder—that name she couldn't care to recall—on Curtis Grimmett's radio show. How pleasurable it is to find the brain so efficient, the memory parcel dispatched from the warehouse exactly when required. It must have been the name that did it: she didn't want to talk about these books to twelve-year-olds. A Big Kid was how she felt, in search of other Big Kids.

It took the group administrator three days to approve Rebecca's request to join Harry Potter for Big Kids. Connie was in a meeting, so she didn't need to wait until she was home to find out what these other Big Kids were all about.

She scrolled through the most recent messages and saw immediately that she was living in interesting times. The previous day, 2 December, the administrator, Jenny71, had sent out a declaration of independence:

Dear all,

Now that the dust has somewhat settled over the dramatic events of Election Day, there's something I'd like to share with all of you at HP4BK, before we announce it to the rest of fandom. The accusations against Athena, the deletion of her fics by fandoms. net, their refusal to re-upload her fics after she'd offered an unconditional apology and excised the controversial passages, and above all, the hate and vitriol that's been directed at her over the past few weeks—it's made many of us reflect deeply on the state of fandom as a community. The truth is that fandoms.net was at best a temporary home. We need a space where the best of the Harry Potter fandom can thrive, where fanfic and discussion can coexist, a home where we don't have to share space with other fandoms—where the best fanfics are read and reviewed by genuine fans. That's why we're launching GryffindorCommonRoom.org. I know the name is long, but we really wanted to show that this is a safe, warm, welcoming space to read and talk every evening. I'm guessing it'll be known pretty much universally as GCR, so we've bought the domain name gcr.org as well. HP4BK will continue, don't worry—GCR isn't adults-only.

Snogs,
Jenny

The group had been created only the previous March. But on that first evening of discovery, reading only a week's worth of messages—the equivalent in words of a longish novel—she marvelled at the intimacy that had been established between people who had never met outside this world. This meant that, in cheerful violation of the stated rules, many messages had little to do with Harry Potter, or used the books as an excuse for something more personal. She saw, too, that she would be popular here. All she'd have to do was say she was English, by birth, and sound it, which involved little pretence. Even the American members sounded like the kind of Harry Potter nut that she'd be, if she were to be a Harry Potter nut. But she felt the *effort* it would take to have this intimacy extended to her: the commitment, the hours. And something well-fixed in her—had she been born with it, or learned it at Harvard?—wanted to know, in advance, whether it would be worth it. Whether these people would be worth knowing; whether it would be worth them thinking that they knew her. Who said she needed new friends, anyway, new intimacy? She just wanted to talk about these books. She would join this new site instead.

At GryffindorCommonRoom.Org, she found not one but two distinct sites: Gryffindor Tower housed fanfic, and the Common Room was a discussion forum. A handful of threads had been opened, but almost all the posts were on a single topic: 'R/H vs H/H: the Deathmarch, Round 1'. She'd first picked up a Harry Potter book less than a month ago, but she could work out what those letters stood for. The battle was between those who wanted Ron and Hermione to get together, and those who favoured Harry and Hermione.

The teams or parties referred to themselves as 'ships', presumably a reference to 'relationship'. They took this metaphor as far as they could: the Ron/Hermione crowd were 'the Good Ship R/H', their antagonists the 'HMS Pumpkin Pie.' There were certainly references to pumpkin pie—and pumpkin juice—in the books, but what did this have to do with an imaginary romance between Harry and Hermione? Evidently this lot had been around long enough to have inside references that everyone bar her understood.

For a 'deathmarch', this one was strangely incoherent. No one could decide if the question was which of the two couples was most likely to end up together in or by Book Seven, or which of the two made a 'better' couple—more compatible rather than more romantic or compelling. The Ron/Hermione side kept trying to press their claims to likelihood only to be frustrated by Team Harry/Hermione's insistence on compatibility. The whole thing was like a presidential 'debate': success lay in delivering your message and sticking to it, no matter what the question. When she'd read all eighty-five replies, she refreshed the page. There'd been ten further replies, three of them by a single H/H poster: chudcannon26.

There was none of the intimacy of the Yahoo! group here. None of the lightness, either. The tone was evangelical. But why, she asked Annabel, was her earnestness allergy not getting triggered?

This was the sort of question Annabel liked. It allowed her to cross her arms and grin with the delight of omniscience: *You don't understand you like I do. Let me tell you the truth about yourself.*

'This whole 'earnestness allergy' thing,' she said. 'It's just another one of those stories you like to tell yourself about yourself. You need to outgrow these progressively, like kids outgrow the tooth fairy and then

Santa Claus. *You* are earnest, you've just been waiting for something to be earnest about. Like those people who say they 'don't believe in love' and then make the rest of us sick when they do fall in love.'

Annabel had always said she didn't believe in love.

She hadn't started posting on GCR yet, which meant that her Pottermania was something hermetically enclosed at home, shared only with Annabel. Connie's presence in the office foreclosed the possibility of Potter conversation with the other associates. But the following weekend she was to visit Lydia and Christine in New York. Christine she could take or leave. Christine had never inspired anything you could call a feeling in her; and if the converse wasn't true, it was only because she and Connor had hooked up once or twice before he met Rebecca. But Lydia was still in the habit of calling Rebecca her 'best friend'. And it was books that had given their friendship depth. Sometimes she worried that without books, there would be no friendship to speak of. It seemed a shallow foundation, or at least an unsatisfactory one.

Unlike Rebecca, Lydia *lived* books: she was assistant to the publisher of a prestigious literary imprint, Gramercy Press. A shared love of Harry Potter might extend their friendship by years. The thought of all those conversations waiting to be had warmed her, gave the discovery of these books even greater value.

But in New York it turned out that Lydia scorned Harry Potter.

'You can't possibly be *enjoying* that crap, Bec,' she said. 'You of all people! Harold Bloom took her down in grand style in the *Journal* a few months ago. I'll send you the piece—your regard for Rowling (she pronounced it to rhyme with 'scowling') won't recover.' And then Christine, who worked in private wealth management and had never been known to have literary opinions, chimed in. 'Don't tell me this is your way of *coping* with the break-up. Reading children's fantasy books and then *fan fiction*, am I saying it right, about those books? Seriously?'

On Sunday evening Lydia accompanied Rebecca to the bus terminal—even waiting with her in the Greyhound queue. What, then, had she been itching to say? 'I'm sorry about Christine, she can be so harsh sometimes, but she means well. And you know she and Connor used to be really close. Don't tell her I told you this, but she spoke to Connor a few days after he sent you that email—breaking up in an email, who *does* that? He was like, Rebecca never really opened her true self up to me. He said he'd come to find you cold and distant. That you were "all surface", apparently. And that this new girl was warm and "emotionally accessible". Can you believe that? Such a load of bullshit psychobabble. First he breaks up with you, and then he speaks about you behind your back in that way! To one of your best friends! Christine and I are going to have no more to do with him. I'm so sorry it happened in this way, Bec, but in a way I'm glad that you're no longer with someone so obviously unworthy. I learned this neat phrase from this British girl in the office: you're well shot of him.'

It was easy enough to resolve to ignore Lydia and Christine and everything they said, but she was too disarmed by the sheer justice of Connor's diagnosis of her, at least until she spoke to Annabel, who said, 'Emotionally accessible? That just means he's realized he's more comfortable with a girl on his emotional and intellectual level, which is, at best, the third floor, and I'm thinking of the Prudential Center here.'

Still, you had to wonder at it all. She and Annabel, twenty-three, the ink of their Harvard stamps as fresh and potent as it would ever be, employed in demanding—in terms of time if not thought—jobs, spending their evenings either reading children's books or arguing about those books or, increasingly, reading fan fiction inspired by them.

If she thought of her twenties in those socially determined terms, of *experimenting* in the quest to *find herself*, she couldn't possibly justify her involvement in this. But she didn't need to buy into those clichés. For some people, their twenties were a time of anxiety, driven by a paralysing uncertainty about the future. Every decision asked to bear a weight that it could not quite hold. But it was also the last time where you could do what you enjoyed with no consequences for anyone but yourself. She ought not, really, to validate her own decision to bury herself in Harry Potter by the fact that Annabel had done so too, or that the hundreds of thousands of others who had were, in the main, normal, sane people. But she couldn't help herself. Annabel and the rest were how she knew that it wasn't her, it was the books. There was a universalizing magic here that her four years of literary education didn't equip her to understand. Scanning her memories of lectures and seminars provided no clues. Even Shakespeare hadn't been 'Shakespeare', the Bard, the only truly universal presence in literature, until two hundred years after his death. She'd read that Harold Bloom article—it was easy enough to see that Rowling wasn't a literary genius in the classical sense, but that only compounded the mystery. There was something almost accidental about her magic.

When she wasn't talking about discrimination in college admissions, it was easy to forget that Annabel was Chinese. She'd never joined any of the Chinese or Asian-American social groups on campus. Particularly around mid-terms and final exams, she complained unironically about 'Asian pre-meds' who ruined the grading curve, a memorizing army of cyborg ants. She did speak to her parents, who lived above their tiny restaurant in South Boston, in Mandarin, but she always left the room to take their calls.

Rebecca had been waiting for Annabel to come home so that she could show her GryffindorCommonRoom and the Deathmarch. Their own Harry Potter conversations had tended to focus more on individual characters and what might happen in Book Five than romance. She wasn't sure whether Annabel would get really into the ship debate, or find the whole thing ridiculous. She was shocked to find herself hoping it was the former. But as she watched Annabel read the first few posts, which were the longest—debaters setting up their position, before they moved on to minutiae—she saw not fascination or contempt, but discontent. Or was it outrage?

'So, Bec, which side are you on?' said Annabel, looking up from her screen.

'Well, I'm not really sure that I have a side … I kind of want to post as some sort of wise neutral and be like, you guys are arguing at cross purposes. There are two separate debates here—likelihood and compatibility. Ron/Hermione is more likely, Harry/Hermione are more compatible. But then again, it seems like it *would be* more fun to pick a side. So I guess Harry/Hermione. Ron is kind of an idiot, isn't he? I just don't think he's good enough for Hermione. And arguing for compatibility is way more interesting than arguing over likelihood. Rowling will just settle the latter one way or another.'

'But don't you see what's missing in this whole debate? What's being deliberately ignored?'

'They seem like they have every angle of this topic well covered.'

'You've read the books. Tell me, does Harry have any romantic interest in Hermione? And, for that matter, does Hermione have a boyfriend?'

'Well I guess you could call Viktor Krum her boyfriend. And no, he hasn't, but they aren't even fifteen yet. He has plenty of time to fall for her.'

'Bec, I can't believe you're not getting it either. Why are we sitting here debating two imaginary pairings when Harry already has fallen for someone? Fallen hard, and stayed fallen for almost two years?'

'You mean Cho? But she chose Cedric …'

'Yes, but we saw that she *would* have said yes to Harry if he'd asked her out first. And now Cedric's dead—J.K. Rowling got him out of the way, she's cleared the path for Harry.'

'But come on, Annabel, Cho? We hardly know her! Harry hardly knows her. She's just a pretty face.'

'Weren't you just a pretty face when Connor fell for you? He asked you out, what, fifteen seconds after meeting you? Jesus, no, you still don't get it.'

'Get what?'

'Sexually speaking, we know two things about Harry Potter. Well, actually three things. One, he's straight. Two, he isn't attracted to white girls. Three, he is hugely smitten with one particular Asian girl, Cho Chang.'

'Not attracted to white girls? How do you figure that?'

'Who are the two girls he asked to the ball? Cho Chang, Parvati Patil. In both cases we know it was about pure physical appeal. Plus, he's the only wizard at Hogwarts whose tongue doesn't end up on the table every time Fleur Delacour—pale and blonde—walks into the room.'

'So what you're saying is …'

'That the same way that so many white girls at Harvard hated it when a white guy was attracted to Asian girls—'yellow fever', as they called it—the Harry Potter fanbase are in denial about the fact that Harry Potter, who is more than a character, who represents all that is most heroic in the world, is in love not with his white English best friend, but with a Chinese girl. It's against the laws of nature as they see them. These are people whose grandparents, maybe parents, thought miscegenation laws were a good thing. And so they concoct this irrelevant debate. J.K. Rowling doesn't deserve fans like these.'

'What about Ron and Hermione? She's with Viktor now, but she wanted Ron to ask her.'

'Oh, there's no *debate* there! It's so obvious that they're going to get together. It's a pity, because Ron is such an idiot, he will never ever understand or appreciate her, but the books will end with them married; Harry will be best man, and he won't be gazing longingly at the bride.'

Annabel was back in Cleveland the following week, and Rebecca spent those four evenings wandering GCR, the threads that now covered everything from flints (errors, inconsistencies and contradictions in the books) to botanical symbolism—*what* did it mean that Harry's wand was made of holly, and Hermione's of vinewood? A formal division emerged on the forums between Canon and Fanon. The former meant the books themselves; the latter fan fiction and fan art. Fanon—how Laurent Kameni would have laughed at that term; how her father would, if she ever let him know about this side of herself. Had he even heard of Harry Potter? This was the first time Philip Nicholls and

Laurent had ever coexisted in a thought, the first time in a year she had thought of Laurent in any context. Maybe it would have been worth it to see where things went with Laurent, if only to take him home to Toronto and watch the two men react to each other.

At IvyEdge, she had been able in the quieter days before Thanksgiving to surf fansites, but now, with regular admission deadlines at the end of December, she and her colleagues were editing essays and application materials non-stop. She pleaded unsuccessfully with Connie on behalf of two applicants who had written essays on Harry Potter: 'How Harry Potter Changed My Life' and 'Harry Potter and Meta-ethical Thinking'.

Connie had reserved for these two boys her ultimate humiliation. She had them come into the office and watch as she put their essays through a paper shredder. 'Go home and start again,' she said. 'And don't waste my time, the admissions officer's time, and most importantly, your own time, by writing another essay about witches on broomsticks. And you, Derek,' she said, addressing the meta-ethicist, 'don't give me this *meta* crap. If that's what you want, you can go to the UMass Amherst Honors College and feel smarter than everyone around you for four years. Harvard isn't shopping for pretension.' She carefully poured each shredded essay into an envelope, and handed them over to the boys. 'Keep this on your desk as you write your new essay.' In four weeks their applications would be in the mail, and they could enjoy that blissful three-month affliction, senioritis. And be free to live in Harry Potter. Rebecca walked them out, to an approving nod from Connie—the pretty redhead was supposed to play good cop. 'For what's it worth, I really liked both your essays,' she said. And passed them a Post-it note on which she'd scrawled a URL.

6

In the first weeks of the twenty-first century, Kannan had two troubles, each unfamiliar but, in its own way, a recurrence of something he had thought himself past, or at least set aside for so long that its revival must violate some statute of limitations. When walking down the street, either to work or to the grocery store or in Cambridge, he would see someone walking towards him, from a distance of fifty yards or so, sufficient, in this country, for identification, and recognize them as an acquaintance from Northeastern or tailgate.com or a cashier from a store he often shopped at. As the walker came within greeting distance, he would see that it wasn't in fact that person, just an unknown look-alike. And then, a few minutes later, he would run into the person for whom he had mistaken the first walker, never in a place where he had seen them before.

The first three instances he could dismiss as coincidence, no matter how intriguing Grimmett found the whole thing. But not eight times in a month, one of them a college classmate from Bangalore who was only in Boston to accompany home a grandfather who, on the last stop of a grand tour of his American cousins, had turned off the nightlight and fallen on his way to the bathroom, landing on a veena-case and fracturing his spine. Surely, he said to Grimmett, there couldn't be a more humdrum premonition: advance notice of an unplanned meeting with someone to whom he was totally indifferent. But the sheer meaninglessness of it was no consolation. The only solution was prevention: while walking, he needed to take in no specific details whatsoever of the faces or figures of those around him. This way he could wholly eliminate the possibility of recognition, while maintaining the minimal level of awareness required to avoid a collision. Other pedestrians would be as tangible as primitive video-game characters; he would register only their height and, perhaps, their gender.

It was a technique he had developed in 1997. Midway through his first semester as an RA at Northeastern, he began to notice that, with one exception, whenever he saw a student from his floor out on campus, the moment of mutual recognition was followed by the student either turning away while beginning to giggle or, more commonly, suppressing a laugh with all the ceremony of one attempting to hold back a sneeze. The exception was Brian Hanahan, a junior who had appointed himself liaison between Kannan and the students, who met Kannan's gaze with an expression of unimprovable solemnity. He knew Brian to be a Catholic and, as the first time he saw this version of Brian was a Sunday morning, he thought of it as his 'church face'. Now, as he recounted this period to Grimmett, he learned that Brian had been deploying a 'poker face'.

Two weeks of this had compelled Kannan to initiate the avoidance of recognition. He wasn't sure whether his technique had anything to do with it, and couldn't know how long it took, but he knew that it was safe to look around him once again when Brian began to harass him, almost daily, with gestures of unexplained friendliness that he did not want, but did not resist. First, he was invited to accompany Brian and his friends to a Celtics game. This was, Brian explained, the worst ever

Celtics team, and they needed all the support they could get. 'It's like, imagine if Mick had vocal nodules and Keef developed Parkinson's and the Stones went on tour anyway, but they were so awful that they didn't sell out anywhere. A *true* Stones fan would still go to see them. And the Celtics are at *least* the Rolling Stones of basketball. The Lakers are the Beatles, they're Hollywood, the team for people who can't tell the difference between zone and man-to-man. The Celtics are the real classic team, but they're struggling right now.'

The Celtics' struggles meant Brian could afford miraculously good seats. At Fleet Center, the Celtics hosting the 76ers, Kannan, reluctant ball-handler for his school and PU college teams, felt himself not moved or even entertained but disoriented, the ten men before him a ceaseless blur from another space–time in which classical mechanics were laughably irrelevant. Brian and his friends were less impressed. It was a measure of the two teams' ineptitude that their star players were both rookies. The Celtics' was Antoine Walker, who combined the build of a young rhino with the aggressiveness of a middle-aged Lab. On the other side was Allen Iverson, the only player on the court constructed on a human scale, which in this setting made him a mongoose, twice as feisty for his lack of size. 'Pass the fucking ball!' Brian yelled out each time Walker or Iverson bricked another long jump shot. 'Basketball is wasted on these two,' he said to no one in particular. 'They just don't get it. They have all the physical tools, but they'll never grasp the essence of basketball.'

Next, Brian offered to take Kannan to the gym and to have a bodybuilder friend show him round the free weights.

'Free in both senses,' he said, 'and Derek's a personal trainer, his time is usually expensive.' How happy it must make him, thought Kannan, to combine a pun and a rhetorical appeal to Indian parsimony in one phrase. But before he could say no, he saw his father's figure hanging over himself and Santhanam like a cancerous prophecy. His brother was further along; in this, he decided, he would not follow. Three months later, he could look at himself in the mirror, the inheritance of belly fat disclaimed, the upper arms and thighs thick with new muscle, and feel two new things: triumph and gratitude.

While still a student, Brian had parlayed his gifts of theory and analogy into a gig as the first blogger at tailgate.com, then a Geocities page. It was Brian who introduced Kannan to Eric and Brendan.

And in the summer of 1998, seeing that Kannan was the only person in the office unmoved by Griffey, Sosa and McGwire's pursuit of the home run record, Brian had given him *Harry Potter and the Sorcerer's Stone*, leaving it at his cubicle without either description or explanation. Kannan had time to wonder, later, at how Brian should have known about the book at all, that early, back when this world was only open to children.

They had never been friends. Kannan had understood from the outset that his overtures had some motive short of friendship. He had only opened the book out of some unformed notion that Brian's interventions in his life were rarely without consequence. What that motive was, he thought little of. The workings of minds like Brian's, or Eric's, or Brendan's—why be curious about what you could never understand? It wasn't a matter of East and West. He cared passionately about Harry's mind, after all, and Hermione's. Later he would come to know Grimmett's. But with Brian, maybe with all Americans his own age, it was enough to figure out how to respond to what was said or done without bothering about what might drive it. If it was important, they would tell you, eventually.

A few weeks after *Prisoner of Azkaban* came out Brian was poached by NewsCorp to run a new basketball site, based in LA. Eric and Brendan said he was a traitor who would get what he deserved: a second life as a Clippers fan. At the farewell party he asked Kannan if they could step outside for a moment.

In the street they stood for what must have been the longest episode of silence of Brian's life. Kannan counted six Lincoln Town Cars go by. Left to Kannan, who knows how long it could have stayed unbroken?

'I'm glad you stayed,' said Brian, finally. 'For the party. Thank you.'

Kannan said nothing: he knew that one didn't need, at moments like this, to find the right platitude to fill the space. Silence worked just as well. The American would go on regardless.

'I should have said this a long time ago. I guess I was never going to say it at all. I confessed it, all those years ago; but my girlfriend says that's not good enough. She's really opened my eyes about the Catholic Church. She says confessing to a priest is a way to chicken out, morally. And that it's not enough to try to make it up in other ways, either. You've got to confess to the person you wronged.'

'Confess *what*, Brian? Who have you wronged?' Kannan hoped that he didn't dwell on wrongs received—what a waste of time—but he was conscious of not forgetting them, either. From Brian, for whatever reason, he had received only one good turn after another.

'Do you remember when you first moved into our hallway, my junior year, as an RA, and that people used to laugh at you when they saw you on the street?'

'I'd forgotten, but yes.'

'Well, that was because of me. Do you remember recording a voicemail message?'

'No … well, I must have, but I don't recall.' No one was supposed to remember doing a thing like that.

'You did, and that was how I wronged you. My buddies and I thought your message was hilarious, both the stuff you said and the way you said it, your accent. You were trying so hard, it was like something out of a 1960s movie making fun of Indians. Peter Sellers. We used to call you late at night hoping you wouldn't pick up. Then we figured out the times when you were away from your room, so we were guaranteed to get the answering machine. Jesus, we even used it as a way to impress girls. Successfully, at least once. Then I recorded it so we didn't have to keep calling you—it took me a while to think of that, actually. And I played it to all of Northeastern and beyond. When people saw you on the street, they had it playing in their heads. And it was wrong, and it was cruel. Because it wasn't your fault you spoke like that, you were just trying to have a normal American voicemail message. I'm not asking for your forgiveness. I'm confessing to you now so that maybe in time I can forgive myself.'

Later, Kannan would reflect on the centrality of *myself* to all this; to the crime itself and, even more, to the confessing of it. Standing on the sidewalk with Brian, he had wanted to escape the tyranny of thought, to remove himself mentally if he couldn't physically; to go back to counting town cars until Brian went back upstairs. But he saw that Brian sought a response, for *himself*. What is saying you're not asking for forgiveness but soliciting it by dishonest means?

'It doesn't matter,' Kannan said. 'It was so long ago. I'd honestly forgotten about it. And you've done so much for me. Harry Potter, tailgate, it was you who first taught me how to work out … those things I haven't forgotten. Good luck in LA. Don't be a Lakers fan.' As Brian reached in for a hug, Kannan kept his arms by his side, and Brian pulled away; Kannan had succeeded in passing off his revulsion as awkwardness.

Now, almost two years later, he wondered if the premonitions were really an omen, and he was meant to be in constant anticipation of running into Brian.

His second trouble was tangible and comprehensible, and more worrying for it. He was to visit Bangalore, for the first time since leaving for Northeastern in August 1996. The emails had arrived in mid-December, the first from Santhanam and the second from their father, exactly half an hour apart, like scheduled news bulletins. Santhanam's said only: 'I have bought tickets for you to visit India, 16–21 Jan, and am FedExing them over. Excellent match found for you. More to follow from Appa.' His father's consisted of the extended biodata of a girl. He saw that her name was Malathi Venkataraman, and that she had been born in 1979. He closed the email at this point; he would read the rest if and when he had to.

Santhanam had visited Bangalore once a year since he joined Dell. Kannan knew nothing of the details of these visits. Lately, Santhanam's emails spoke of little else but the activities of the Vedic Expositors and Defenders of America, whose Austin chapter he had founded. But he was sure that if Santhanam had wanted to, he would have been married himself by now. As elder son it was his right to go first, and in any case he was so much more than just first in the litter.

Unlike Kannan, Santhanam had the freedom to do as he pleased, and yet the privilege of being considered the model son, respectful and obedient. He had always had this, but since graduating from Carnegie Mellon he had also paid for it. Their parents had thought $5,000 a year a handsome remittance, had hoped for nothing more. Santhanam had started with $10,000, a quarter of his salary after tax; later, when Kannan graduated, he had upped it to $15,000. In a letter sent to their parents and copied to Kannan, he said that as Kannan lived in a more expensive city, and had less certain prospects as an employee at a start-up, it would be unfair to expect him to contribute. Kannan had wondered when and in what form his brother would cash this cheque. Now he saw that Santhanam had meant that he would have to contribute in other ways. Kannan's marriage had been on Santhanam's mind as far back as his advisory letter of 1996. Pulling out the letter to confirm this, Kannan found that marriage did not, as he had thought, have a sub-heading of its own, but found mention in several places, particularly the section on employment, which ended thus:

There is a highly positive correlation between the job you obtain—measured by salary, location or company brand name—and the wife you go on to obtain. I doubt you have given much thought to marriage. But all that time you have spent with your friends shopping for porn videos at National Market means you do possess manly desires. If you start flirting with some American blonde, you will soon become a laughing stock. But if you get a good job, you can make a good match with an attractive, educated, modern girl.

That is the only way you can express those desires in a decent and respectable manner.

Add the cost of his airfare to the $15,000, then. Perhaps this was Santhanam's way of dodging the question of his own marriage. Was he hiding something—an American girlfriend, even an American wife? No, he would have paraded such an acquisition. Kannan considered his options. Visiting home ought not in itself be such a terrifying prospect. He had no curiosity about the girl, but he was curious about his parents, and their changed circumstances. Santhanam had flown them over to the US once, in 1997, but they had not come to Boston, so as to avoid the expense of a hotel. Instead, Kannan had gone to Austin for a long weekend, and as he watched Santhanam being fawned over, he wondered briefly if this was what it was like to be the sister of an Indian son. Going home without Santhanam around, seeing himself talked up as eligible, as a catch: there were worse circumstances. He could consult Grimmett beforehand, draw up a list of pretexts under which to decline the marriage offer. But he went back to Santhanam's email, and back again to the old letter, and thought of Brian, and he had no relief from the certainty that the tides of his life were once again changing without his say-so.

If he didn't manage to quite take Santhanam's place, he profited, nonetheless, from his brother's absence. For the first time he was conscious of his mother really looking at him. She took in his broad calves and visible triceps—the latter sight, he hoped later, might have hit her with the threatening unfamiliarity of her husband's sex organs on their wedding night—and asked if he had become non-vegetarian. No, he lied, but I have been working out. Working out *what*? Surely she thought it, but she didn't ask. Before the hours with Grimmett he had never thought of it this way, but conversation had always been a lack in his family life. That he was now treated with no contempt, either overt or implicit, did not alter this. But two days with his parents and grandmother reassured him that his lack of regard for them was not a petty reaction to their preference for Santhanam but a reasonable accounting of their characters. The absence of conversation or any other form of intimacy was enforced, in part, by the derelict state of his Tamil: when a question was put to him, he replied only in English, not even Tanglish.

He arrived on a Thursday, and was informed that on Saturday the girl and her father were coming up from Madras by the morning Shatabdi. The girl and her father had asked that she be able to meet Kannan alone before the congress of two families. Whatever the request's merits, said Kannan's father, the man had no place to make it. His mother put it down to the softness of a father who had only daughters. But it had been agreed to leave it to Kannan who, because he had refused to allow himself to pay any attention to the question, could never have thought of such a proposal, but consented to it with a surge of ascending relief. Meeting the girl alone would give him many more potential justifications for rejection, justifications that could not be challenged empirically. And the encounter itself might even serve as a kind of test of where he stood, of how far he had come.

Until then, he was free to roam the city, in pursuit of privacy and of any Internet connection that beat the 32k VSNL dial-up his father used. At home, he found a periodical called *Bangalore This Fortnight*— it came free, of course—that devoted an entire section to the city's possibilities for 'Pub Hopping'. Rather than contact Vinay or Ashok, both of whom now worked in Bangalore, he set out alone, hopping between not pubs but the cyber cafés that were growing across the city like German measles. Some were specially designed for gaming; others offered cubicles enclosed on three sides and thus ideal for porn. None of them served coffee or made any other attempt to live up to the second half of their name. Most young men he saw typed so quickly and looked at their screens with such unwavering intensity that they must have been working on MS or job applications, or cramming for exams.

Any of the cafés was good enough for him: fandom demanded little bandwidth. But he rarely stayed in one longer than an hour, marvelling each time at how little effort it took to find another. Even for a student of computer science, the Internet had, in his time in Bangalore, been little more than a rumour.

Santhanam had told him to expect the city transformed. He had never thought of it as *his* city, less out of a reluctance to lay claim than out of the lack of the attachment that such a claim implied. Now he saw that it had been his city, in the sense that it was gone. The new city was a blur of headlights and construction dust. The buildings that had carried over from one Bangalore to the next had acquired new facades, in various shades of Alucobond. The newly built offices of the IT services firms were more likely to be plate-glass, but they must have come to regret the extra expense: everywhere, he saw broken windows, the legacy of protests against the kidnapping of the actor Dr Rajkumar, the chief deity of Sandalwood. The year before Kannan left for Northeastern, KFC had been forced to close its first Bangalore branch by a mob of picketing farmers. But KFC was back, and the lines outside it and Pizza Hut suggested that Kannadigas had made their peace with foreign junk-food chains or, more likely, had been outvoted by invading migrants. Four and a half years had been enough to remake Bangalore, and yet the new version felt provisional, as if it lacked whatever solidity the memory of the old city seemed to possess. He thought of his journey in reverse. The man who left Boston in the summer of 1996 would have returned at the start of 2001 to find every fire hydrant still in place.

Friday mornings, American time, were a quiet time in fandom, a trend Kannan put down to the need to catch up on all the work left undone earlier in the week. The youths in the Cunningham Road cyber café were less monkishly focused than usual; there were even a few girls. Perhaps they were there to email US-based potential husbands. He might as well read the rest of Malathi's biodata. Assuming that her father, and not she, had written this document, he was either an unassuming man or an excessively confident one: he refused to stray from the narrowly factual. She had obtained a first division in her PUC and BA, and was currently finishing her MA, but as the subject was English, this was not proof of either brains or focus; indeed, all it proved was that as a girl she had the privilege of not having to earn a living. The duration of her study of Carnatic vocal music was listed, along with the name of a teacher that meant nothing to Kannan. Her height was given as 5'2 ½", hopefully measured barefoot, but there was no description of her appearance, not even of complexion and, infuriatingly, there was no photograph. He skipped over the horoscope section: he knew it had already been confirmed to match his. He couldn't see the point of the document: it offered him grounds neither for pre-emptive refusal nor anticipation. At dinner he was told that this was Malathi's first time in Bangalore. He was expected to plan the meeting. Where did you take a new visitor to Bangalore? He flirted with the possibilities of deliberate perversity—Tao Fu had survived the cyber café epidemic. 'Take her to Cubbon Park,' his father said. 'There are more trees there than in all of Madras.'

The girl was a little over five feet, in between short and average, but she stood and walked with a short person's determined uprightness. In America she could have worn stilettos. She wore a turmeric salwar-kameez with a dupatta of a slightly brighter yellow—the effect was, if not exactly plain, then certainly less than he expected of someone dressing to impress a potential husband. It had been impressed upon him that he was not a suitor: this was not a swayamvar. It was up to him and to his parents to proceed with the match. Whether the girl saw things this way was uncertain, especially as her face and eyes seemed impenetrably calm. Her features even, her nose narrow, but it was all set a little too close together: you couldn't, by any standards strict enough to be meaningful, call her pretty. She was just short of pretty. You could say she was condemned to be so. But even a girl of unremarkable near-prettiness was sure to have been catcalled, to have received notes from boys from other colleges, to have been told she was beautiful. Kannan had never received any sort of approach, nor even a compliment. Along with everything else, Santhanam had been granted a complexion the shade of a Parle-G biscuit, while Kannan's was Cadbury Dairy Milk. The girl was darker than Santhanam, but distinctly fairer than Kannan.

They entered Cubbon Park, moving past a statue of Queen Victoria towards the red-oxide monuments of colonial Bangalore. Kannan made no attempt to play guide. He had been to Cubbon Park as a boy, had ridden the toy train on a school outing, but he knew nothing beyond the fact that they would eventually come to the high court, a building he was certain no member of his family had ever entered. She was silent because she had the woman's privilege of not having to initiate conversation. Kannan had spent the first hours of the morning not planning this meeting, but visualizing it. He was sure that he would think only of what she might be thinking of him. But as they walked he found his mind blank, not out of anxiety or nervousness but of mere inactivity. He neither thought nor attempted to think. Was conversation even expected of him? By their request, the girl and her father had placed him in a zone where expectations, for once, were ambiguous, or at least undefined. Other than a certainty that it would be inappropriate to touch her, an urge that, in any case, he did not feel, he might even be free of expectation, but that might be even worse than its familiar encumbrance.

And then, on the steps leading up to the high court, he paused and began to absently stroke the mane of a gold cement lion that he had ridden on his boyhood visits to the park, and she spoke. In the park, it was the content of her words that proved decisive, but later he would fixate more on the fact of her having spoken first. He would decide that he was in no place to say what the act meant about her character, but it certainly meant that he had been lied to. The walk in the park *was* a swayamvar: if they had passed the morning in unbroken silence, Malathi would have gone back to her father and refused to marry Kannan.

'I have heard that you excelled at computer science and work as a software engineer,' she said. 'I don't know anything about computers, so I won't understand anything about your work. I have no head for maths or science.'

'My work is quite boring, you don't need to bother about it.'

'But I was hoping we could find something else to talk about. Do you have any outside interests? I am sure your work gives you very little free time.'

'Well, during my college days, I liked to watch movies with my friends. And ever since moving to the US I have made time to work out at the gym.' The replies came out like muscular twitches—he was aware of them while not intending them in any conscious way, almost as if he was hearing himself speak in the third person.

'I studied English because I love to read books. But the books in my BA and MA course have been quite boring. Do you like to read?'

Now he began to feel himself in active control once again. He could form a thought before voicing it. Outside the office, he had spoken of Harry Potter to no one but Grimmett. That next step had been meant for the week after his return, when Grimmett was to host an offline meeting of the Boston Gobstones Club, in the pit by the Harvard Square T station. Why talk of it now? Only because there was nothing to lose, as the name would mean nothing to her, and because the alternative was to say that he didn't read, and seem dull.

'Yes, I do. I love J.K. Rowling. The Harry Potter books.'

All this time she had done him the decency of avoiding eye contact. The person speaking looked ahead at the high court, or at the ground; the other did likewise, only looking at the speaker with discreet corner glances. Now she looked straight at him, and he was forced to confront her unrestrained delight, her irises dancing, her smile stretching too far for her small face, the smile of someone who had just received her Hogwarts letter.

'Really? You like Harry Potter? Harry Potter is my favourite thing in the whole wide world,' she said. 'This is wonderful.'

Unprepared as he had been for this, he began to let himself go. It was almost two o'clock, well past lunchtime, when he realized that they ought to head back home to Malleswaram. Malathi knew the books at least as well as he did. She was even aware of fandom, had read some fan fiction, but hadn't been to GCR or HP4BK, or read the real classics. So much for her to be introduced to. When, after over an hour of Harry Potter talk, he had put to her the most important question, she said, 'I feel so sad about how Hermione and Ron are going to end up together. I pray every day that Ms Rowling changes her mind, or is just trying to trick us, and that it doesn't happen.' Back at the flat it was evident that no one need bother asking either of them about their morning. Business was swiftly concluded; her father proved remarkably easy to deal with. The wedding was to be in Madras, in early March. With her MA to finish and the visa to be obtained, it would be several months before she joined him in Boston.

It was only later, on the flight back, that he attempted to sort through the events of that morning, and his impressions of her. He tried, with fleeting success, to focus on things other than Harry Potter. His initial assessment of her looks had been unfair. When she spoke her eyes had plenty of kalai, the luminous intelligence that, according to their grandmother, Santhanam had been given Kannan's share of in addition to his own. After five years at Stella Maris College her accent was, if not quite convent school, then a great deal more clipped and impressive than any of his own relations'. She could read the news on the radio. What of his own? In his letter of five years ago Santhanam had, to Kannan's initial puzzlement, included a whole section on the matter:

14. Accent

You will find, if you make a success of yourself, that when you return to India you will encounter a lot of jealousy. Those who can't make it to the US bitterly resent those of us who have. People will find ways to insult and abuse you. One of these is to mock your accent.

They will say, 'Look, the fellow has gone and got himself a fancy American accent.' All this when half of them can barely speak English and when they do, sound like braying donkeys. In India people have a colonized mentality. They think speaking properly is sounding like a Britisher. Which is why the whole world thinks we sound like pathetic servants. All you should care about is speaking in a way that allows Americans, such as your professors and your co-workers, to understand you clearly. In America, it is considered rude to make fun of someone's accent. You will have to make changes to how you speak to be well understood: once you have succeeded, you should ignore any remark an Indian passes about your accent.

On this visit no one had remarked on his accent at all. That didn't mean it wasn't changed. He had found at Northeastern that while his classes presented no issue—a majority of students in his programme were ESL, and computer science required little conversation—the position of RA, on a floor comprised entirely of white Americans, required him to attempt modifications. The answering-machine message that had so amused Brian—it had taken Kannan thirty-eight goes to record it to his own satisfaction.

His parents were more used to him speaking in Tanglish, and had probably been taught by Santhanam to regard an Americanized accent as both functional and aspirational. He hoped that Malathi wouldn't change her accent in America.

7

Rebecca had known since accepting Connie's job offer that she would receive two weeks off at the start of January. IvyEdge's leave policies were modelled on a school or college rather than a corporation: there were plenty of holidays, but these were mandated and inflexible. And hers had been meant for Connor, for a warm-water trip, Costa Rica or something like it. They'd been putting off choosing a place, but she had begun quietly to invest in this first vacation alone together notions of decisiveness. Its course would suggest, in a way that her dissatisfaction at each phone call could not, where they were headed.

And now time opened up before her: bonus time, that by-product of misdirected plans, like a new segment of earth risen between continental plates, waiting to be filled up. Two weeks.

If, as Annabel would advise if asked, she were to travel on her own, programming the trip to her tastes rather than Connor's, she'd pick a European country she hadn't been to, perhaps a former Eastern Bloc member whose architecture had survived World War II. But she would end up submitting to the predictability of unstructured travel: the futile wrangling between the main sights and a flaneurial walk, ending always with the sights, and at 11 p.m. she'd find herself in one of those hybrid bar-clubs full of grimy, buff young backpackers ready to seduce her—in the offhand European way, not the eager American one. Every night she could 'take a lover'—how Lydia would love that phrase and how Annabel would mock it—from a different country. As if there were any better way to make the trip about Connor than a series of hook-ups.

She decided to spend the weekend at the end of her break with her parents in Toronto. Until then, she would hibernate, in her apartment with the still, soporific warmth of a bakery, and read one fanfic after another. Anyone could see the madness and futility of it. She could feel the shape of those days about to be lost. For we don't have a fixed supply of days. Activity works on days like a stimulus: each day spent productively points forward to countless more like it. The psychological energy thus generated allows for nothing but forward motion. Do nothing, on the other hand, or feel yourself to have done nothing, and your only thought at the end of the day is that you've lost another one.

All this she knew, and it meant nothing.

Her first explorations of this new world had not been promising. At Gryffindor Tower, the authors were listed alphabetically by username from A-Z. Beginning with M, selecting a name at random, she would read the one-paragraph plot summary, and then the first chapter.

The vast majority of fics tended to take off where *Goblet of Fire* had ended, and closely follow the books' school-year structure. All the talk on the forums was of a delayed release for the new book. Depending on whom you believed, JKR was either burned out from writing *Goblet of Fire* at Stakhanovite speed, or was proof that even geniuses suffered from writer's block. Or, as everyone hoped, she had found love. Any which way, the annual ritual of a new Harry Potter book could not be observed in 2001. It was rumoured that the release might be pushed all the way to 2002. This meant two full years where the only way to read about Harry's fifth year would be to read fan fiction. For both authors and readers, these homemade Book Fives were a way to get through the day. Some fics were pure wish fulfilment, involving an American

exchange student who clearly embodied the author's most optimistic
self-perception and who would win Harry's heart.

This was a form of literary addiction quite without precedent. In
1841, she had read, the ship bearing the final chapter of Dickens's *The
Old Curiosity Shop* was stormed at New York Harbor by hundreds of
fans demanding to know whether Little Nell was dead. But what was
striking about that scene was that they had been able to wait months
to find out. Dickens obsessives didn't even think of writing their own
versions.

But these Book Fives weren't written by Big Kids. Their authors were
teenage or younger—you had to be thirteen to join GCR, officially, but
your self-declared age was received on trust. Novelty value aside, they
held nothing for Rebecca. If this was all there was to fandom, she'd
never have stayed.

The GCR thread that changed everything was called 'A Fanon
Canon'. It had been created by chudcannon26, one of a handful of
users that she had identified early as prominent and distinctive. She or
he—she thought he, but knew better than to presume—was earnest and
passionate even by the obsessive standards of fandom, but Rebecca was
most struck by his or her persistence: on the R/H vs H/H Deathmarch,
chudcannon26 replied individually to every single user on the Ron/
Hermione side, refuting their arguments with specific references to the
books. All this done in the sure knowledge that not a single person on
the other side was open to being convinced.

It was time, said chudcannon26, to begin the collective curation of
a list of the fanfics everyone should read. This 'Fanon Canon' would
comprise the fics that would, decades from now, stand alongside the
books as the enduring core of the world of Harry Potter. chudcannon26
began by proposing three favourites of their own. These would be the
first fics Rebecca read from start to finish—or, rather, from start to latest
chapter. Like Dickens, these writers published serially, but, constrained
by the real life of jobs and families, their output was irregular. In

each case, Rebecca noted the average lag between past chapters and calculated that she had to be prepared to wait at least a week.

These fics whose next instalments she would have been happy to await at New York Harbor were really novels that happened to be situated in the world of Harry Potter, written by people with literary talent and ambition who chose to use a pre-fabricated fictional world and set of characters, not because it was easier than developing their own, but because it guaranteed them a readership. They dealt with the lives of Harry and his friends in the years after Hogwarts. The true substance of their fics was relationships—friendship and romance. Their authors were, she could tell, virtually all women between twenty and thirty-five. They allowed her, in a way that the books could not, to truly escape into Harry's world.

The fics that she chose—she had shortlisted two dozen to read in ten days—had one other thing in common. They all involved, or built towards, a romantic pairing between Harry and Hermione. This had also been true of each of the three fics with which chudcannon26 had opened 'A Fanon Canon'.

To Rebecca, her preference for Harry/Hermione fanfic was inevitable; the fact that chudcannon26 shared her taste had only advanced the discovery. Hermione combined moral and intellectual firepower to a degree Rebecca didn't think she'd encountered either in fiction—apart from Dorothea Brooke in *Middlemarch*—or in life. And, unlike Dorothea Brooke, she wasn't even annoying. Ron had a 'good heart', whatever that meant, he was 'loyal'—except that he wasn't when it mattered. He lacked both talent and imagination, and as the youngest of six sons, he was tortured by phoney crises of masculinity. He might love Hermione for what she could give him, but he could never really respect her, much less understand her. The fact that J.K. Rowling was clearly set on a Ron/Hermione pairing in the books only made the other life of fanfic more urgent and necessary.

As her current favourite writer, Perdita, had written Rebecca in a response to the first fan email she had ever sent, it didn't really matter whether Harry and Hermione got together in the books. 'We who sail this ship see them as the deepest, most mutually fulfilling, lifelong romance. And that isn't usually something that happens to you at age fifteen. We're in this for the long LONG haul.'

It was through Perdita that Rebecca understood that she had started to think of Harry and Hermione not as characters in a book series but as people that she knew, whose future she felt invested in. The existence of fanfic liberated them from the confines of the books. In fifteen years of novel-reading, she'd never thought of character in this way, even before the literary-theoretical education that was designed to purge any residual naïveté about fictional people. To do so now wasn't embarrassing; it was thrilling. Still, she wondered about that 'long LONG haul'. How long exactly did Perdita think all of this was going to last?

Perdita's ongoing epic was called *Time Regained*. It had been the first fic on chudcannon26's list.

Set a decade after the defeat of Voldemort, it was part thriller and part love triangle. Harry, Ron and Hermione had reunited to save the wizarding world from a resurgence of the Dark threat; but the story's core was the human relationship between the adult Trio—one relationship as well as three. Like all fanfic, each chapter of *Time Regained* opened with the disclaimer that it was based on characters and situations that belonged to J.K. Rowling, Warner Bros, Scholastic, Bloomsbury, Raincoast, and others, and that no profit or copyright infringement was intended. But in the literary sense, Perdita could justifiably claim to own her characters.

Each chapter ended with a series of acknowledgements: to the fandom friends who had read her drafts, assisted her research or supplied music recommendations and pep talks. One of her minor characters was Indian, and twice she thanked chudcannon26, 'for Harish'. All of these friends, she was sure, were people Perdita had only ever known online.

It had taken one chapter for Rebecca to be hooked, as a reader. Three more for her to decide that she wanted to be more. She wanted to be thanked at the end of each chapter; she wanted to know Perdita.

Enjoying a work of art had never before provoked in her the desire to get to know the artist. Except that this wasn't quite the same as writing to a conventionally published author. She and Perdita were both part of the same substratum of Harry Potter fandom, as well as on the same ship. So this could be the fan letter as an invitation to friendship. This person, she knew already, was someone worth being friends with. She began by talking about *Time Regained*, how it had the qualities of the long nineteenth-century novels she most cherished: vividness, the unselfconscious depiction of character, an unapologetic pleasure in storytelling. It was long, she said, not out of the notion that length was the barometer of ambition, or because of a surplus of displayed erudition—'Admission: I didn't even get halfway through *Infinite Jest*'—but because it took its own time.

Rebecca's email had begun 'Dear Perdita', as it was sent to an address that had evidently been created for fandom use alone. The reply was signed 'Michelle', who turned out to be a trainee nurse practitioner in urban Philadelphia, not yet thirty. Emails were exchanged first daily and then every few days. They were spontaneous, unconsidered, but had the detail and intensity she associated with letters.

They discussed canon and fandom, of course, their favourite fics and shipping, but also other books and music, and their lives. Michelle had grown up in Chicago, essentially working class but with parents whose lives were defined by Willow Creek, an evangelical megachurch to which she continued to belong. She didn't say how this sat with Harry Potter or *Time Regained*. In the Nicholls household, Christianity was something other people did, and would eventually, one hoped, grow out of—a knowledge of it wasn't any more necessary than of alchemy or homeopathy or bone-setting. She set aside the question of Michelle's faith—she couldn't understand it any more than she could, say, the experience of having some incurable disease. But it deepened an instinct, provoked by several references in *Time Regained* and fortified by her literary and musical tastes, that Michelle was black. She couldn't figure out whether this was subtlety and deductive reasoning on her part, or whether such a judgement, in the absence of any direct statement, was monstrously inappropriate. But when Michelle confessed to having never possessed a passport, and seeing England as a quaint place, 'almost as if it existed in history, and in literature, but doesn't really exist in the real world, if you know what I mean?' Rebecca replied: I was born in London, I grew up partly in Britain, I'd be happy to help out if you ever need any Britpicking.

'You're *hideously* unqualified,' Annabel said. 'You left England as an unformed child. Britpickers are supposed to know *contemporary* Britain, and slang and stuff like that. Sure, you sometimes speak with a British inflection, but that's a mark of pretension, not authenticity.'

Annabel was just jealous that the volume and schedule of her work didn't permit her to fully enter fandom. For once, Rebecca decided to take her neither literally nor seriously.

In Toronto she told no high-school friends that she was in town. She scarcely left the house, except to accompany her mother to Karma Co-op. A long weekend spent catching up after months apart passed so swiftly, she almost didn't notice how exhausting it all was, trying to provide narrative form to her life. For Liz Nicholls, no amount of information was ever satisfying. For a garrulous person, she had a remarkable appetite for listening. But her listening was attention without contemplation: tell me more, how awful, tell me more. Rebecca wondered now if she had ever had the thought before: that here was someone to whom no detail of her life was boring or irrelevant.

Occasionally Liz's attention shaded into concern. Twice this revealed itself directly: she asked if Rebecca was quite sure that she had reckoned, fully, with how much Connor had hurt her, rather than suppressing the question or distracting herself, and, later, whether working at IvyEdge was spiritually damaging.

'You know I'm not at all about spending your time usefully, always moving forward, any of that materialist nonsense, but sometimes you can be moving backwards without realizing it, and by the time you do it's too late to change or even get out.'

But at other times, perfectly innocuous remarks left the unexpected aftertaste of worry. Rebecca wondered if she was picking up on something deeper. But as she had never previously been able to accuse her mother of subtlety or implication, it must, instead, be a projection of her own discomfort with concealment. She was giving Liz the fullest possible account of her life in Cambridge—without mentioning Harry Potter.

The snow and his daughter's visit had been insufficient to keep Professor Nicholls out of the office. On Sunday, an early dinner before her flight back to Boston, he addressed her directly for the first time.

'Well? Are you going to take him back?'

'It isn't up to me. But if you mean would I take him back if he came crawling back on his knees, no, of course not.'

'And have you learned your lesson? Is this the last time you plan your professional life around a man?'

'Darling, that's unkind,' said Liz.

'Perhaps I can put it another way. If you have learned your lesson, which I'm sure you have, as an intelligent woman, why are you sticking with the plans you made to suit a man who has left you? Why are you staying in Boston, and applying your intellectual and emotional energy to doing all you can to entrench the inequality of opportunity? They aren't paying you nearly well enough to blind you to the social consequences of your work.'

'You know nothing about my work, Philip. You haven't asked me a single question about my job while I've been here. These aren't a bunch of stupid rich kids! They're people who need help fully expressing their talents. It can be really fulfilling. And personally I think helping teenagers unlock their potential is a lot more *consequential* than studying political theory.'

She looked to her mother, but not in expectation.

'By addressing me as if I am a potential recruit to your company, I suppose you mean that I insult your intelligence. Which is fair: everything I just said, you knew yourself before you took the job, and I'm sure six months at it have only hardened those thoughts. And if there is some compelling reason for you to stay in this job, you aren't obliged to share it with me, although I confess to being quite mystified.' At which point her father did something she had not thought him capable of, and changed the subject. 'Why don't you tell me more about your life in Boston? How is living with the Chinese girl?'

'Annabel's away on work a lot, so I'm mostly alone during the week. But I'm really glad I got to live with her; she's surprisingly chill, and we have a lot of fun.'

'I can't imagine you get out much in this weather.'

This was small talk. What on earth had Liz said to him? Up until now Rebecca had been quite conscious of her act of withholding. For all that Harry Potter had consumed somewhere between seventy and eighty-five per cent of her waking hours these two weeks, she didn't see that it was essential information. It didn't constitute *news*. There was no way of explaining it that would convey anything like the nature of her experience. It was a mark of how unsettling her father's behaviour was that she spoke up now.

'We stay in most weekends. Annabel and I have gotten really into the Harry Potter books. And the broader Harry Potter fandom.'

'The what? Aren't those children's books?' Liz, this time.

'They were written for children, originally, but a lot of adults read them too.'

'Your father was saying the other day that these books are taking over the world, and that it's a perfect example of the infantilization of literary culture, especially in the English-speaking world.'

'Well he hasn't read them, has he? Since when is it ok to make grand literary pronouncements over books you haven't read? I thought that was the practice of post-structuralists who don't care what the text actually says?'

'My, Rebecca, you really have come back ready to take offence. Since when do you read children's books instead of literature? Is this some reaction against your education at Harvard?'

'A lot of what Annabel and I have been reading, what I guess animates this online community we're sort of part of, isn't the books themselves, although those are great, but fan fiction.'

'Fan fiction?'

'Stories, well, novels really, written about the Harry Potter characters and universe, but by other people, by fans.'

'Like the sequels to *Gone with the Wind*? But isn't the author of Harry Potter alive? And churning new books out at a Dickensian rate, while the market is hot?'

'No, these aren't sequels. It's difficult to explain. I can send you some good fan fiction if you're interested.'

'These sound like cover versions of famous songs, done by fans, with the lyrics changed. So you spend your days reading either children's books or, well, *tribute stories* written by fellow adult fans of these books, and you propose your mother and I do the same?'

Best to end this now, even though she would send her father a printed version of *Time Regained*. Perhaps she could try one more thing: 'In Boston, the guy who sort of runs the Harry Potter community is called Curtis Grimmett.'

'Ah yes, Steve Vogler told me that old nutjob was still going strong on Friday nights. He has quite a following, for some reason. Are you a regular listener of Grimmett's?'

'No, but I think I'm going to write to him.'

'He's a notorious Anglophile. He probably just likes Harry Potter because it's British. So that doesn't mitigate anything.'

'I wasn't saying it did! But this isn't infantilization or Anglophilia. Millions of adults love these books.'

'If you're justifying your taste that way, you ought to move on to the serious big numbers. *Atlas Shrugged, The Prophet, The Bridges of Madison County.*'

'You haven't been keeping up, Philip. Harry Potter has outsold all of those.'

'Which tells us, of course, that the arc of literature moves ever upward, even if it moves slowly.'

'What do *you* think I should be reading? I spent four years reading the classics. I feel kind of cut off from contemporary literature.'

Professor Nicholls, unlike his wife, with her impatience with things that hadn't actually happened, read a great deal of fiction; the evidence was on his nightstand and on coffee tables and sideboards. The paperbacks moved around the house like migratory birds.

'I think in this case, what is needed is not simply any old *good book*, let alone that nauseating idea, a *good read*, but a more targeted antidote. Let me see. Why don't you read *Disgrace*, by the South African J.M. Coetzee? And move on from that to Philip Roth's latest, *The Human Stain*. Both came out in the last year or so. And are at the far end of the spectrum from Harry Potter, whichever spectrum you might have in mind.'

She made a show of pulling out a notebook and writing the names down.

'I suggest these books because they offer the best kind, indeed the only worthwhile kind of *realism*—an unflinching grappling with the highest stakes and most uncomfortable questions. They wouldn't simply engage you, they might even *ground* you, repair your relationship to reality.'

'My what?'

'I'm worried that this obsession with children's fantasy novels and fan fiction thereof is representative of a wider issue.'

As a teenager, she had often wondered how much of what she told Liz was passed along to Philip. It was probably all of it, but she doubted that he paid much attention and, in any case, she couldn't see where this was going.

'While you don't hold any religious or "spiritual" views, even of the New Age variety, you're suffering under at least one delusion, and that's not counting the Harry Potter thing. I'm referring to the theory, although the word "theory" adds a wholly undeserved air of gravitas, of menstrual synchrony.'

'What, are you a biologist now? And keeping track of my periods?'

'Don't trivialize this.'

'*I* keep track of my periods, more scientifically than anything you do, as does Annabel, and it's unmistakable. Our periods are syncing. And it's a proven theory! The original study was in *Nature*, in the 1970s.'

'That "study", and once again the appellation is inappropriate, was thoroughly debunked. It was, at best, pseudo-science. And tell me: did you experience synchrony all those years you lived with Annabel and the other girls? When you shared a bedroom with Lydia?'

'No.'

'Why ever not?'

'I don't know, why don't you tell me? Enlighten me with your long experience of menstruation.'

'Perhaps because then you had no time for delusions. Liz and I might not have endorsed your choice of boyfriend, but you were impressively unsentimental about the guy. That was then.'

'So you're saying that, having observed something in my life, and made a conclusion on the basis of clear evidence, I should throw all that out because it doesn't fit the accepted science? I thought you were all about rationality and self-reflection?'

'In this case, what you're doing is interpreting facts to fit a theory you find attractive, which supports your sense of growing closer to your roommate. Liz will tell you, if she hasn't already, that she had a similar delusion herself when the original *Nature* article came out. Thousands of women suddenly realized their cycles were in sync. And it was all a mass delusion.'

'How is any of this *any* of your fucking business? Even if you were to have a sex change, you wouldn't menstruate. This isn't an experience you're ever going to have access to or understand. This isn't your world.'

Philip Nicholls rose and began gathering the dishes, which had always been his primary contribution to housework. 'I've always said, and believed, that it isn't my job to tell you how to live your life, and if, in the course of this conversation, I've violated that standard, I regret it. I've been thinking lately about whether I've been a little too indirect in my means of getting through to you. Not instructing you doesn't mean not telling you what I think: I believe in your moral autonomy, but also that I have plenty to offer you. But it doesn't seem like I have any great gift for directness. I apologize.'

Loading up both arms like a rickety conveyor belt, he left for the kitchen. The two women said nothing. Not for the first time, Rebecca longed for a mother capable of taking her side.

Grimmett had chosen Wednesdays, at midnight, for the weekly offline meeting of the Boston Gobstones Club, and had scheduled the first meeting in January, so as to keep the numbers down. The online membership was now in three figures, at least fifty of whom posted more than once a week. Grimmett didn't want them all to show up. 'This may be a hard analogy for you to follow, given the nature of Hinduism,' he said to Kannan, 'but think of this as being like the Catholic Church before Vatican-II. I'd rather my church be pure, made up of the truly devout, than large but impure.'

Grimmett hoped for a turnout of at least a dozen but under two dozen. They made sure to be the first people there, walking up from the People's Republik in Central, where Grimmett had drunk bourbon and compelled his friend to do the same. There was the problem of the weather. In January, the cold might depress turnout even beyond Grimmett's target. Tonight, the air fuzzed with snow, and as they took their positions and waited, Kannan was unable to keep his friend's face in steady view. If you were the type to go out on a night like this, it wasn't to stand around and talk Harry Potter. It was made for flightier entertainments.

If anyone did show up, would they recognize Grimmett? He was a public figure of a kind, but not having ever read the *Globe* and not owning a television, Kannan had no way of knowing whether his friend's face was a known one. He moved to stand beside Grimmett, the T station to their left and the Cambridge Savings Bank behind, and pulled out from his backpack his copy of *Goblet of Fire*, to ensure they were recognized. The sight of the book moved Grimmett to tears. 'A couple hundred yards away from here, maybe less, we stood in line, 7 July, and that book is the reason we met!'

Kannan had reflected more than once on the fact that he had never made someone cry, and that Grimmett was sure to be the first. That didn't mean he knew how to react.

Across Mass Ave., outside the southwest entrance to Harvard Yard, Annabel gave Rebecca a nudge. 'Look at those two,' she said. 'They're hugging like men without arms! Like double amputees.'

'Like World War I veterans meeting again after many years. So physically awkward, yet so loving.'

'I don't know if I'd call it loving, but it's definitely awkward. And the Indian guy has a Harry Potter book, they're definitely here for the meeting. I wonder if the other guy is Grimmett?'

'We'll soon find out. But I don't want to be the only other people there; let's come back in five minutes.' By the time they returned, Grimmett and Kannan had been joined by several other Gobstones members. Annabel and Rebecca made twelve and thirteen.

'I think that should be it,' Grimmett said. 'Let's begin.'

'But no!' said a woman who looked to Rebecca to be older than Grimmett and thus surely the oldest person there. 'Remember what

Professor Trelawney said at Christmas dinner at Hogwarts. When thirteen dine together, the first to rise is the first to die! Shall we wait for one more person?'

Rebecca looked from the woman to Grimmett, determined not to allow any eye contact with Annabel, whom she knew to be gesturing at Rebecca with her eyes, saying some variant of let's get the fuck out of here. Grimmett looked mildly at the older woman.

'As I recall, Minerva McGonagall had a great response to that line,' he said. 'Kannan, could you remind me?'

'We'll risk it, Sybill. Please sit down, the turkey's getting stone cold.' It came out slow-footed but sure, in an accent that sounded clumsily Americanized. The slowness was clearly unconnected to the effort of accurate recollection.

'That's right. And I don't want to go down some kind of theological tangent, but let's just say I'm on McGonagall's side here,' said Grimmett.

He opened the floor, but asked that there be no personal introductions—he was sure they'd all get to know each other through their contributions to the group. The discussion took in the various paths the group could take. Should they become a kind of book club, choosing a particular fanfic each week? Should they ban ship debate, given how saturated fandom was with it? A consensus formed around dividing each meeting into two halves: the first to discuss canon, the second fanon. The book club idea was rejected on the grounds that it was too prescriptive: a wonder of fanfic was that you could find exactly what suited *you*. Instead, there would be a round-robin of pitches, where each member told the others why they should read a particular fic.

Supplying Grimmett with the quote he had wanted was Kannan's only contribution. At two minutes to one, Grimmett declared the meeting closed, but Annabel, like one of those students who stays back after a lecture to sweet-talk the professor, tugged Rebecca along to meet Grimmett.

'I just wanted to say that I've been listening to your show since I was in middle school,' said Annabel. 'My parents didn't like my going out on Friday nights. Listening to *The Lonely Hour* rather than studying was all the rebellion I could manage. Then one night, last fall, we were driving to Cape Cod and we tuned in kind of by accident. That was the first either of us had heard of Harry Potter, and that's why we're here.'

'I'm touched,' said Grimmett. 'At my age, to introduce even one uninitiated person to the joys of Harry Potter brings great satisfaction. That my show led to the two of you being here ... now that really is something.'

'I don't know whether it was for better or worse, but that show of yours has transported both of us, Rebecca more than me even, to a place I had no clue existed. I never thought I could ever be part of a *fandom*.'

When meeting new people in a group, it took Rebecca a few minutes to get the melody of a conversation, as if she needed to tune her instrument to Annabel's. Now she had it. 'I went to see my parents last weekend. They're very high-minded, literary people, and I was almost too embarrassed to tell them how deep I'm lost in fandom. When I told them, they didn't get it all, but I really feel it's they who are missing out, not me who's crazy.'

'I'm no religious man, but you could draw an analogy with a new religion,' Grimmett said. 'The early Christians in the Roman Empire, say. I don't mind the word "fandom", after all I can hardly deny that I'm a fan, short for fanatic, a word whose origins lie wholly in the realm of religious devotion. But when people outside fandom use the word, it's always pejorative, as if we're members of some infantile cult. When it's them who have no idea what they don't know.'

'I hate to ask something really practical,' Annabel said. 'I didn't want to bring this up during the meeting itself. But is there any way you would be open to moving these sessions to the weekend? I'm in Boston this week, but I can't be the only one who travels for work during the week.'

'Annabel, I'm sure you are the only one,' said Rebecca. 'Annabel and I went to Harvard, which tends to warp your perceptions a bit. As a consultant, she has to travel Monday through Thursday most weeks. But most people in the real world have probably never even met a management consultant.'

'I doubt most people know what that even is,' said Grimmett. 'My own notion of it is very faint, and it's supposed to be my job to know a little bit about everything. Kannan might know, though,' and he tapped his friend on the shoulder, 'as he has a greater connection than I do to corporate America. I'm sorry about the time, but I don't think we can move it; please do come when you are here, and the other weeks you'll have to live vicariously through your friend.'

And then he swivelled his head from Kannan to Rebecca to Annabel and back again, stopping at Rebecca this time, in the manner of someone who is about to change the subject without yielding the floor. 'Now that the meeting per se is over, I think we can allow for personal introductions. I'd like you to meet Kannan properly. He's the real Harry Potter expert here; in his native India, I'm sure this would be thought an enormity, given our respective ages, but I'm more or less his student in these matters.'

If it were Kannan's place here to produce some bit of real or false modesty, he either didn't know it or didn't care. To Rebecca he looked a person who would rather be anywhere other than where he stood, which was odd for such a devoted fan. But then he extended a hand first to Annabel, said, 'Nice to meet you,' with a credible smile, and then to Rebecca, although he didn't turn his gaze from Annabel to her as he did it. This absolved her of the requirement to speak next.

'I'm sure we already have met, in the Yahoo! group,' said Annabel. 'What's your screen name?'

As Rebecca half-expected, Grimmett answered, not Kannan. What exactly was his role here? The line about Kannan being his teacher seemed obviously to imply that he hoped it was the inverse. Were they friends? The double amputee hug seemed to rule out anything sexual, although she shouldn't be so presumptuous in making a judgement like that. Was Grimmett looking to protect Kannan, or was it just his nature to speak whenever the chance arose?

'In the circumstances, I think we can say that isn't too personal a question,' he said. 'I lived for many years in England, where I came to learn, the hard way, about all the nuances of what is and isn't an unacceptably personal question. Our standards here are laxer, of course. But Kannan, don't tell her. Why don't you try and guess?'

'How the heck am I supposed to do that? Hmm, okay, if you're asking I guess that means it's a deducible name. I don't think there's anyone with an Indian-sounding name. Let me see. chudcannon26? Is that you?'

'That's very impressive,' said Kannan. 'How did you know?'

'Well, Mr Grimmett'—and Grimmett did not suggest an alternative form of address— 'said you were a real expert, and we've all seen on the group that you have the books basically memorized. And I thought maybe "cannon" isn't a million miles from your name, although I'm not sure I caught quite the right pronunciation.'

'It's Kannan,' said Grimmett. 'K-A-N-N-A-N, although the spelling will lead you astray. It's really quite easy—kun-un. Both syllables rhyme with "fun".'

'You can call me Cannon if you like. It's not as easy as Curtis says it is. People have said my name a lot of different ways.'

'Well, I feel like I already thought of you that way, through your posts,' Annabel said. 'But Rebecca here is the one who pays them more attention, I'm sure, as you're shipmates. I'm pretty grossed out by all that Harry/Hermione stuff. My ship is Guns and Handcuffs.'

'Oh, we're more than shipmates,' said Rebecca. 'I'm in your debt, in a pretty serious way. Your Fanon Canon thread is how I discovered Perdita and *Time Regained*. Which is how I came to fall in love with fanfic, and to ship Pumpkin Pie.' Kannan didn't say anything to this, didn't even look as if he was thinking of whether he ought to, but for the first time he looked intently towards her. She thought he was looking straight at her face without allowing even a flicker of eye contact. It looked a difficult trick to pull off.

'Oh no, you're the one who put her on to that pre-adolescent trash,' said Annabel. 'She says she's in your debt, but now I know whom to blame.'

'Kannan will be more than glad,' said Grimmett. 'His approach to these things is—although he might reject the word—evangelical. To convert people like you to Pumpkin Pie is one of the reasons he started that thread.' Kannan didn't have a chance to respond, because Grimmett went on. 'What are your screen names?'

'We both went for our places of birth,' said Annabel. 'I'm southbostonchung, which is a mouthful, I know, but you won't have noticed it; I just read fanfic, I don't post. Rebecca's is fancier, of course. She's bayswater1977.'

On a usual weeknight Annabel hoarded every minute of sleep. Now she looked like she wanted to stay, so it was Rebecca who took charge.

'Well, we'd better be going,' she said, 'but it was lovely to meet you both, and I'm looking forward already to next week.'

Kannan and Grimmett watched the girls walk away, arm in arm, their perpendicular elbows locked together, and with their near-identical grey coats and black leggings they looked like a Hindu swastika. They evidently didn't lock arms to be safe in the snow, for they walked quickly, at a pace, surely, that precluded conversation. Neither man spoke until they had walked past Widener and were out of sight. Kannan was waiting for Grimmett. Would his friend speak first of the meeting, or of what had come after?

'Well, well,' said Grimmett. 'What did you make of that? That Chinese girl is, through no fault of her own, I'm sure, of a type I'm somewhat allergic to. Hillary Clinton-like, you know. Her friend had more charm. And attractiveness?'

'I thought she was a vision,' said Kannan. 'I noticed that her nose was ever so slightly turned upwards. Is that considered attractive?'

'By some people, yes.'

'I couldn't look at her while we were talking because I was scared I would just look at her nose. And her hair. I wish it were daylight, so that I could pin down its colour.'

'Well, I thought she had a wonderful voice, and accent. I couldn't quite put my finger on what it reminded me of. It was well met, that's for sure. And I'm not sorry her Chinese friend can't make it on Wednesdays, unless that holds her back, too.'

Dearest Kannan,

My father isn't usually given to dispensing advice. But today before leaving for work he suddenly stopped at the door and said these two things, out of the blue! He said that emails (he calls them 'electronic mails') were the best way for us to communicate until I join you. That even though you get cheap calling cards in the US now, it's strange to talk to someone on the phone when you don't really know them; it puts a kind of pressure on the people involved, which writing does not. And he said that I shouldn't try to use these emails as a way to 'get to know' you. We have our whole lives for that. Not just in the sense of having time, but that you never stop getting to know your husband or wife. All we need to do is 'stay in touch', he said. That's one of those fortunately vague phrases that one can make mean anything!

Do you remember when we were in Cubbon Park and you said that one of the things you liked about America was that you didn't have relatives around you giving you 'free advice'? Of course I agree, but I think that when someone gives it so rarely, then advice, when it comes, is a form of love. And I think it is good advice.

What do you think? If you'd like to talk on the phone, I'd be happy to. Why would I turn down a chance to hear your voice? But if you agree with Appa, then we can email as often as we both like. I know that I've only spent a few hours with you and shouldn't make any assumptions, but something tells me that you'll feel as he does.

I've been thinking about how it's not just that we hardly know each other. So much else is unknown, to be determined. Only a generation ago our parents knew exactly what to do and how, what would happen and when. It was scripted. I couldn't have called you by your name. We would have exchanged our first letters after marriage, if, for instance, you had to go away on work. If for some reason we were allowed to write before marriage, my mother, were she alive, would have dictated the letter!

Now it's up to us: whether and how often to write, what to call each other, what to say. And I may have (almost) two degrees in English but I can't begin to express how exciting I find that: the thought that our lives will be this shared searching for what we want and what we ought to do.

Impatiently awaiting your reply,

Your Malathi

PS: I have been reading *Time Regained*, but I'm only halfway through (it's longer than *Goblet of Fire*!), so you'll have to give me a little while to tell you more.

8

Every potential contribution to fandom was now fraught with opportunity. But Kannan was used to seeing his posts in this way, not so much in Gobstones, but in HP4BK and GCR, where each post was a chance to make a certain name for himself, to establish a position in a world. It was an instinct he had never felt outside fandom, a lack that he dimly knew made all the difference between him and Santhanam. So he was not unprepared. This was opportunity on a different scale; he could accept that. He could accept, too, that even if each post made the best possible impression, the cumulative effect of those impressions might not get him even a tiny fraction of the way to what he wanted—whatever that was. She had given him no grounds for optimism; she had given him nothing.

One of the girls on his floor at Northeastern had been a neuroscience major, and she had once explained to him that the more times you tried to recall the details of an incident, the less accurate the memory became. Memory wasn't like a video cassette that you could rewind and watch again; each viewing polluted the original memory with false additions or modifications. He didn't doubt this theory, based as it surely was on solid science, but he thought he could disregard it when it came to a memory that was only a day old and, if he excluded the Gobstones meeting and restricted his field of view to the two-on-two interaction, had lasted maybe eight minutes. Every potential ground for optimism turned out to be a false positive. 'Lovely to meet you,' she had said, but that was just American insincerity, diction that seemed to have made its way from customer service into everyday conversation. Her choice of words was the blandest possible. She had been so unmoved that this was all she could come up with.

Then there was the matter of her 'debt', as she had called it. At the time he had barely registered what she was saying, only that she was addressing him, and knew who he was, online. Later, he had thought it signified a triumph. Unlike 'Lovely to meet you', it referred to something substantial and specific to him. But she had said 'debt', and that word belonged to the realm of accounting rather than intimacy. Here, too, there was nothing for him to hold to.

Kannan was in the unfamiliar position of being home at five o'clock. When he wasn't heading straight from work to meet Grimmett, he rarely walked straight home. Instead, he would head south from tailgate. com's Kenmore Square office, along the Fens, past the Museum of Fine Arts, before looping back to his apartment in the South End. It was a walk he had first developed at Northeastern, although these days he took care to stay at least three streets away from campus. The exact path varied, but, still mindful of Santhanam's letter of four years ago, he never ventured into Roxbury. Santhanam had never been to Boston, but he seemed to know all about which neighbourhoods it was safe to enter at what time of day (Roxbury: never).

He told Grimmett about these walks, but described a fictitious arc that started northeast rather than southwest, taking in the river and Beacon Hill. It wasn't that his friend wouldn't approve of the real route. But the walks were the only part of his day, and his life in this city, that were his alone; they had begun as an exultation in aloneness, and as Kannan had shed other forms of aloneness, he knew that he should keep this one. He didn't tell Malathi about them for a different reason. She would have so many questions that he'd be unable to answer. The walks were for thinking about the fandom evening ahead, and for escaping thought altogether, noticing only the feeling of each stride against the pavement, sometimes counting the steps it took to cross a street. He couldn't tell her about the shops and restaurants he passed, or the cars or trees or people, least of all the buildings. At best he could name the streets, and direct her to an architectural guide to Boston. She wouldn't like that.

Today he came straight home because it seemed that fandom couldn't wait. But once at his desk, he saw that he'd made a mistake. He didn't know where to begin. In a fandom sense, he'd thought himself prepared. But this wasn't just a matter of advancing in fandom.

Of course there were girls Kannan had found attractive, in college, and in his Bangalore locality. He had been as good at discreet staring as the next man, likely better. But not only had he never got beyond staring, he stared less intently than the other boys, and he never lingered on a particular girl long. He knew these things because boys talked, even Vinay and Ashok; even they rated girls, and made ranked lists, and devised strategies, and occasionally actually approached girls, always accepting the first rebuff. Kannan joined in the rating and ranking; it would have caused more trouble not to. But he was happy to get no further. Even Vinay and Ashok had more experience than he did of situations like this.

He could go six months these days without thinking of either of them.

These thoughts were a way, he now saw, of dodging the real questions—of what he was to do, and of what might come of it. He looked around his living room and tried to place Rebecca in it. Where would she sit? His parents and brother had never visited him, but the apartment was true to the virtues they prized: cleanliness and economy. The dining table, a cheap plywood affair, and its four chairs had been given for free by a graduating student. He never sat there if he could help it—thus far he could always help it. He couldn't offer her his swivel chair. That left what he thought of as Grimmett's chair. For two years, the whole room had stood empty bar the dining table and desk; when Grimmett entered his life, hived off part of his aloneness, he'd asked him where he bought his armchairs, and bought one to match. The four times Grimmett had come over for a drink, that was where he'd sat, and that was where Rebecca would have to sit. But when he placed her there, he found that he couldn't settle on an image of her. Her face, that nose, came clearly to mind, but nothing below the neck. He tried instead to look not at her but as her: look at the room as she might.

The only objects of any substance, the only luxury, were the large combination desk-bookshelf and swivel chair at which he spent his evenings. He'd spent his first signing bonus on them; by then he knew that unlike Santhanam he wouldn't send money home, and that if he was going to spend his life at home on the PC, he should do it in comfort. The bookshelves held the British and American editions of the four books, plus books about J.K. Rowling and Harry Potter—all of them unsatisfactory—and spiral-bound versions of the fics he liked most to reread. Malathi would know what to make of this room, what to do with it. Rebecca—even with Grimmett's chair, how would she interpret its emptiness? She might think he was still moving in. That would be the easiest story.

But how could he see as she would, or devise a strategy, when all he knew of her were those eight minutes? The Gobstones meeting itself had told him nothing; he hadn't known that she was what he should be paying attention to. Then he saw that now, in the short term, fandom wasn't yet a way to impress or charm her. It was a way to pursue her in another sense: of investigation. He had one crucial piece of information: her screen name. The first step was to go to GCR and Gobstones and read or reread every single post by bayswater1977.

This pursuit was only more futility. There were exactly twelve posts: nine on GCR, three on Gobstones. None were longer than a paragraph. None were controversial, or original, or notable in any way: they either expressed agreement with another user, or affection for a fic or a character. Not one of them was worth rereading. No wonder her screen name had meant nothing to him. All that he could tell was that she wrote in formal sentences that sounded more like Grimmett or J.K. Rowling herself than any American he knew.

Other than his trip to Bangalore, this was the first day in 2001, the first since late November, that he had avoided his friend. There were days when they couldn't meet—on Thursdays Grimmett often had too much work—but on those days they spent at least an hour chatting, in the form of rapid-response emails rather than instant messenger. These exchanges always took place in the evenings; Grimmett knew how little Kannan worked, but still he could not countenance disturbing him at the office.

Unlike so much—everything else—in their friendship, this format hadn't resulted from a plan or preference of Grimmett's. One night in their first month of knowing each other, Kannan had written to congratulate Grimmett on a Gobstones post. Grimmett had replied within minutes, and twenty emails later Kannan signed off with: 'this was fun'. He'd never expressed to Grimmett the private pleasure he felt at this form of communication that was uniquely theirs. The thrill of waiting three minutes after he'd pressed send to refresh his inbox and find the reply was something that the instant-messaging millions could not know. Sometimes, instead of waiting at his desk, he would get up and walk to the window, and see before him not the South End of Boston but a grey owl on the horizon, bringing with it Grimmett's reply.

Today he'd come home to an email from Grimmett, setting up an exchange about last night's Gobstones, and ignored it. It wasn't so much, as he was sure Grimmett would think, that he needed the time to sort through his thoughts on his own. It was more the matter of defining Grimmett's position. For all that it had been Grimmett who had pointed first to Rebecca's charms, thus enabling his own confession, his friend was not competition. But, equally, he wasn't sure that Grimmett had anything to offer, practically speaking. He could never have gone anywhere in fandom without Grimmett. But this was another realm, to which Grimmett was condemned to be denied entry. He did not know how he knew this, only that he did.

If Grimmett presented neither threat nor assistance, that left the question of what he owed his friend. Here he was much less certain. He had told Grimmett nothing about the purpose or principal event of his trip to Bangalore, saying only that his brother had been promoted and had insisted on the unwanted gift of his first visit home. The next visit, for the marriage, would need some new excuse.

What about when Malathi arrived in the US? Could you conceal a wife from a best friend? There was an implicit contract in which Kannan was entitled to keep much more of himself away from Grimmett than the other way around. How much more, he couldn't say. He couldn't prevent Grimmett from seeing Malathi in anthropological terms. He might silently reproach Kannan for the manner of the marriage, or he might see it as wonderful, the fulfilment of Kannan's destiny as an Indian man, of his family history and his particular place. Kannan was entitled to not give him the chance. But he owed Grimmett this much: if he was going to turn his own involvement in Gobstones, and in fandom more broadly, into pursuing Rebecca, Grimmett had to be informed. His ownership of his own life in fandom was partial; Grimmett had always had a stake. And Grimmett was American and could at least prevent him from misunderstanding her words.

That Thursday, he thought of online fandom in these instrumental terms, and of Harry Potter itself only once. Before yesterday's meeting, he had written up a list of potential discussion topics for Gobstones. One prompt was the question: if you could possess one magical object, other than a wand, which would you choose? Grimmett found this sort of question infantile: he had said, many times, that they had to avoid any question that involved imagining ourselves in some way capable of *physically* entering the magical world. 'That's the kind of thing that gives escapism a bad name,' Grimmett said. 'I'm trying to redeem escapism.'

But Kannan thought he could make a case for this question as a permissible exception. Magical objects always served some particular, limited purpose: this was yet another example of JKR's genius, of her ability to keep humans, rather than magic, at the centre of the world. And he could stipulate that, as a Muggle, possessing the object wouldn't give *you* any magical powers: you wouldn't be able to fly on a Firebolt any more than on your own household broom. An honest answer to his question could be revealing, even uncomfortably so. For a moment, the fact that he thought of this suggested he was capable of sustained thinking on matters other than Rebecca. But this idea that had, only yesterday, possessed such autonomous glamour now refashioned itself as another way to advance in her consciousness.

When he first arrived at Northeastern, it had taken only a few days for him to see just how ill Santhanam had judged his taste. It didn't matter that he didn't have the confidence to approach an American girl; he didn't have the inclination. More than anything, it was the white skin that repelled him: a thick, insipid, powdery whiteness that recalled his mother's coagulated payasam. Not that he was some contrarian admirer of darkness. The phrase 'dusky beauty' was a form of linguistic affirmative action, a consolation prize for those who could not truly be beautiful. Fairness was still to be prized, but not up to the point of whiteness. What justified this exception? Surely he hadn't been tricked by the light, which in Harvard Square at midnight had the disorienting quality of an aircraft cabin after sunset. She was white, an undeniably pale white, but he was sure her whiteness, admittedly made up, was finer, more definite than other women's. It was a self-justifying but unfalsifiable thought, at least until next Wednesday. Today, Thursday, was the day by which he had promised Malathi he would write. It was a slow period at work, he had said; he would have plenty of time to email. This remained true, but she would have to wait. If, as chudcannon26, he meant anything at all to Rebecca, she might notice even a day's absence from the forums. And even the most pessimistic view of things allowed that, after meeting him, she might look at his posts with new interest.

He couldn't know exactly what would make an impression on her. But just posting on a thread he knew she followed wouldn't do. She might miss it and, in any case, what new was there to be said on the Deathmarch anyway? How could you stand out when every possible argument had already been made a dozen times? He would start a new thread: one that she was bound to see, because everyone would see it and talk about it. He had wanted for months to start a debate on the idea of One Big Happy Weasley Family. OBHWF—no fandom cow was holier. He had wanted to wait until he was more sure of his own position in fandom; he didn't want to be thought of as an attention-seeker. But he couldn't afford such worries now.

In the week between the first and second offline meetings of the Boston Gobstones Club, Rebecca resolved to pull away a little from fandom. She didn't need to follow the alcoholic's approach of unrelenting self-denial: this was a legitimate hobby, but one that needed to be reined in. At IvyEdge, Connie was determined to prevent the affliction of senioritis from spreading from the applicants to their counsellors. March would bring the anxious pilgrimage of parents and juniors to Boston for the college visits that marked the formal opening of the application process. For selected applicants, Connie offered free guided tours of Harvard, MIT, Wellesley, Tufts, Brown and BC: a loss leader intended to decisively win a family's trust. Rebecca had long suspected that these tours were a primary reason for her own hiring.

Until then, she was tasked with selling IvyEdge to prep-school headmasters and headmistresses across New England. Connie had decided to soften her adversarial attitude to her clients' schools. As an upstart in an underdeveloped market, she had seen high-school counsellors as her primary competition. When pitching parents, she would insist that the profession of college counsellor attracted only the most clueless and apathetic.

But she had come to recognize that working with, rather than against, schools was the only way for IvyEdge to truly scale. Her new sales pitch was that encouraging students to use IvyEdge would allow schools to employ fewer or part-time counsellors at a time of recession. And schools that brought in sufficient business would be offered discounts that they needn't pass on to their students. It was one thing to delegate the preparation of the pitch, but Rebecca wondered at Connie's decision to send her out to these schools, callow and twenty-three, rather than go herself. It spoke to a self-awareness that she hadn't credited Connie with. The absence of self-awareness, like hypocrisy, is only noticed in other people.

If work required more of Rebecca than previously, it wasn't this that compelled her to pull back. She had begun to perceive a certain narrowing of her life, less than monomania, but a too-specific concentration of her psychological energy, what her mother would call imbalance.

This concern pushed up against the idea that balance and emotional diversification were all she had ever known. Could she accuse or credit herself with total immersion in anything, ever? She'd never felt the consuming obsession of first love that, whether it lasted a few days or a marriage, appeared from books and those around her to be the most universal human experience short of birth and death. Not in high school; not with Connor. Some part had always been held back. It wasn't that she failed to commit. She had always been reliable, steadfast, attentive, but she was unable to forget in the way that immersion demands: forget everything other than the object of the obsession.

All she remembered of her first real date, aged thirteen, were various scenes from *Father of the Bride*—she could summon, just about, the face of the boy next to her, the bumps from the razor he hadn't really needed to use, but she couldn't say whether they had held hands, or how any of it had felt. It probably hadn't felt like much. On stage, whether in high school or college, she never sealed herself off from life outside. She had once come up with a thesis for an essay on *To the Lighthouse* while delivering a speech as Rosalind in *As You Like It*. The *Crimson*'s reviewer had called her the production's 'most convincing presence'.

The thrill of the new that she felt on entering fandom might have been less fandom itself than the feeling of immersion, and the new knowledge that she too had the capacity for it. Why pull back now and award victory to the dull good sense of her former life? In part, she wondered if Harry Potter was an aberration; balance and restraint made up the major part of her character, and were always going to reassert themselves.

What handed them their decisive advantage now was her discovery of the limits of fan fiction. Before Toronto, she had identified and finished twenty or so well-done adult fanfics, and assumed there would be countless more. Now her explorations only bored her; she seemed to have already read all that was worth reading and, *Time Regained* aside, none of it was worth rereading.

She made the mistake of saying as much to Perdita. She thought her new friend might be flattered to be described as the only writer of any value in all fandom. Codswallop, said Perdita. There's so much good stuff out there. Athena Alice above all; she's our Cervantes. Then Rebecca cautiously raised the matter of Athena Alice's plagiarism.

All fanfic, said Perdita, was copying anyway. That was why authors had the right to ban fanfic, to declare it theft. Anne Rice had done that, famously. They were conscious, always, of how generous and indulgent it was of JKR to allow them to use her creations; after all, wasn't it the highest aim of every writer of fanfic that, late at night in Edinburgh, her daughter safely asleep, J.K. Rowling would get up from her desk, where she had been struggling over a key chapter of Book Five, and place herself in her favourite armchair by the fireplace, in search of inspiration or, better still, diversion, with a printed-out version of the fic that everyone was talking about? (These details came from a Scottish member of Harry Potter for Big Kids, hufflepuffofmidlothian, who claimed to have delivered pizza to Rowling's house.) If you had qualms with plagiarism, you might as well ban fandom. Let's face it: Athena's success had made a lot of people jealous.

Rebecca left it there. She didn't want to be thought one of those who had been made jealous.

What was new about reading fanfic, anyway? She had always devoured novels with greater speed and enthusiasm than anything else. Put the question to him in these terms, and her father would say: you're the same as ever. It's only the quality of what you spend your time reading that's changed. She walked down to the Harvard Book Store and picked up *Disgrace* and *The Human Stain*.

That Thursday night, having read no fanfic at all, Rebecca logged on to GCR for a last look before bed. There she found Kannan, chudcannon26—she didn't quite know whether she was supposed to think of these as one person or two—in the form of a new thread that had been active less than two hours but had already turned into a shitstorm. The topic was an acronym: OBHWF. chudcannon26 had opened proceedings with this post:

This thread is meant for the discussion of one of the most popular concepts in fandom. OBHWF, or One Big Happy Weasley Family. OBHWF is based on four assumptions. One, that the Weasleys are J.K. Rowling's ideal family. Two, that independent of what JKR thinks, it is impossible to imagine a better or happier or more loving family. Three, that Harry has already chosen them as his family, since he doesn't have one of his own. Four, that the Weasleys would be even bigger and happier and more perfect if their children marry the right people. So OBHWF is a product of shipping. The central pillars are Ron/Hermione (I refuse to call this the Good Ship) and Harry/ Ginny. Many people would add Fred/Angelina, as well as maybe Bill/Fleur and George/Katie (or Alicia). Percy/Penelope is taken for granted and Charlie (for now) is not paired off. But many of us do not support OBHWF for various reasons. This is not restricted to those like me who sail the Pumpkin Pie. The idea behind this thread is to debate whether OBHWF is destined to happen as well as whether it should happen.

Some of the responses suggested the imminent issuance of a fatwa. One user, Hobgoblin, replied individually to every single anti-OBHWF post, ending each time with: 'If you don't love the Weasleys, you don't deserve Harry Potter.' Some got more personal. 'Fandom is no place for people like you,' said nantucket1966, addressing Kannan. 'If JKR were to read this, she would be so upset that she would wonder why she bothered to write at all.' Curtis Grimmett, one of the few people in fandom who posted under his own first and last name, was nowhere to be seen.

Rebecca's scepticism was well-founded, the evidence gathering with every post, but she found herself fighting back against it. It was almost a law in her generation, and at Harvard it was the whole of the law, that naive idealism was either to be exorcised in high school or else sufficiently coated in irony. The old notion that idealism was the only proof of humanity in a young person, and that you needed to be hit with life and responsibilities and a mortgage before giving it up: that was an unmourned delusion that had served only to justify the silliest excesses of post-adolescence. If chastity and continence are what I need, I don't want to wait for them.

But the idea of a Harry Potter fandom in which Ron Weasley was the most widely beloved character, in which Molly was the perfect mother, in which Hermione was surreptitiously disliked and thought of only as a future daughter-in-law … OBHWF had to be stopped. There had been holdouts at Harvard, of course. She had seen them march for the Tutsis and for a living wage for the custodial staff. But to find an activist impulse rising within her was like waking up to find that she had grown a horn overnight.

Rebecca had posted on 'A Fanon Canon', and on threads where Harry/Hermione shippers pooled their warmth and sentimentality, but this was her first contribution to a debate. What could she say that was new—or worth restating? She fell back on the tactical memory of high school debate: ignore the other side, focus on the judges. If there were neutral readers, let them see that the OBHWF-sceptics were reasonable and decent, and wrote good prose. She included no criticisms of the Weasleys themselves. Instead she built her case on Perdita's insight: the idea of One Big Happy Weasley Family grew out of the coupling of Ron and Hermione. Yes, they seemed likely to date as teenagers, but how could we assume that they would get married? If OBHWF was what as subtle a writer as J.K. Rowling had in mind, then why had she given Harry and Hermione all the ingredients of long-term compatibility? She ended with a personal plea to certain posters—'on both sides,' she said, but she meant Hobgoblin—'I'm not naming any names, but surely we can all calm the f**k down? This is just a fandom thread, not a family feud.'

She couldn't help checking the replies before work the next morning. There were two that addressed her directly, both asserting that compatibility, which was in the eye of the beholder, was what a Harry/Hermione shipper with no real arguments fell back upon. Hobgoblin hadn't even bothered to reply. But, alone at the office, Rebecca checked GCR again. She had a message from Hobgoblin. Not on the thread, but a private Owl:

Subject: Your vile post!!!!!

Do you really believe after all JKR has said, since before *Goblet of Fire*, that Harry/Hermione has a chance in hell of happening?

If you like this ship and want to keep supporting it in Fandom, that is fine, but as for trying to prove it is actually going to sail, despite what the author has said, is unbelievable!!!!

As for the question you ask, reread the books and you will see that Harry and Ginny have been written to be compatible, NOT Harry and Hermione.

And before you read, take off those 'Pumpkin Pie'-tinted glasses that distort canon and misinterpret stuff like 'Hippogryffs', 'teacups', 'Pig flying' and 'toast'.

> If you think I am rude then I'm telling you that anyone that uses foul, filthy, language like the 'f' word at me deserves much worse.
>
> I have reported your post for swearing and let me tell you, you give Harry/Hermione shippers a worse name than they already have!!!!!!!!

As Rebecca read this, she absorbed only individual words. On the second reading she began to grasp its message, but it made no deeper impression. Later, she thought she must have read this message more times than Connor's final email; it was much shorter. What would Annabel make of it? Annabel never laughed—when she felt especially triumphant she made a sort of grin with clenched cheeks—but to this she would say: serves you right, you should just stick to reading fan fiction, and stay away from this ship debate bullshit. Except I guess it's worth it, for the laughs. Oh, and this guy Hobgoblin is no older than twelve. Don't you have to be thirteen to be a member of GCR? Dude's lying about his age. Rebecca resolved not to show Annabel the Owl.

The Annabel-in-her-head was right about Hobgoblin being a child who was only worth ignoring. As much as she loved the books, why need she care about any of this, anyway? Maybe it was enough that she *did* care. And that, instead of deleting her GCR account and writing the past three months off as an amusing waste of time, she might find a better way to be in fandom, might salvage something more enduring from it.

What she needed was a guide to this world, someone other than Annabel to argue away her misgivings and help direct her attention. Would seeking out Curtis Grimmett in this way be like befriending one of her professors in the quest for life advice? But while Grimmett was, in a way, entirely unlike her father, professorial, this was an opportunity to stop thinking like she was still in college. Wasn't this where the human potential of Harry Potter fandom lay—in its suspension of the usual hierarchies and assumptions and prejudices? Befriending Grimmett might end up being what her involvement in all this was *for*.

Her first email to Grimmett said only that she wanted him to know how much she had enjoyed the Gobstones meeting, and she hoped he wouldn't mind if she wrote to him from time to time. There were questions and occasionally insights that came to her over the week that she'd rather put to someone she knew offline than to the forums.

As she pressed send she wondered if she had written to the right person. Kannan sailed the Pumpkin Pie and he had introduced her to Perdita. Not only was there no evidence of Grimmett sailing any ship at all, but it was impossible to conceive of him in relation to romance or sexuality, real or imagined. He seemed to have come from a world where those things didn't exist, where all births were virginal. Kannan was, surely, only a few years older than she was. His skin had the firm evenness and his face the settled definition that marked that tragically brief phase where someone is no longer maturing, and not yet ageing— their prime. The 26 might be his birthday, but it might be his age.

Every important concern she'd ever had about fandom must have occupied his mind, too, at some point. Not just about fandom, either; who knew how enriching it might be to see how someone whose background and temperament could not be more different from hers was grappling with *his* twenties? But she thought she knew how Grimmett would receive her email, and what would follow. She'd go home some weekend in June and tell her father about her new friend. With Kannan she had no way of knowing anything. That first email might be the last, unanswered and, the next week at Gobstones, unacknowledged.

And the fact that Kannan resisted her perceptive faculties ought not to intrigue her. She'd seen how these things worked from the other side. In her first two years at Harvard, the time before Connor, men were forever describing her, to her face and otherwise, as mysterious and enigmatic. When Connor first began to pursue her, Annabel warned him against it. The fact that something seems mysterious doesn't make it worth investigating, she had said. Sometimes that seeming mystery just conceals an emptiness, which is the case with Rebecca.

Unlike Grimmett, whose eccentricity was of a piece, the different bits of Kannan—his background, his accent, his build, his relationship with Grimmett, his career and his place in fandom—refused to fit together. But was there more to the interest and attention he provoked in her than the mere fact that she couldn't quite *get* him? The bit that she knew, chudcannon26, was earnest, uncompromising, committed, formidably supplied with facts. These weren't qualities she had consciously found appealing in the past—but why need that be relevant now? She was more than ready to set aside the tyranny of self-justification. You were aware of an interest in someone, and you tried to explain that in reference to their attributes. In the long run, you might tell yourself, or others might say of you, that you had a type. These things weren't knowable; they were stories that didn't need to be told.

She had written to Grimmett in the quest for friendship. With Kannan, she knew only that she wanted to know, and even if everything she found bored or repelled her, well, maybe there was no such thing as *worth knowing*, no such thing, really, as wasted time. The only question left was how. She wouldn't write to him yet, not until that presented itself as a surer means to knowledge. She would have to do something or the other at Gobstones.

9

Thursdays were Grimmett's day of work. The mornings were spent on the following week's show: finalizing a topic and arranging guests. The afternoons and evenings were for research for the following day: at his age, his ability to retain information in terminal decline, most of his preparation was done in this concentrated burst. Formerly this had meant a trip to a public library, either Boston or Cambridge; these days he rarely needed more than his desktop. On Thursdays he met Kannan later than usual, if at all, often for as little as half an hour.

And then, before bed, he put on an episode of *Desert Island Discs*, the lambent star at the heart of radio's greatest constellation.

When he accepted that he had moved back to America *for good*—the phrase still made him shudder—he promised himself that no calendar year would pass without at least one visit to Britain. And he kept his promise, but as the years passed, and his British life receded further, he was less and less drawn to old haunts, or to old acquaintances from Birmingham or London. Nothing so pathetic as nostalgia, that basic inability to accept that life moved forwards. Instead, he conceived of these two-week trips as supplements to an American life. He thought rigorously about what his Boston lacked, and it was this that propelled him each time to the same bookshops and galleries and shoemakers, and to Italian restaurants run by actual Italians. But he came to see that the most significant difference between Britain and America, or at any rate between *his* Britain and his America, was that in America one could not listen to Radio 4. With each year, he grew more disinclined to leave his hotel room, and he timed his meals for programmes he could live with missing. This was how he came to properly discover *Desert Island Discs*.

For years he consumed two episodes per visit, each time marvelling again at the perfection of the format. Most radio was music *or* interview, but music as a way into a life; this was what radio was *for*.

The first time he heard Sue Lawley host *Desert Island Discs*, Grimmett knew he couldn't wait a year. He needed to be able to listen year-round, to possess every episode, for posterity as much as pleasure. He had an old colleague from the publishing house that he suspected could use the money. Every month, for a fee that might seem lavish to the ignorant, the tapes arrived.

What was it about Sue Lawley that had such an effect on him? As a fellow interviewer, he could identify with admiration her fearlessness— the willingness to ask the sort of question that was on every audience member's mind, but that the typical celebrity interviewer could or would not ask—and her penetration, the ability to get to the core of a castaway's experience or character. She had an infallible sense, too, for the rhythm of an episode. Every week he waited to see if she would, for once, get the timing of a record wrong. She never did. Lawley might discomfit her castaways with her directness, but she did so only temporarily, for she knew exactly when to move from cross-examination to sympathy, and in this movement she expanded the possibility for moments of genuine feeling.

But, in truth, it was her voice. He was sure it was the voice itself, not the accent, for it wasn't the sort of quality you could acquire through practice. It was a voice, if you liked that sort of thing, to deliver sexual punishment. It was an unbreachably firm voice, but with hidden reserves of kindness, deployed only once or twice per episode, such as when discussing a bereavement. After offering her castaway their book and a luxury, she always said, 'Thank you very much indeed for letting us hear your desert island discs.' Grimmett hated when the castaway replied. It was never anything more edifying than, 'It's been a pleasure, Sue,' and it meant that hers could not be the last voice he heard before bed.

As he grew to know Kannan in the summer of 2000, Grimmett never saw in his new friend a potential admirer of *Desert Island Discs*. He would find it too foreign, too fusty, the wrong kind of sentimental. He wouldn't have heard of any of the castaways or recognize much of the music, which tended towards the romantic and classical. To put it accurately: he just wouldn't *get* it. And his not-getting-it would upset Grimmett; would mar the perfect sympathy between them. Grimmett was terrified of upsetting Kannan. But to be upset by him, that was a far greater horror.

But then the rumours began to circulate on the forums. J.K. Rowling was to be cast away in early November. Quotes from the interview—revelations about her life or future books—would find their way to newspapers and the forums well before Grimmett's tapes arrived. But you couldn't reduce an episode of *Desert Island Discs* to a few quotes or a summary. To be able to listen to the whole episode was, for an American, a privilege to be treasured, and to be shared only with Kannan.

He told Kannan nothing of the show's history or its part in his own life. He only explained the format. It could scarcely have begun any better. Lawley was a little glib in asking JKR how she was 'coping' with success, but otherwise a model of balanced restraint. Perhaps this was less a conscious decision than the only human response to this castaway. JKR combined unaffected grace with easy charm, and she was funny, which he hadn't taken for granted, because people with a gift for making children laugh tended to be insufferably unfunny adults.

Kannan listened to her in pure rapture. He probably wasn't even aware of Sue Lawley. Thankfully, he knew nothing of Grimmett's anxiety, his fear that *Desert Island Discs* might show JKR up in some way.

Even her musical choices were excellent—and Lawley couldn't have spent any time in fandom, for she didn't ask JKR if the Smiths's song 'Girlfriend in a Coma' had inspired her decision to Petrify Hermione in *Chamber of Secrets*. Her last record was Mozart's *Requiem*. And now it was time for her to choose her book. What would she choose? Grimmett had spent hours going over the possibilities. He hoped it wouldn't be a children's book—they knew her favourites already. This was a chance to be surprised, to get to know some new aspect of JKR.

She asked for the SAS survival handbook. She could hardly have been more perverse if she had revealed that Sirius Black actually was a murderer. She had broken the rules of *Desert Island Discs*, if not the letter than the spirit. He had always thought this—choosing a book that offered practical help with survival or escape—the foulest possible violation of that spirit. But this was worse even than that. The woman whose imaginative capacity surpassed that of all other known human beings had just done the most unimaginative thing. For an instant Grimmett felt like a child who has just seen an idolized teacher make a spelling mistake.

But then Kannan said, 'SAS? What does that stand for? Do you have a copy?'

'No, but that's easily remedied.'

'I don't think I'd read it. I don't even think she was serious. But just because she asked for it.' And Grimmett saw that his friend had just passed forty-five of the happiest minutes of his life. For this alone he could be glad for Kannan's sake, not just his own, that they had met in line outside WordsWorth.

'While you wait on the handbook,' he said, 'take this tape.' Kannan didn't protest; how could he know that from this day on, Grimmett's set of Sue Lawley episodes would be complete bar one?

The two women they had met at Gobstones had said they had heard about Harry Potter on his show. Were they radio listeners? People their age weren't, as a rule, unless they commuted by car, and he wasn't on at a commuter hour. They'd probably never even heard of *Desert Island Discs*. Now, and for some reason this had taken him almost twenty-four hours, he placed Rebecca's accent. Last night he had noted the absence of any regional markers, but that could mean her family had moved around the country, or that she imitated TV rather than her peers. But now he saw that it was an American accent that had been formed overseas. He was almost sure she had lived in the UK. It is rather depressing to find that our instincts have run ahead of our rational faculties, have diagnosed something quicker. He ought to have seen all this last night.

Kannan had been captivated by her. This was unfamiliar terrain. Kannan had never spoken of sex, and of love only in the context of Harry and Hermione. The accent could have done nothing for Kannan. Nor could any of what she had said. It was her face, then, or rather her face in relation to that head of red hair.

There are two kinds of love at first sight. One is a visceral sexual attraction that, in the short term, provokes obsessiveness, but soon enough, in the face of new evidence, either flames out, leaving no ash behind, or is kindled into something enduring and substantial. The other, though its origins, once again, may lie in nothing more than red hair and an upturned nose, takes over like a transplanted pair of eyes. Every subsequent event or piece of information is assimilated or repurposed for the task of confirming the initial attraction, and thrown out if it can't be. If this love is unrequited, nothing can disprove the notion that you are condemned to be without the love of your life. If it is returned, if not with love than at least with consent, then perhaps, one day, the new vision will alter, the discarded bits of evidence will break out of the prison in the mind for unwanted thoughts, and will flood the consciousness, and it will have been so many years since you fell in love that you will see that love not as a delusion but as a cancer.

For Kannan's sake, please let it be the first kind. Even with the best and most careful intentions in the world, it was impossible to look at this young woman and not think that at Harvard she must have been successfully courted by some blonde, lacrosse-playing or crew-rowing son of the Northeastern establishment, not necessarily WASP these days, maybe Jewish, clubbable, diligent, now a junior banker on Wall Street, with the emotional security and narrow certainty about life's prospects that was the privilege of his class. Maybe she had grown tired of this fellow and traded him in for a hipper alternative who played indie rock and had read David Foster Wallace. Grimmett didn't get about enough in the world any more to be sure of it, but self-segregation, above all in matters of love and marriage, had always seemed to stand between his country and true multiculturalism.

Back when there were just two races, the ethnic mixing that had produced people like him was described as a *melting pot*, even though one race was barred from the pot not just by custom but by law, unless it was a rapist doing the melting. Now, white men sometimes took Asian, Hispanic or, more rarely, Black wives, by a form of consent rather than force, but with only a slight dilution of the traditional inequality of power. Something similar, he had read, was true of the Indian caste system: a man could, in certain circumstances, marry a woman of a lower caste, but the reverse was proscribed, so severely that the offspring of such a marriage were deemed outcaste, or Untouchable. These things worked more implicitly here, of course. A white woman dating or marrying outside her race would meet only parental disapproval, which could work as a form of encouragement, and perhaps not even that. Young women like Rebecca were beholden only to predictability, to the notion that freedom ought not to alter the basic form of a life. There was nothing more noble than emancipating someone from the belief that they could never be reproached for doing what was expected of them.

Rebecca wrote to Grimmett at lunchtime the next day. He saw the email just as he was setting out to meet Kannan.

> Dear Curtis,
>
> I just wanted to thank you for Wednesday night. Online fandom is wonderful, of course, but this felt necessary and, at least to me, new and unexpected. It's not a book club, not a support group—not that I have any experience of either—what is it? A community of feeling, I guess, except few shared feelings can be so intense. I was struck by how every single person there was someone I would never otherwise encounter. Or rather: I might encounter each of them every day, on the bus or the T, or ordering right before me at Starbucks, but never know that we shared the same private preoccupation, might even be waiting to get home to read the next chapter of the same fanfic.
>
> Anyway, there are times when I wish could discuss my HP-thoughts and questions outside the forums, with someone I can actually put a face to. If that's something you wouldn't mind, I'd like to be able to email you.
>
> Thanks again,
>
> Rebecca/bayswater1977 (you said on Wednesday that you lived in London for many years, but didn't say where; my parents were in Bayswater when they had me)

Bayswater; it was only a mile southwest of the Maida Vale bedsit in which he had spent his London years. Shorter than the walk to Central Square to meet Kannan, which constituted his daily exercise. But it stirred nothing in him, no visual memory, no personal association. He might remedy that on his next visit.

When walking to Central Square, Grimmett never cut through Harvard Yard. The students already had to put up with jabbering swathes of Asian and European tourists, even in January. He still passed plenty of students, of course, as he walked south down Mass Ave. the campus to his left and the Square to his right, but he never noticed them. Today—it must have been Rebecca that made him do it—he stopped outside Johnston Gate. A pair of students were walking out, holding hands in a complicated way: her left all the way across her in his left. But for her hair being dyed blonde rather than red, she could have been the Rebecca of a year ago. *He* was a type: square-jawed and bulky, a lumberjack shirt visible beneath his jacket, Doc Martens. The jock-god apparently still beloved in New England in what was now the twenty-first century. Not a type that had ever moved Grimmett. They were so wrapped up in each other that Grimmett was sure they would not register him or catch him staring.

People like this, he ought to have remembered, always catch someone staring.

They looked at him simultaneously: the girl kindly, the boy mild and confused. But then he regained his poise, so quickly as if Grimmett had imagined the confusion, and he was the one who spoke first.

'You look lost.'

Look at the state of our young people, thought Grimmett; at the very most, he should *ask* if I'm lost.

And then her: 'Are you visiting Harvard? Do you need us to help you find where you're going?'

Grimmett was not short of private urges that remained unfulfilled. Some mortified him; some only made him feel silly. He never knew whether they were unfulfilled out of better judgement or cowardice. Now one of these, long dormant, rose up from the hold and overwhelmed him. And he didn't suppress it. After all, this couple clearly thought he was a tourist.

So it was, that after thirty years of practice in the shower and in his sleep and before a mirror, Curtis Grimmett at last pretended to be English.

'Ah, yes. I'm terribly sorry to bother you.' Even better: he was living up to their idea of what an Englishman must sound like. 'I'm here for a conference on, on, um, Athenian democracy. Could you direct me to Boylston Hall? Thank you ever so much.' All that came to mind was the name of a building that he had once visited to interview a professor of French literature.

Carrying on the pretence meant walking through the Yard. He didn't look back at the couple; they didn't interest him apart from what they represented for Rebecca, for Rebecca and Kannan.

Even he could tell what Rebecca's email signified. That it was a departure. The normal course for a woman like Rebecca was not to willingly seek out the likes of him, certainly not in this way. There were two possibilities, and each of them pleased him, so much so that it didn't matter which was the truth. Either Rebecca was not as he presumed, and nothing like the girl who had just directed him to Boylston. Or she was like that, had been on that course, but now she wanted different. And what could be more different than a friendship with him? Well, something more than friendship with Kannan.

Grimmett exited the Yard. Later, he reckoned that if some student had seen him at that moment, they'd never have taken him for a tourist; the sheer energy of his cranial activity must have spilled over onto his face, invigorating what remained of his hair; he might have looked like a mathematician who has just unlocked an elusive proof, or a novelist who has found his ending. What he had was a question so new and potent that even Harry Potter seemed trivial by comparison. Rebecca and Kannan *must* be together, just as Harry and Hermione must; but here the justice of the universe seemed at stake. And anything Grimmett did to effect this would more than justify his own existence. The question was: what did he need to do?

But no gambit presented itself, not even a bad one. And as Grimmett passed the Plough and Stars, where he had taken Kannan for their second set of drinks, he had his crash. The first correction was minor enough: how could he think himself fit for purpose as a matchmaker, as a romantic engineer? But this was only the foreshock. The earthquake itself so disarmed him that he was compelled to first hold on to a lamp post and then sit on the steps leading up to an ATM until his breath began to settle. How could he do this again? How could he have learned nothing? There he was, trying to shape Kannan's life, treating him as a chess piece—*gambit*, he wanted to vomit at the word—all of it unasked for, unwanted.

The aftershock was merely depressing. He could not learn. He was incapable. He could only restrain himself.

What revived Grimmett, and thus preserved him from having to either pretend to be okay or invent some explanation for his guilt, was an alternative that arrived not as a way to redeem his guilt, but to redirect his energy. He wanted to give Kannan a gift. Not something like romantic help—as if a romance with Rebecca was in his gift—but something that he alone could conjure, something that would allow Kannan to be not simply happy, but happy with himself. What this might be, he had no idea; but he was certain one would appear soon.

By Friday afternoon, as he waited for his friend whom he hadn't seen in over forty hours, Kannan was conscious of no longer being under enchantment. When he woke that morning, his computer left on overnight, the OBHWF thread open, he checked the most recent posts, but didn't stop to think of whether she had seen the thread and what she might make of it. By noon, in the office, he had begun to draft his email to Malathi, and found it even slower going than an important GCR post. And at one o'clock, catching up properly on the thread, he read the long post by bayswater1977, laying out the limitations of OBHWF with moving precision, and didn't even read it as Rebecca. He thought, instead: this is a person who gets it, and a teammate worth having.

When meeting in the afternoon, Grimmett and Kannan always took the same table at 1369 Coffeehouse in Central Square. Grimmett took the seat facing Mass Ave. Kannan faced only Grimmett. Like most of their arrangements, this had been established by Grimmett, uncontested, but never codified. As he waited, Kannan realized that unless he took Grimmett's seat instead, he would miss Rebecca if she were to walk by. That he didn't marked the passing of the enchantment, or at least his consciousness of that passing.

Grimmett arrived, congratulated his friend on the success of the thread, and began to talk about tonight's show, on the prospects for peace in Sri Lanka. He didn't expect Kannan to have anything to contribute. He hoped, in fact, to educate his friend, whose ignorance about the other countries of South Asia was pristine. Grimmett had met people in Lowell who had never been to Boston, so he didn't judge Kannan too harshly. He suspected, however, that unless the subject was Harry Potter, Kannan wasn't in the habit of listening to *The Lonely Hour*, so he might as well get all the information in now.

In the first twenty minutes he only permitted himself one digression. 'That girl we met the other night, Rebecca Nicholls, wrote to me.'

'She emailed you? Or sent a GCR Owl?'

'An email. It was a delightful surprise. She just wanted to thank me for such a pleasurable meeting. Delightful manners. Oh, and perhaps you'd figured this out, but she's the author of that eloquent post supporting our position on your OBHWF thread. She was born in Bayswater, in London.'

'She told us that, didn't she? She told us her screen name, or rather her friend did.'

'Ah, of course you're right. You're kind of enough to forget, I think, that I'm in what they used to call late middle age, and easily confused.'

And that was all they said of it. Of course, Kannan was still curious about this girl who looked as she did and who got it. But with the lifting of the enchantment, other things—the OBHWF thread, getting Grimmett to okay the question about magical objects, replying to Malathi—felt more urgent.

He went back to the office to finish the email. He wasn't sure if Malathi had Internet access at home, or how often she checked email. Saturday went by without a reply, as did Sunday. There were emails from Santhanam and his parents, about his wedding in a month which required almost nothing of him. He was to spend two days at home before they all went to Madras. Vinay and Ashok had been invited, but he was sure neither would come. On Sunday evening, Santhanam called. He was in an odd mood: his voice was laced with an unbecoming warmth, like sambar with added sugar. He wanted to know all about the meeting with Malathi. Kannan resisted the temptation of terseness. Why not display his enthusiasm, even play it up? The thrill of impending matrimony was, he had begun to suspect, one that Santhanam would never know.

After asking the appropriate questions, Santhanam became himself again.

'I have made enquiries,' said Santhanam. 'Both before and after you met her. You know that her mother is long dead, of course.'

'Yes, of course, that was made clear from the beginning.'

'Apparently the father is devoted to his daughters. They are all that matter to him in this life. And vice versa.'

'We didn't talk about him much, but I got the sense she adores her father.'

'He is a fairly successful man. Nothing big, but he has a decent business. Plywood. With his own house in Mylapore and some land in his village near Coimbatore.' Santhanam often liked to come to the point first by implication, as if to test Kannan, or to highlight his want of subtlety. That Malathi's family was more prosperous than his, a great deal more, he knew already. Business, with its uncertainties, its lack of a guaranteed pension and its refusal to correlate with or reward academic success, was as foreign to his family as mutton biryani. His father usually mentioned businessmen in the context of tax evasion or black money. Malathi's father stood apart from his caste, for whom Santhanam's life was a template. Besides their tiny flat, Kannan's parents had no other assets to speak of, although they had avoided the liabilities that came in the form of daughters. All this he knew, but he didn't see Santhanam's point, and said nothing.

'I am surprised that you haven't wondered why they were so keen on you. The girl is still quite young, she doesn't need to rush just yet. My sense is that the mother's death meant they had to adjust their horizons. Especially in a place like Madras, these things really matter. So you should be aware of your luck. Hopefully there is no ostentation at the marriage. It is a criminal waste of hard-earned money. And it means less to go around when your father-in-law dies: he is not *that* rich.'

Santhanam's jibe was not wholly unfair. That the match, on paper, had so swiftly been considered satisfactory might be down to her family circumstances. But her lack of a mother could not explain the events in Cubbon Park.

On Monday morning he woke, at last, to a reply. She wrote from a cyber café. The Internet at home had been down for the past several days. But it would be restored soon, and then she could really get back to work on *Time Regained* and the other fics he had recommended. They had two computers at home, one for her father and one for his daughters, and with her sister married, that meant she had her private PC, but they shared an Internet connection. It helped that the chapters were so long; she could load a chapter, log out of VSNL and only log back in when she needed to load another chapter, without wasting precious minutes. And if her father asked why she spent so much time on the computer these days, she could point to all the wonderful online resources that she was using to study for her MA finals.

Before leaving for the wedding he would send and receive eight more such emails. Occasionally he wondered if Malathi wanted more from him, more detail, greater variety, deeper revelation, but he felt most at ease when he was writing about Harry Potter. Once she wrote, 'I don't know if it's the way you talk about it, or how much Harry Potter contains within it, but just from talking about these books I feel my knowledge and understanding of you advancing after each email. I hope I'm not imagining this.' Kannan took this as licence for him to continue in the same way as before.

It wasn't that he restricted himself to Harry Potter. He told her about his apartment, and about his workouts, and about Brendan and Eric and even Brian Hanahan, describing him as a source of unexplained generosity. When she asked about Santhanam, he described his feelings towards his brother with a candour he'd never previously exercised, not even to himself. It was only Grimmett, really, that he never mentioned. At first he said to himself, some things aren't easy to write about, to explain to someone who doesn't know the context, who has no way of understanding. It isn't just me; nobody could have the right words. It's best that she see all this for herself. But then he felt a correction arriving, so definitive that the original thought faded irrecoverably. There was no need to excuse his omission. He didn't owe her an account of Grimmett or of their friendship. He was marrying her, not merging himself with her. Indian marriage, arranged marriage, the only kind of marriage he had seen first-hand, did not impose the requirement of confession.

Dearest Kannan,

I hope you don't mind that I continue to start and end these emails as if they're letters. I like your habit of just beginning, with no formality, and not signing off. It suits you, is true to you, just as this is true to me. When I said, all those emails ago, that I was excited about our shared search for the right way to do things, I didn't mean for one minute that we both had to do everything the same way.

What you say about Santhanam has led me, for the first time in my life, to feel grateful for my own sister. Whenever I make a new friend and they learn about my mother, they always say: you're so lucky to have an older sister. She must have been your rock, seen you through that time. When nothing could be further from the truth! When Amma died, my sister was totally wrapped up in her own self. It's not the cruelty of hindsight that makes me say that a part of her enjoyed being made much of in school. And occasionally over the years, when Amma has come up in conversation and she, wanted a weapon with which to hurt me she's said things like: you didn't really know Amma, you were too young. I was ten! But I've gone off track; what I really meant to say was that, unlike your brother, she never thought it her purpose in life to direct mine. She allowed me to develop in my own way. And now she is helping in a hundred different ways with this wedding, but at no point has she interfered. She neither encouraged nor discouraged me from getting married, and all she's said about you is 'He sounds like a nice boy'. I hope you don't mind her saying 'boy'. You know that's how it always has been: boy until marriage, man after.

I wonder sometimes if the difference between your relationship with your older sibling and mine is one between male and female sibling pairs. But even if it is, it isn't that things are condemned to always be the way they've been thus far. You're not going to like this suggestion at first, in fact you're going to hate it, but I can't help myself. Why not introduce Santhanam to Harry Potter? I can't think of a greater kindness that one person could do another. From your descriptions of him, so tough-minded and practical and cynical in his view of the world, it's exactly what he needs. You've said that your life in America is quite solitary and that Harry Potter has been your greatest source of happiness. Isn't Santhanam alone, too? When I construct a picture of him from your email, even though you only wrote a few sentences, I feel sure somehow that he isn't happy. Could even he resist J.K. Rowling?

You didn't say it in so many words, but I'm sure of this too: you don't suggest things to Santhanam, only the other way around. I think he'll be so surprised at your doing this that, if only out of curiosity, he will open *Philosopher's Stone* and start reading. And you don't need me to tell you how it is with that book. He might never thank you, but once he's read three chapters, his life will have changed.

Please, please, once you're no longer irritated, at least think about it.

As ever, your Malathi

10

Through that first winter of Gobstones in the Pit, Grimmett would watch his friend's confidence and authority swell, his performances gaining depth and colour like pastis as water is poured over it. He was familiar with the process, he had seen it online, but that did nothing to diminish his exultancy. As they walked over to the Pit for the fifth meeting, the last of February, he told Kannan that he was going to let him moderate, and Kannan began the discussion by introducing the question about magical objects. Grimmett wasn't even disapproving. No one had replied yet, or thought out loud, but the successful introduction of a question to a group can be heard as well as seen, on a frequency that wouldn't show up on a recording, but is audible to everyone present, an unexpectedly pleasant collective tinnitus. Then the answers began to come in.

'I'd like the Mirror of Erised,' said an earnest young man, black and, Grimmett thought, rather beautiful, the oval face sitting on a birch-trunk neck. He was new to Gobstones. 'I know it would drive you crazy, but I feel like by showing me my heart's desire it would help me know myself, without which you can't know anything, really.'

'I can see that, but wouldn't you want to throw the Mirror away after looking in it once? For your own sanity. Otherwise you'd end up spending all day staring at your heart's desire,' said a woman whose name Grimmett thought might be Krista. She had emailed him; she worked at the post office. 'I'd want something to help with cooking. But if you want something specific, I guess I'd say Floo Powder. I can only get away to see my mom on major holidays and the way Amtrak and the airline companies fleece you, it's like poisoning someone and then raising the price of the medication to treat the poison. This way I could just hop into my fireplace and hop out of hers.'

Kannan thought this an unsatisfactory answer. You couldn't travel by Floo Powder unless the fireplaces were on the Floo Network; had she *read* the books? And he was certain that neither Krista nor her mother had real fireplaces. But he'd had her down as one who might fail to understand the subtleties of the question, so he didn't contradict her in the hope that she might be the only one.

Next up was the elderly woman who had been most relieved by Annabel's unavailability. 'I'd like an Orb. I feel like the other media of Divination require real skill and an Inner Eye. But with the Orb you can just look in it and who knows what you might see?'

The youngest member of Gobstones was a precocious junior at the Cambridge Rindge and Latin School. 'Since I can't fly a broom, which is what anyone with a soul would want to do, could I have a Pensieve?' she asked. 'It would be incredible to be able to watch your thoughts and memories like a movie, to relive them.'

'You stole my answer,' said Kannan. 'Now I have to come up with something else.'

Grimmett and Kannan faced the others, who stood in an intended semi-circle that had turned into a wide-bottomed boat. Rebecca was at the end closest to Kannan, which meant she went last but for the moderators, and had plenty of time to think. Now it was her turn.

'This is almost like cheating, but I feel like all the good answers have already been taken, although I can't wait to hear what you guys are going to say. But I'm tempted to spin off another question from your question.'

'Please go ahead,' said Grimmett. 'A question that doesn't inspire spin-offs or deviations isn't worth asking.'

'Well, I don't know how interesting or relevant this will be to everyone, except for you, Charlene,' addressing the Cambridge Rindge and Latin girl, 'but I graduated college less than a year ago, and I work with high schoolers now, so I thought of looking at your question from a different angle. After all, the Trio are going into their fifth year; they'll be taking their OWLs soon. So here's my question: imagine you were taking a test, whether in high school or college or whatever. What one magical object *or* ability would you want? A Quick-Quotes Quill, to write the essays for you? Polyjuice Potion, so your brainy friend could impersonate you? A Time-Turner, to give you more time to study?'

Kannan was so irritated that, surprised at himself, he wondered if he was resentful of Rebecca's eloquence. But no, Rebecca's question had style, but no weight: what did it matter how someone might cheat on an exam if given three options?

'A Quick-Quotes Quill, for sure,' said the woman who longed to practise Divination. 'I never had strong fingers. I remember when I was in high school, my fingers ached like arthritis every time I had to take a test. And those quills are so creative! You could write a novel with them.'

A man whose roommate had got him through college by doing his math problem sets asked for Polyjuice. Charlene wanted something off-menu. 'What would be *really* cool and useful would be the ability to read minds,' she said. 'Like often, in my AP Literature class, I end up staring intently at my teacher's temples, hoping to get the ideal answers out of her telepathically.'

'But witches and wizards can't read minds,' said Kannan, his poise now precarious. 'It's one of the abilities they've never been shown to have.'

The young man who had wanted the Mirror of Erised intervened on behalf of moral seriousness. 'I feel like the only acceptable answer is the Time-Turner. That way you study harder and do well through your own effort. The rest are just cheating, plain and simple.'

'How is the Time-Turner not cheating?' asked the man with the clever college roommate. 'It's just like using steroids in sports—they're meant to help you recover faster and thus train harder. Athletes who use steroids actually put in *more* effort than those who don't, but aren't they cheating?'

'I don't know about steroids, but at least the Time-Turner is closest to doing things the right way. And I feel like the Trio would never cheat.'

'Are you kidding?' asked Rebecca. 'Ron totally would. Not because he's unethical, but because he's a typical teenager. If you gave him the chance, he'd jump at it. Harry might have some reservations, but he'd give in, especially if it were Potions or Divination. Of the Trio, only Hermione would never cheat.'

Her remark about Ron would have caused bedlam on the forums. Here, though, OBHWF partisans were either absent or subdued in the face of superior force. Or maybe it was impossible to summon the same vitriol when you were arguing with someone face to face.

After Grimmett had called the meeting to a close Rebecca lingered, half-joining a group of members waiting to speak to Grimmett about this or that. Kannan, who stood free by Grimmett's side, didn't get any further than wondering what might happen if he were to walk up and claim her attention now and, moreover, what he might have done if he'd still been under enchantment. In that scenario, he'd have pulled out his copy of *Goblet of Fire* and pretended to check something until she left. Now he had no terror of what might happen if they spoke, but no urge to speak either. Eventually, she bored of waiting for Grimmett, and said, half to Kannan and half to the group in general, that she'd see them all next week.

As always he went straight to bed; he never checked online fandom after Gobstones. But Rebecca had stayed up, because he woke to an email from her. She had replied to him on the Gobstones list; there had been her post on the OBHWF thread. But had she ever addressed him directly?

> Hey Kannan,
>
> I wanted to apologize for somewhat hijacking, or at least diverting without permission, your discussion tonight. I know my answer wasn't at all in the spirit of your question; but it was the first thing that came to mind, and I think maybe that it spoke to how clever your question was, in the way that it used the books as a means of revealing something about each of us. By next Wednesday I'll think of a proper answer, which I'll share with you, even if the group has moved on.
>
> Read any good H/Hr stuff lately? *Time Regained* aside, I've been pretty underwhelmed.
>
> Sorry again,
> R

He knew himself to this extent. If he didn't reply immediately, he never would. Summoning all the Americanness he could access, he wrote:

> Don't worry about it. See you next week.

The lie was totally unconscious. It didn't occur to him until days later, when he was on a flight to Bangalore.

Vinay sent a regret email. 'Vry sorry 2 miss ur upcoming nuptials, but work is v busy rite now. Wish best of health & prosperity to 2 u and ur bride in ur married life. Pls let me know whn u are next in blore.' A few emails in 1998 aside, they hadn't spoken in five years.

The only American to be informed of the wedding was Brendan. Kannan needed the company's help with Malathi's visa paperwork.

Eric and Brendan had decided the site needed a complete redesign to increase traffic. They had begun 2001 bitter and depressed. Timing was everything, and it didn't make a difference whether you were off by a month or a decade. Mark Cuban was a billionaire with an NBA team. Brendan and Eric were ten times the man he was; they had built a site with a dedicated user base five times the size of Cuban's broadcast.com. But they had been a year too late. Brendan's father, who owned a long-term storage business, told them to stop feeling sorry for themselves. What will happen to America if we become a nation of young men who want to con investors into buying a house of air? Build a real business that you can call your own. Make it profitable and when you hire someone for a real, sustainable job, you raise an entire family. Brendan and Eric weren't buying this, but they weren't temperamentally suited to moping either. There'll be another boom to follow the bust, said Eric, and when that time comes we'll be all the more valued for having survived the first time. Hardened by fire.

Yet, Mark Cuban hung over them like the dweeb from high school who shows up to the reunion with the prettiest girl on his arm. That guy had an NBA team! 'But it's just the Mavericks,' Brendan said. 'A team whose history would fit on a fridge magnet. And they'll never amount to anything. It's a football town.'

'If it had been us,' said Eric, 'If we'd been a year earlier with the site we've built, we could have bought the Celtics. And made them great again.'

By telling Brendan about the marriage, by humouring him with as many details as he might want, Kannan hoped to postpone the website overhaul. He wasn't up to it, technically he might not have been up to it even two years ago, but now he wasn't up to it in any sense. Either he needed to rebuild his capacity for the work he was paid for, or to convince them to hire a couple of new developers or to outsource the whole project, or he could start putting his resume out there. It was a resume that added up to more than he did, but not one that would earn him another job in which he could hide in plain sight. For now, time would do.

'You're getting married?! Congratulations! Wait, aren't you pretty young to get married? How old are you, remind me?'

'I'll be twenty-seven soon.'

'Right, you're a few months older than me. Not that young, I guess. Just feels old to me cause you know, it's *marriage*, right? It just feels so distant. Kids, responsibilities, getting an actual job. Who's the lucky woman?'

'Her name is Malathi. She's finishing her master's in English literature.'

'Oh, so she's the English major to your geek. Yin and yang. That's great.'

'Thank you.'

'But wait, I didn't know you had a girlfriend. Is this, what do you call it, you know what I mean …'

'An arranged marriage? Yes, our parents arranged it. That's why I went home last month. To meet her.'

'That was the first time you met her?'

'Yes.'

'And you're getting married a month later? What's the rush?'

'The date was set by our parents. Her father didn't want a long engagement. You ask why the rush, but I guess the thinking there is, why wait? When you've decided to get married. But I like her, I'm excited about her coming here.'

'I guess it's just foreign and not so easy for someone like me to understand. But this is all great. We'll have to have a party to celebrate once she comes.'

What *was* the rush? Six weeks ago he had flown home fixed upon rejecting a proposal and now he was flying home to get married. Santhanam didn't provide any precedent, and his cousins on both sides were unhelpfully younger. Some norms were force-fed to you daily as a child, like cod liver oil, others you were expected to absorb by diffusion, but sometimes you learned of a norm in the form of an instruction. He had never found that it made any difference. And even in their community, he saw, this case was different, because it wasn't as if there was an opportunity for them to spend more time *getting to know each other*, as someone like Brendan or even Grimmett might demand. Marriage was the only way she could come over to the US.

He met Santhanam in Frankfurt airport. They shared connecting flights to Bombay and onwards to Bangalore. He'd never needed to ask his brother for advice and wasn't going to start now. But he could indulge his own curiosity while displaying a greater quantity of subtlety than he had ever been credited with, which was a low bar to cross.

'When my boss was granting me leave, he asked me why the rush to get married? Since we only met a month ago.'

'And what did you say?'

'I said I was happy to get married.'

'I hope you don't let silly questions like that get into your mind. People will say things like this in India also. They want something called Modern Arranged Marriage. Your parents introduce you but then you date, like Americans, spend six months "getting to know each other", which probably means having sex also. It is a fool's errand. How can you modernize arranged marriage? It's like saying, let's modernize God. The whole point is that it works and has been proven to work for thousands of years. You either do it properly or you reject it altogether.'

Kannan didn't think he had ever been to a marriage. There had been receptions, of course, three or four times a year, but these were glum affairs, as they could be counted on to bring his parents' silent loathing into the open. His mother, condemned to keep her vanity hidden the rest of the year, wanted to show herself, to arrive early and leave late, to imbibe enough attention and regard to see her through until the next time. His father's preference for home-cooked food had hardened into a refusal to eat anything else.

'How can you be so stubborn?' she used to say. 'They have called five hundred people. Will they all die of cholera?'

'I have regard for my own health, even if these days one cannot expect a wife to care for her husband's health. Who knows where they have got the food from? These days they don't even bother to hire Brahmin cooks.' Neither Kannan's mother nor anybody else ever raised the objection that the part-time cook they employed at home was non-Brahmin.

It rarely took more than fifteen minutes, once at the reception, for his father to ask if they could leave. Whether the reception was in a banquet hall or on a lawn, the format was identical. The bride and groom stood on a raised platform. To the left of the platform was proof that in the right setting, Indians could queue just as well as their former colonizers. You waited your turn, went up on stage to bless the couple and, if you were important enough, have your photo taken, and moved on. Often the queue for blessings emerged on the other side of the stage as the queue for dinner. By the time Kannan was sixteen and had joined PU college, his first thought on entering a wedding reception was to gauge the size of the crowd and the length of the queue. If the reception was hosted by a non-Brahmin colleague of his father's from the bank, rather than by a relative, then a long queue meant he had enough time for a discreet and delicious non-vegetarian meal.

Was one's own wedding to be enjoyed or endured? As so often, he couldn't bring himself to know or, particularly, to care. The details of the ceremony and reception were governed by rules, most of them inflexible. None of it had any bearing on what was of real interest: the course of his life with Malathi. Since he had no guests of his own, his obligations consisted only of behaving himself, which required less effort than not doing so.

Malathi's father had dispensed with the optional luxury of an evening of classical music, so there were only two events on a single day:

the muhurtam in the morning, followed by lunch, and the reception in the evening. The previous night, at dinner in his father-in-law's house, with Malathi's extended family, he was amazed to be subjected neither to interrogation nor even to serious observation. Santhanam did most of the talking. The house was large by Mylapore standards, and on two levels. Malathi and her sister had each had their own bedroom. Even Kannan, to whom the individual details of houses were as vague and unimportant as blades in a lawn of grass, noticed the number of knick-knacks, not that they looked expensive, although who was he to say, but to be confronted with figurines, dolls and even paintings, when he had grown up in a flat as bare as a village schoolroom, was to feel himself abroad. Santhanam pointed out later that there had been no idols and no gold, only trivialities. It must be the work of the man rather than his late wife. Kannan didn't get to speak to Malathi that night. He wanted only to avoid conveying any of his apathy. The marriage ceremony itself might, for her, be full to capacity with weight and meaning.

Kannan had spent eighty per cent of his life in educational institutions, but when he first read Harry Potter, it was Harry's school life, rather than magic or England, that he found most foreign. Grimmett often said that part of the books' appeal was that they grounded wild fantasy in a set of experiences that most children could relate to. But Kannan's only moment of recognition came in the form of Professor Binns, the ghost who taught History of Magic. Binns had died, turned into a ghost, and floated over to teach his morning class as if nothing had happened. Kannan thought, exactly, this is what all my teachers were like. Binns was Harry's only ghost professor: in engineering college in Bangalore, Kannan had only one teacher who could not fairly be described as a ghost.

He taught physics, and the job was a holding one as he applied to PhD programmes in Europe and the US. He began each class not by taking attendance, but by walking up to the blackboard and writing, from memory, a quotation from a famous physicist with some connection, often oblique, to the day's material. Unlike anything on the syllabus, many of these quotes had stayed in Kannan's mind. He thought now of how Einstein, according to this lecturer, had explained relativity:

'Put your hand on a hot stove for a minute, and it seems like an hour. Sit with a pretty girl for an hour, and it seems like a minute. That's relativity.'

Kannan spent his marriage day sitting with what he had decided was a pretty girl, but this wasn't why it had passed so quickly. If you think time speeds up only when you are most alive and engaged, you've never spent a day as an automaton. The accidental magic that he had felt at work in Cubbon Park; it was as if the kalyana mantapam had been proofed against it. There seemed to be no link between everything said that day and over email, and this. The wedding ceremony asked of him only that he follow instructions so undemanding as to be secure against idiocy. At the reception, he stood on the stage with his wife and was congratulated by a cavalcade of strangers. He was aware of it all happening, as he would have been if watching a live telecast of his own wedding. But the thing about being an automaton was that not only did time flit by, it left no residue. The hours in Cubbon Park had gone by at two speeds: Firebolt-quick in real time, but replayed in his head with the meandering slowness of an overloaded river boat. On the flight back to Boston, this time on his own, he found that he couldn't even remember the colour of her sari.

There was no question of a honeymoon at this time. When she moved to the US, they could go to Niagara Falls, which he had a dim notion was where you were supposed to go. Maybe by then he would have introduced her to Grimmett, who would have better ideas. Who knew what she would want? What she would turn out to be?

In lieu of a honeymoon, the bride and groom had been left alone to spend a night together in Madras, not at Malathi's house, but in a three-star hotel on Bells Road: the venue for the reception, a few minutes' walk from Marina Beach. This had been Santhanam's idea. 'You will not see your wife for several months. It is better if you part on terms of some intimacy.'

Wedding receptions empty like train compartments: a few passengers get off at various minor stops, before a mass ten-minute clear-out at the end, leaving behind the cleaning staff. As the exodus began, Malathi asked Kannan if she could go up to the room before him. This was the first point at which he felt compelled to decide and thus to think. How long did he need to give her? 'Go ahead,' he said. 'I'll come up within half an hour.' She couldn't know that it was he who needed the time. In Boston he would have stepped outside, even better if it were freezing, the wind forcing calmness upon him like electroshock therapy. Here he could think only to lock himself inside a bathroom stall. Fortunately, the gap between the door and the ceiling was well above head height; no one would notice that he was standing.

Kannan had first seen sex when he was sixteen, in his first year of PU college. A classmate's parents were going away for the weekend and he wanted to show off his latest acquisitions. Kannan wondered why he had been invited: he was pitied, perhaps, although he didn't know for what. There were six of them in that room. The first film was American, the story of an eighteen-year-old boy being fought over by three thirty-something cougars. The host took it upon himself to provide both commentary and direction. A minute into the first sex scene and he was panting like an overworked bullock. 'She's so hot, so fucking hot. If none of you mind, I need to jack off,' he said, using a phrase Kannan didn't know. He whipped his penis out with the effortlessness that is only produced by assiduous rehearsal. Two others followed him. That left two boys whose shame or awkwardness overpowered the urge to show they were man enough, and Kannan, who hadn't looked away from the screen. For many months afterwards, he could not look at his parents in the same room without thinking about it, the many dozens of rounds of intercourse it must have taken to produce Santhanam and himself. Their apartment, their style of living had no space for the unknowable. He knew that there was no better past, no time at which relations between his parents could have allowed them to look forward to a night of sex with anything other than dread. If his mother had been unlucky enough to produce daughters, the torture might have continued years longer. He wondered why she hadn't insisted on stopping after Santhanam. Maybe even when you had a son, you wanted another as an insurance policy.

What about their first night together? Surely they could not have hated each other yet, although his mother had entered the marriage convinced that no man could match up to her father and that this one suffered especially by the comparison? Maybe that first sexual encounter had been enough to keel disappointment over into disgust.

It was almost forty minutes before Kannan knew what he wanted to say and could leave the stall. He found his wife changed out of her reception sari into a white nightie with a pattern of strawberries and other fruit that she would meet for the first time in Boston. Her jewellery was off, too, except the thaali that he had tied round her neck earlier that day, although he had no memory of it.

'You must be very tired,' he said.

'Aren't you tired?'

'I'm tired, too, although the day flew by.' As he had hoped, she said nothing to this, or at least nothing immediately. This allowed him to say what he had prepared.

'I can't wait for you to come to Boston. I think you'll really enjoy life there. And when you come the weather will be perfect. My job isn't so stressful. We'll have a lot of time to spend together.' Here Kannan encountered the distance between drafting a list of things you wish to say and actually delivering them in the course of a conversation. Do you attempt an uninterrupted monologue? Even with a cooperative interlocutor, very few people can do this, and the days spent listening to Grimmett hadn't taught him how. But any other way means giving the other person turns at the wheel, and little or no chance that you stay on the course you'd originally mapped. He would have to try the monologue.

'I hope you know how happy I am to be here with you … as my wife,' he said. 'But I almost feel I won't believe it fully until you're with me in Boston. Things have happened so quickly. And what I mean to say is, do you mind if we don't, if we don't, if we don't, if we don't make love tonight? I'm sorry if that seems like a strange thing to say. But I think to do all that once, and then to not see each other for three months, would not be nice. When you move we can take our time, everything can happen easily and naturally.'

Later, on the flight back, he would think of how much she had helped him, not so much by what she said but by how quickly she said it, how decisive her tone. She must have understood the debilitating cruelty of silence, both the anxiety that making him wait for a reply would induce, and that even the most reassuring reply would feel false for the fact of it having taken so long.

'I understand,' she said. 'I think what you say is right. But won't you kiss me?'

They kissed with an awkwardness that was only physical, and almost comforting because it was shared and sure to be temporary. By the time she wriggled out of his arms to find a more comfortable position, he was asleep.

11

The time apart had been good for Grimmett. He had the glow of the man about to unveil a discovery. If he could look at himself, he would have been reminded of the scientist in Wright of Derby's painting, who has suffocated a bird by placing it in a vacuum pump, before a gathering of awestruck onlookers. Grimmett had seen the painting in the Tate Gallery in 1975 and went back to it on every London visit, following it from the Tate to the National. He took in all the faces before resting, every time, upon the scientist's countenance, which could lazily be called impassive but really bore the worldly calm that was the mark of true confidence. Wright of Derby had caught the moment where scientific inventions had begun to take the place of miracles; and isn't it in the nature of miracles that they appear almost commonplace to the miracle-maker, at least in the performance? But Grimmett was unlucky in his choice of audience. Back in 1369 Coffeehouse for the first time in over a week, Kannan could sense that his friend had good news, but he could summon no anticipation.

'Before you tell me all about India,' Grimmett said, 'I want to tell you something very important. I've been working on this for some time but

I am finally able to reveal all to you. I'm sure you detest guessing games as much as I do, but I want to confirm that this really is the surprise I hope it is. Do you have any idea what I'm talking about?'

'I'm confused. Do you want me to guess or not?'

'Yes, I apologize for being so circuitous. Take a guess.'

'I don't know, do you have a new idea for Gobstones? Are you going to start a fanfic site?'

'No, no, there's no need to address me in the second person in that way. That sort of thing I could hardly do without you. A new site—*you* wouldn't need *me* for that.'

He left it there. He was clearly desperate for Kannan to guess. He had begun to look nervous.

Kannan had seen Grimmett excited, passionate, ecstatic—but nervous? It was unlike Kannan not to humour him—to say that their friendship was constituted by Kannan humouring Grimmett would be unkind, but not wholly untrue. But today Kannan was not up to it. He was back in Madras with Malathi; and in the Boston Public Garden with Malathi, three months in the future; and on GCR, drafting a post about Ron's lack of respect for women. In *Goblet of Fire*, JKR had introduced a word for people like him. He had 'splinched' himself—left part of him elsewhere. He wasn't sufficiently *here* to play guessing games with Grimmett.

Grimmett was refusing to take his eyes off him. Was it really necessary that he have coffee with this person every single day?

'I don't have time for this, Curtis.' As he said this he didn't wish he could take it back; but he knew, at once, that he had never spoken like this before. Not just with Grimmett; not since arriving in America. Which meant that he had no way of anticipating how Grimmett might respond.

'You know, Kannan, you and I might disagree on this, but I think there are limits to the Internet, especially when it comes to really building a community. Actually, we wouldn't disagree. After all, look at our friendship. It couldn't have been this way if we'd stayed glued to our keyboards.' Grimmett had taken refuge in blabbering. It allowed both of them to ignore what Kannan had just said. But a part of Kannan didn't want Grimmett to ignore it; he wanted his irritation acknowledged, registered, whether that meant an apology from Grimmett or escalation.

But he said nothing, and so Grimmett continued along the same lines. And then: 'Okay, I'll come to the point. In late May we're going to have an event. A fandom evening. I'll rent a ballroom at the Park Plaza, and invite fans from the Boston area and a few Big Name Fans from further afield. There'll be drinks, and then there'll be the main event: an offline Deathmarch. I'll moderate, with two speakers on each side. For Pumpkin Pie there'll be Clara—and you.' Clara was, Athena Alice aside, probably the best-known Harry/Hermione fanfic author in all of fandom. She lived in New York.

Kannan had made it to twenty-six without ever receiving what you could really call good news. Getting into Northeastern had been better than expected, better than the nothing which was expected, but not cause for exultation. He didn't think he'd ever been the source of good news either. He could imagine how his grandmother had reacted to his birth: my God, this one is dark.

And once again he was elsewhere: on stage beside Clara, about to represent his side. Grimmett was passing him a mic. If only Malathi could be there to see him! But, on the other hand, perhaps not. For all her confidence and liveliness and English, he couldn't be sure that this was a world to introduce a wife to. Not this sort of wife at least.

'If you're nervous or apprehensive, I understand, of course. And I should make it clear that this is yours only if you want it.'

'Thank you. It's an honour. And I know how important it is. I will be well prepared.'

Only now did he properly notice the source of the good news. He ought to thank Grimmett—no, not thank him, but convey the weight of all of this. But he hadn't visualized any of this. He noticed that Grimmett's left arm lay extended across the table, palm down. How long had it been there? Kannan placed his right hand just above

Grimmett's left wrist, and pressed down a little, halfway to a squeeze. Grimmett let him do it for several seconds before slowly withdrawing his arm.

'I knew you would take that attitude. So much for us to look forward to. While you were away I took the liberty of telling Rebecca about this. She's the only one from Gobstones to know; she's going to help us plan.'

It wasn't worth saying anything to Grimmett about having no sexual or romantic interest in Rebecca, let alone introducing the subject of Malathi. He was sure his friend wasn't trying to set things up for him. Not that Grimmett couldn't be subtle, but arranging a thoughtful surprise for a friend, like Kannan's slot on the Deathmarch panel, was a rather different quality from that required for romantic intrigue. Maybe Grimmett was just fond of Rebecca because of her tenuous connection to Britain. Maybe he had designs on her himself. It occurred to Kannan from time to time, but he rarely let it linger: how much of Grimmett's life and mind did he really know?

Gobstones let off a little early this time. A discussion of whether Harry was a Gary Stu—fanfic parlance for a too-perfect hero—had been derailed by a woman who made the reasonable point that Cedric Diggory existed to remind us that Harry wasn't infallible, but then, tipsy on her own pleasure at this observation, proceeded to talk about Jane Austen.

'Cedric Diggory,' she said, 'is Jane Fairfax. She has no fame or fortune, but is even better-looking than Emma and outshines her in terms of accomplishment. And then it turns out that the man Emma wants to marry, Frank Churchill, has been in love with Jane all along. Just like Harry and Cedric and Cho. The only difference is that Cedric is obviously a tragic figure, while Jane Fairfax has a happy ending. Maybe that shows us how brave a writer J.K. Rowling is. Or maybe Cedric has to die to clear the way for Harry to be the hero, because there can't be anyone better than him around.'

'You're right, though,' said Rebecca. 'Jane Fairfax is such a fascinating character. You could even call her a "problem character". Just look at the best Austen adaptation ever: *Clueless.*' There was much appreciative sighing at this. Loving Harry Potter and loving *Clueless* went together. 'Even though they didn't credit Jane Austen, it's a pretty faithful adaptation. And they cut Jane Fairfax out altogether! Hollywood couldn't handle the idea of a character who gives the heroine an inferiority complex.'

This was too much for Grimmett, who in his own fiefdom was being made to watch the wrong sort of Britishness being first compared with Harry Potter—that was bad enough—and then crowding it out. Jane Austen! The wilful blindness to everything that was difficult or important, the insufferable moralism, the relentless contest between the author and her heroines to see who could be more smugly delighted with themselves.

'All most interesting, but let's bring things back to Harry Potter, if no one objects,' he said. 'Does anyone have a new topic to propose? We have, I think, fifteen minutes.'

But no one had anything. No one had read a new fanfic worth mentioning, or been sufficiently outraged by some fandom troll that they wanted to talk about it offline. Kannan and Rebecca aside, Grimmett wasn't sure he wanted to know what any of these people thought of anything. Why had he ever thought than an offline Gobstones would be a good idea? He'd always looked down on book clubs, those gatherings of the well-intentioned and half-literate. Literature was supposed to be a private activity. He'd thought that none of the rules applied to Harry Potter which, in terms of the breadth and intensity of its effect on people, was like no other literature anyone could remember. But with this membership, Gobstones had degenerated into a book club, and even worse than usual for the fact that every week was dedicated to the same four-volume book.

It was a warm evening in March, which in Boston is like a moment of lightness in a Dostoevsky novel, to be fully exploited in the certainty that it is an aberration that doesn't portend any change in the climate. When Grimmett saw that Rebecca was staying on as the others left, he knew that it couldn't be to talk Harry Potter. For that, she would just email him.

She waited for the club's only couple to resolve their weekly dilemma about getting home in favour of taking the bus, and stepped up to Grimmett and Kannan. She looked as if she hardly knew what she was going to say.

'It's such a nice evening,' she said. 'Better enjoy it before winter comes back from vacation in a few days.' And then, as if she needed to account for her doing something so banal as make small talk about the weather, 'The only fanfic-reading I've been doing has been some Britpicking, for Perdita, *Time Regained*. In this chapter she has Hermione say, "It's so nice out today!" I had to tell her that was too American. I know the British are pretty versatile when it comes to talking about the weather, but "nice out" isn't quite right, not for Hermione. I told her to make it, "It's such a nice day today."'

'That's unobjectionable,' said Grimmett. 'We have a tendency in this country to abbreviate. It's almost a pathology at this point. Although the British do say "nice out" and "cold out" too, you know. We got it from them, I suspect. But, you're right, our dear Hermione wouldn't say it.'

Kannan thought there must be a point to all this, there must be a reason she's here. But Grimmett is going to be so happy to chat about nonsense like this that who knows when she'll come to that point.

'I know it's late, but it seems such a shame not to stay out on an evening like this. Would either or both of you like to accompany me on a walk? There's no better time to walk around Cambridge than after midnight.'

This was the sort of situation in which you could rely on Grimmett. He could answer for the both of them, and Kannan would go along with his decision.

'It's certainly past my bedtime,' said Grimmett. 'But that doesn't apply to you two. Kannan, don't let me deprive you.'

'What route would you like to take?' asked Rebecca. 'We could walk around campus, or go down Brattle Street, which is one of the oldest streets in the country, past Longfellow's house.'

'I'm fine with anything. You decide. Goodnight, Curtis.'

Grimmett made a little bow to Rebecca, like a circus animal at the end of its act. Kannan hadn't seen him do this before. He didn't think he'd like to see it again.

Whatever route they took, there was the matter of what was expected of him, conversationally, and you couldn't address that question without first wondering about her plan. She had to invite Grimmett as well, the situation didn't permit her not to, and he knew they had been in correspondence, had a kind of friendship. But it was Kannan she wanted to ask, because otherwise she would have made an excuse of her own, withdrawn the offer after Grimmett declined it. But, unlike in Cubbon Park, silence was not a viable gambit. He'd have to answer to Grimmett for it tomorrow and, more importantly, it seemed a waste of the circumstances. He hadn't gone into fandom in the hope of finding romance, or sex, let alone expecting it, let alone fantasizing about a conventionally attractive white woman asking him out on a walk. Fandom was its own reward, the oldest woman in Gobstones had once said: Grimmett had grimaced, his face for once letting on what he thought of what someone had said. But Kannan had held on to the thought, had repeated it in his head like a shloka. But if these were the other rewards of fandom, as unexpected and as mysterious as they were, it would be perverse to reject them without a little exploration.

He would stick to Harry Potter, unless she forced a change, although he expected that she would do the tour-guiding that was implicit in the original offer. They began down Brattle Street, and he asked if she was allowed to tell him more about the latest chapter of *Time Regained*. She interrupted her own reply to point to a building on the left, a low box on stilts like an oversized rabbit hutch.

'That's the American Repertory Theater. There's a small space in back, the Loeb Ex, where I often acted in college.' To which Kannan asked if she thought Harry Potter would ever be adapted for the stage. 'I hope not,' she said. 'I'm sceptical enough about the movie. I worry that the books would be so constrained by the theatre. It would be like a shirt that's many sizes too small. A few buttons pop and you just look silly. Actually, let's not walk down Brattle any longer. We'll turn right here.'

Shortly they came to a garden in the midst of four buildings, which she said was called the Radcliffe Yard. 'There's the Admissions Office, which was my office of sorts; I used to be a tour guide for them. For most of the kids who apply, getting in is every bit as enticing and magical as receiving a Hogwarts letter. And the Agassiz Theater, where I once starred in *The Taming of the Shrew.*'

Kannan looked around him, taking in nothing but a sense of confused possibility. He thought of Harry and Hermione, on a midnight walk in a spot like this, figuring out they loved each other. If only. What about him and Malathi? She would submit to it totally, for her it would be as if she had walked out of her life into the pages of Harry Potter, or into a romantic movie. But he saw now that he could never play his part to hers. Never? What was never? Not never. Probably never. But definitely not now. What about the part that was being offered to him here? The script said, you may kiss her now, and she won't run away. She might pull away, and look confused, but nothing worse than that, and probably better. He didn't not want to kiss her. To do so might not be the right thing, tactically, but it would complete the scene, would be all the scene deserved. Well, if she kissed him, he would kiss her back.

'But I don't mean to bore you with my college memories,' she said. 'Let's walk on towards Harvard Yard.' Nothing was said for several minutes. He could bring things back to Harry Potter, but he no longer needed to. Then they were through Johnston Gate and into Harvard Yard and the tour resumed. The President's office, Matt Damon's dorm, John F. Kennedy's: it was a checklist, dutifully ticked off. It didn't suit her.

'And this is Widener, Harvard's main library. It was named for a young alum who drowned with the *Titanic*. I always found it a pretty cold and austere building, especially on the inside.'

'Do you still use it?'

'Now? I don't even know if I'm allowed in. Although I do miss it, just the sense that almost every book ever written was in the building I was walking through. Actually, I don't even know if I felt that then, or it's just a feeling I've assigned to myself in retrospect. I was meaning to ask you, what other books do you like? Before you found Harry Potter, I mean. What are the Indian writers I should be reading?'

This was easy for Kannan. It was ground that had been covered so thoroughly with Grimmett that answering her now was easy as copying and pasting a file.

'I never read storybooks before Harry Potter. They are the only books I love.'

Rebecca was satisfied with this answer, or at least satisfied enough not to push further. 'Let's head back to the Square and you can catch the last bus, or a taxi, to wherever you need to be going,' she said. 'Actually, that's presumptuous of me. You might live around here.'

'I live in the South End. Columbus Square. It's a nice part of town; Grimmett says it's getting nicer, although he's not sure that's only a good thing.' He knew what he wasn't saying: if you haven't been, you should come sometime. To leave it unsaid was not to imply it; it wasn't to close it off, either. But it was a choice, with consequences. These things were supposed to be said.

'Ah, I know of it more than I know it. Rapidly gentrifying. I didn't get to know Boston at all when I was in college. I began to think about the city more when I was choosing where to live. Where you live, though, was sadly outside the price range of an admissions consultant. I don't think I've ever been to Columbus Square.'

Another chance: she was practically asking him to say it. Or to say anything, really, that moved things forward. He didn't know, then, or later—was it that he didn't want to move things forward, or that he couldn't?

'Admissions consultant? Is that to do with college admissions? You consult the colleges on whom to admit?'

'No, the opposite actually. We help students who are applying to colleges. Look, it's not a job I'm proud of. It's help for those who can afford it. But that's for another time, I guess. What do you do? I remember Curtis saying something about your being more corporate than he was …'

'I'm a computer programmer.' He paused. What else was he to say? Was he proud of his job? He couldn't say, not because he was or wasn't, but because he'd never thought of it in those terms. The approaching No. 1 bus absolved him of further elaboration. But he wanted to say something further. All he could think of was the way Brian Hanahan had introduced him to Brendan and Eric three years ago.

'Web developer. Walking cliché.'

'Don't be silly. We're two twenty-somethings who hang out on Wednesdays at midnight with a fifty-something radio host to talk about children's books. Whatever else we might be, we're neither of us a cliché.'

As the bus pulled in, a question came out of Kannan like a belch: involuntary, in the moment, but only because it had been building up for some time.

'Your hair,' he said. 'You could be a Weasley. But you don't like the Weasleys. Is that its natural colour?'

'Yes,' said Rebecca.

12

It was easier for Rebecca than it was for Kannan, but neither had quite figured out the giving of confidences and the receiving of advice. For Kannan, after the initial delusion had slipped away and Rebecca had made her unexpected and still cryptic advance, it was no longer a matter of obligation; indeed, he owed Grimmett nothing. Rebecca didn't feel that she owed it to Annabel, either.

For many weeks after the walk, Rebecca and Kannan also had the limitation of having very little to tell. Grimmett had asked, and Kannan had answered: it was short, and it wasn't very interesting. I don't know what she wanted. For several days, Rebecca had thought the walk not worth mentioning. She knew from Grimmett that Kannan had been in the US four years, long enough for his cultural background not to prevent him from seeing the significance of her gesture. After that he had given her nothing, which meant, at the very least, that he had never previously had romantic thoughts of his own about her.

When she did tell Annabel, the following Sunday, it was largely because of the question about her hair. She couldn't talk about the walk while leaving this bit out; any personal embarrassment would be more than recompensed by Annabel's delight in the question but even more in the answer. She couldn't deny her that. But to prevent that question crowding out everything else, she decided to tell the story of the walk while holding it in reserve.

She skipped a description of the meeting and itself and opened by saying that afterwards she had asked Kannan and Grimmett whether they'd like a walk and that Kannan had said yes. And Annabel was out of her chair, and then she was pouring herself a vodka and tonic, not that she needed the drink or the thinking time.

'Before I respond to that, you're going to have to tell me more. How much don't I know? What has happened thus far between you?'

'Absolutely nothing.'

'What kind of nothing? Have you regularly been staying back and talking with him after meetings? Can you tell from his eyes that he's checking you out?'

'No, none of that.'

'He has shown no signs of interest in you at all?'

'Well, the first night that we met them, I thought he was staring at me rather intensely, without making eye contact. But that doesn't necessarily mean anything, especially as it was, assuming I didn't just imagine it, a one-off.'

'Just tell me the whole story then.' And Rebecca did; their online interactions, all that she had observed and concluded about Kannan and Grimmett, everything but Kannan's remark about her hair, and one other thing. She didn't tell Annabel that the reason that she had first written to Kannan was that when she had slightly redirected his discussion about magical objects at Gobstones, she had seen in his face the awful confused pain of an animal in distress, had watched it grow. She didn't want Annabel to think of Kannan in that way.

'And now you want to hang out with them and talk about things other than Harry Potter. And maybe *date* the Indian one. You think he's your type?'

'You know, Annabel, what *is* my type? Enlighten me. Diagnose me.'

'I've known every friend you've had since you were eighteen and met or heard about all the earlier ones too. Even if you don't have a type per se, these two don't fit anywhere.'

'And I have to be constrained in making new friends by the ones I already have? I couldn't have met people like them in high school or college, anyway.'

'How do you know that you would get along outside of the Harry Potter setting? They're just odd. I guess you could say Grimmett is warm, in a way, but they aren't, really, *friendable* people. Are you trying to make some kind of point here, or is this something real?'

'How can one ever know something like that? All I know is they interest me. I'm drawn to them. With Grimmett, and this isn't because he's not like anybody I've ever met, I can tell there's a friendship there, based on affinity, like-mindedness, that was waiting in the air for me to catch. With Kannan, I don't know anything, really, except that, that for once I can't tell how I think what happens next, and I don't mind how that feels.'

Annabel cut her off. 'You asked both of them on the walk, didn't you? Did you expect Curtis Grimmett to say yes? Did you want him to?'

'No, I don't think I wanted him to, but it didn't matter: when I asked, the way he said no, the way he handled the whole thing … it was as if he was being conspiratorial with me. Playing his part, playing along. He said no on his behalf and yes on Kannan's. I hadn't expected that. But it was useful.'

'I'm not satisfied yet. What's so compelling about Kannan anyway? I know what you thought I was going to say: that you're trying to defy expectations, escape a stereotype. What if it's just your own expectations you're trying to break free from? Do you feel imprisoned by your own narrative of your life?'

Sometimes Annabel threw so much at you that it was almost unfair. It would take hours to sort through it all, to separate the straight-to-the-bone insight from the misunderstandings and the unfalsifiable speculation. But there never was time in the course of a conversation itself.

'I don't know that I know what it is, exactly.'

'Is it sexual? A thus far unknown longing for the exotic? He's not bad-looking, actually. Pretty buff, for an Indian guy. Good skin. But not what I'd call your type.'

'There you go again with types. Why do I have to have a type?' So much easier to throw it back than to allow the uninhibited exploration that Annabel's questions really wanted, or warranted.

'There were some better-looking and better-spoken versions of Kannan around at Harvard. Whom you might actually have been able to relate to. You didn't notice any of them.'

'Do I seem like the same person I was then? With the same approach to men?'

Annabel said nothing, she just sat there with both feet up on the chair, her knees level with her collarbone, a position other people generally took when sitting on the floor, but with her meant she was settling in for a long chat. But all she wanted Rebecca to see was that she wasn't even thinking of what to say next. For once, she was giving Rebecca time.

At last Rebecca said, 'I don't want to exaggerate the extent of my interest, even though it is real. And it's hard for me to know exactly where things come from, to separate conscious and unconscious. It's hard for anybody. Maybe there is an element of wanting to surprise myself, but I think there's a lot more to it than that. I just feel that if things were normal, or what I or other people might think of as normal, which definitely isn't these past few months, then no, I probably wouldn't be drawn to someone like him. But so what if this is a little crazy? If everything right now is a little crazy, that might be because I, maybe all of us, have been too closed off to craziness. And I don't think there's anything crazy about liking Kannan anyway. Why do I only have to be interested in people from our circle? In the expected sort of guy? Who always happens to be white?'

'No one said anything about white. No one's ever said that to you, explicitly or even implicitly. Not with friends like yours. *Definitely* not with parents like yours. You don't know what that's like. If I brought home a Black or Hispanic man, my mother would say that she wished I'd never been born.'

'I'm not accusing anyone else. I don't know exactly where these expectations or these ideas of normality come from. I just don't see why I should be imprisoned by them.'

Annabel rose and walked across the room to the dining table, killing her drink in three efficient gulps and before turning back to Rebecca she thudded her glass onto the table, as if about to deliver a valediction that would contain within it everything that needed to be known. In the days when she had been sure she was to get a fellowship to Oxford or Cambridge, Rebecca had imagined each tutorial ending thus, the don compressing an hour's Socratic dialogue into a single remark.

'I'm not saying, nor would I ever say, that you should stick to or go back to dating characterless bros like Connor,' said Annabel. 'But this isn't the way to make romantic choices either. It's not the job of your relationships to make the world a better place.'

Now Rebecca did something she had learned years ago not to bother with, and interrupted Annabel. She'd had her valediction and whatever Annabel might say next, she didn't want to hear it.

'There was something else,' she said. 'I think you'll flip when you hear this.'

Annabel, being Annabel, didn't laugh. Nor did she look surprised: she looked, rather, like someone who has been waiting for many years to open a bottle of wine, and has found her moment. Rebecca had predicted the degree of her satisfaction, just not its particular quality.

'Did Connor ever ask you about your hair? Did he know that you dyed it?'

'He often said that it was a beautiful colour. And there were a couple of names he called me that had to do with it, although we don't need to get into that.'

'Do you think he assumed that you dyed it?'

'I really don't know. I never really thought about it.' She had her suspicions about where Annabel was going with this, but there was no point asking, or trying to divert whatever was oncoming.

'Do you think he, or other men, would be as attracted to you if your hair were its natural colour?'

'That, I have thought about. No, I don't think they would be. Not *as* attracted, no.'

'So tell me, how do you think of your hair? What colour is it?'

'I'm not sure I understand the question.'

'What colour is your hair? That's not a difficult question.'

'Well, *naturally*, as I'm sure you know, it's a kind of light brown. Before I dyed it I always thought it the worst possible colour. As if it had thought about being blonde but didn't have the energy. And couldn't make it back to a solid brunette either.'

'So when you think of your hair, it's brown?'

'No, I think of it as red. That's how it is and how I'm going to keep it.'

'So it wasn't a lie that you told Kannan, was it?'

'Technically it was a lie, because I'm pretty sure he asked if it was my natural colour. I thought you were going to ask why I answered that way. So you're saying it's because in my head I think of that as the colour.'

'I don't know that I'm saying that or not saying it.'

'Why are you making such a big deal of this anyway? No one says anything to all the bottle blondes out there, but I dye my hair another colour and you turn it into a question of identity.'

'Except that it isn't me who did that. It's Kannan. Unless he is so far gone that he was *literally* wondering if you were related to the Weasleys, he thought it was important, and there must be some reason for that.'

Unresolvable arguments are like pimples: all they need to subside is to be let alone, but this is usually too much to ask. Annabel, miraculously, let this one go. Perhaps she felt that Kannan, having proven himself, whether out of social ineptitude or cultural ignorance or admirable brazenness, capable of asking such a question, would in due course reveal why he had asked it.

That is, if Rebecca ever heard from him again at all. Maybe the walk had been too ambiguous a gesture: after all, she had invited Grimmett, too, although only out of politeness, and with the expectation that he would say no. But on the walk itself she had done the conversational running, and had wanted to. However different his sensibilities were, he had to have been able to see that by leading, by asking questions, she was signalling interest, not something specifically sexual, but an interest in him, in seeing more and probing further. This role of prime mover was new to her, she didn't fully grasp its mechanics, but she was sure that it was his turn, and that his silence bore only one interpretation.

Annabel, of course, disagreed.

'Come on,' she said. 'For a guy like him, interest from someone like you is beyond fantasy. Either he's in denial, or he's just too confused to know what to do. Or … well, I don't know too many Indians, but it must happen with them also.'

'*What* must happen?'

'From what I've heard, Indian families are like Chinese ones when it comes to this stuff. Being gay is up there with dating black. Down there, you know what I mean. But there must still be gay Indian guys, right? Statistically. There's almost as many of them as there are of us.'

Not even in her moments of greatest self-satisfaction, which she fancied were years in the past, could Rebecca say that a man's lack of interest in her raised questions about his sexuality.

'You don't even mean half this stuff. You're just saying it to entertain yourself, to make a well-meaning white liberal wriggle uncomfortably in her seat.'

'Maybe he's asexual. Do you think that's actually a thing?'

Grimmett had sent out a message proposing that Wednesday Gobstones have a break. An off-season, he called it. They could reconvene in June, warm evenings with new ideas. No one objected. Passed by acclamation, he said. She and Kannan would be thrown together in late May, at Grimmett's Deathmarch event. By then whatever little she had felt, or thought she felt, or fancied she felt, or hoped to feel, would have dissipated, like a minor illness that cures itself during the long wait for a doctor's appointment.

Malathi had walked past the American consulate every weekday for five years, on her way to Stella Maris, but she had no idea what the building itself looked like. The consulate was a fortified compound with walls high enough that from the road only treetops could be seen beyond. For visa applicants there was no gate; instead, a black doorway built unobtrusively into the white wall, a door that opened only from the inside to let one applicant or family in and swiftly closed again. On most days the anxious, disorderly queue leading up to the door stretched L-shaped down Cathedral Road and could be seen from Stella Maris.

And now she too had to join the queue. Kannan had suggested that she aim to join him in Boston at the start of June. Everyone in Madras knew that a US visa could never be taken for granted, and Malathi was inundated with unsolicited advice about the visa process. Her father instructed her to ignore it all—most of these friends and relatives had never even been to the US. He himself had left India but once, on a doomed business visit to Singapore. On his return, he informed his wife and daughters that he ought to have followed the old injunction that barred Brahmins from crossing the seas. Yet he had chosen to send Malathi off to America—but first, to be properly coached for her visa interview, to the home of his wife's cousin who, with two married sons in Atlanta, was the acknowledged expert in these matters.

'The most important thing,' said Latha perima, 'is confidence. If you appear nervous, the visa officer will sense that you fear a rejection, and will wonder whether you are hiding something. The slightest suspicion is enough to finish you. They may ask you strange or confusing questions, but you have to stay poised. Dress as you would for a college function: neat, not fancy. Arrange your documents in the proper order

in a ring-binder. And pray every night that you will be interviewed by
an American officer—preferably a man, they are much kinder. The
Indian ones are a bitter, resentful bunch. They hate to see Indians
moving to the US and will make it as difficult for you as possible.' And,
this time in English, 'But don't worry too much about all this. I'm sure
you'll get your visa.'

On this mid-May morning on which the only people outdoors in
Madras were those with no choice, the visa queue was several-hundred
long, filled with young men whom she took to be aspiring master's
students. The air was thicker with nerves than water vapour—if fear
was grounds for rejection, most of her fellow applicants might be better
off saving themselves the trauma of the interview. After nearly an hour
in line she reached the black door, and moved through security and
document checks before taking her seat in the interview waiting area.

She sat at the corner of an empty row so as to eliminate entirely the
possibility of conversation. But with over fifty applicants ahead of her,
and having been firmly barred by Latha perima from bringing a book—
'You'll be so lost in your book that you won't even notice when your
number is called and you'll miss your interview!'—people-watching
was her only means of passing the time. The waiting room had several
TV screens, each showing a subtitled video depicting a different kind
of visa fraud, and highlighting both the inevitability of detection and its
consequences. No one appeared to be watching the videos, and at one
point a consular official—the tallest and pinkest person that Malathi
had ever seen—arrived to reinforce the message.

'I'm just here to remind all of you that entering false information
on a visa application is a felony. Well over a third of you are here
with falsified financial documents. Others may have fake birth or
marriage certificates. If you commit visa fraud, not only will you be
caught but, make no mistake, you will never, ever be allowed to enter
the United States.'

As the official was speaking, Malathi recognized two old school
classmates two rows ahead of her. Both had studied electrical

engineering, and were presumably here to obtain student visas. She scrupulously avoided eye contact—she had never spoken to either, and wanted to avoid being confronted with awkward recognition or, worse, blank, humiliating non-recognition. But, unable to summon any curiosity towards the other, unknown applicants in the room, she began to watch her classmates as discreetly as she could. Eventually one of them—Bharat, she remembered his name—had his number called. He had arranged his documents not in a ring-binder but in loose sheets and as he rose the sheets sprayed out of his file in an unruly cascade. After gathering the sheets, he walked up to a window directly in front of Malathi. She could see that his interviewer was an Indian man. She had been told that most interviews lasted four or five minutes, but Bharat's was past the ten-minute mark—he seemed to have had to refer to every document in his file—when she saw the interviewer slide his passport back to him. Bharat walked out without a goodbye or even a gesture to his friend. In his face, Malathi had seen the decisive embrace of defeat. Nothing ever again was going to be as he had hoped.

And now it was her turn, to take her immaculately arranged documents and strangely unshaken confidence to the counter at the end of a long corridor. Her interviewer, a dark-haired man, had his back turned to her. As he turned and sat down, she saw that he was unmistakably American, scarcely older than her, with a smile of nervous but genuine kindness. He began with the questions she had been taught to expect: the name of her husband's employer, how long they planned to be in the United States.

And then: 'What is your husband's annual income, ma'am?'

The question was so unexpected that she could make no response at all—nor even conceive of one.

'Let me rephrase that. What is his salary? How much does he make?'

She had to say something. 'I don't know. Is that information not with you?' She knew she had made a mistake as she asked the question.

'I hope you understand, ma'am, that you are applying for a spousal visa, a kind of dependent visa. Under this visa you will not be allowed to work—your husband's salary will be your household income. Do you understand that?'

'Yes.'

'And you don't know what that income is?'

'No, sir. But I know that it is more than enough for us.'

'So you have a sense, then? Roughly how much?'

Once again, she was silent—and she wondered now how she could ever have thought this man kind.

'I have to admit that I have some concerns, ma'am. I'm not sure we can send you off to the United States without your having any sense of your financial circumstances there. How long have you known your husband? Did you have an arranged marriage?' They had irrevocably departed from Latha perima's script.

'It was an arranged marriage. I have known my husband for …' The phrasing of the question allowed her some leeway. She decided to choose the date that she had first heard of Kannan from her father. 'Eight months.'

'And you agreed to marry him without any knowledge of his income? Isn't that against the whole logic of an arranged marriage?'

'Our parents arranged the marriage, sir. We—we belong to the same community. Don't worry, I know that he earns more than enough.'

'When and where was your wedding? How many people attended?' As she began to answer—she couldn't understand the point of the question, but she could answer it fairly easily—he raised his right hand: 'Never mind.'

He began to examine her passport and application form in a perfunctory manner that suggested that he was only pretending to read as a cover for thinking. She knew that she had long since lost her poise and confidence—surely he could tell that she was one question away from bursting into tears. Why had he been so obsessed with Kannan's salary? What business of his was it? On the other hand—and the thought felt foreign and wrong, but she could not dismiss it—perhaps he had a point: how could Kannan, and her father, conspire to keep that information from her? But there was no conspiracy—they had not seen any need for her to know, and she had seen no need to ask, and that was bad enough.

Her interviewer raised his head to face her once again. 'I can't help but think that I'm making a mistake here. I am genuinely worried about your going so naïvely to join your husband in the US. But I'm giving you the benefit of the doubt and granting your visa. You can come back and collect your passport this afternoon.'

And now she would have to tell the story of the morning to Kannan. In recent weeks the flow of his emails had tapered off like a river in summer, to the point where it can be crossed by foot. At first she could allow herself to write twice, even three times, before he replied. He was her husband, not someone whose heart needed to be won through coyness and stratagems. But after a while this was inconsistent with any acceptable level of dignity. And she hardly wanted to annoy him.

He had never bothered with excuses, not when the average gap between emails grew from a day to three days to a week, not when his emails were two-thirds shorter than hers, not when he didn't respond to any of the news she'd shared or even the questions she'd asked, unless those questions were points of information. He had never described his work as onerous, but perhaps he was underplaying it to reassure her. She had heard of the dotcom crash that had forced thousands of young programmers back to India in defeat and humiliation, like miners who had arrived too late to a gold rush. Maybe Kannan's employers had fired so many people that he had been given additional responsibilities. All she knew was that he was going to take part in a public debate about Harry Potter. Surely the preparations for that couldn't be what was taking up all his time.

In another life, the deficiencies in their correspondence would have left her looking at the move to Boston with trepidation, even dread. But in this one, she was counting down the days to her departure, because her father wanted her gone. Not that he would ever say such a thing. But no one could miss it, the edgy restlessness that became him like sneakers beneath a sari. Before her marriage she had always thought that her presence in the house sustained her father. By finding her Kannan, he had done his duty, but to have to give her up in the process showed that the performance of duty could be as wrenching as some traumatic dilemma. Perhaps that was it, then: now that she was married, no longer his, he wanted her out as quickly as possible because to enjoy her presence would be improper, and to concede himself a little enjoyment would be to concede everything.

Her unrequited emails to Kannan had, serially, confessed that, as much as she loved Harry Potter, she struggled to match his commitment to fandom. She had even put *Time Regained* aside: it was entertaining, in a way, but she didn't think it shared any of the spirit of the books. And did there really need to be *that much* sex, in such detail? For her part, she was looking forward most to the movie of *Philosopher's Stone*.

But none of this could explain his near-silence. That wasn't the man she had married.

She did the goodbye rounds of friends and relatives, one a day on average. They took on the air of condolence visits. With ten days to go to her departure, she resolved not to keep emailing Kannan, except when necessary—such as to remind him of her flight details. That left vacant the several hours each day that she had spent thinking about whether to write, what to write, writing and rewriting.

It was in one of these unfilled hours, sitting at her PC, that it occurred to her that she ought to write a fanfic. She wasn't sure whose sake she would do it for: hers or Kannan's. Malathi had spent a life reading novels without ever trying to write one. This was different, because it didn't require the ego that a novel of one's own did. And if it worked, if it was good, or good enough, it would be a gift to Kannan, but it would be more than that. It would be a way of getting their life together in America off to a propitious start, of showing how much they shared. Start as you mean to go on.

She had no plot or characters in mind; nothing except the sense that rather than try to imitate JKR, or attempt a sequel to the books, she should use what JKR had given her—the world of magic—and expand it to the world she knew. She couldn't write about England while only knowing it from books.

Ideas began to assail her like hawkers who have got hold of a new tourist. She could barely listen to them one at a time. How caste might interact with the magical dichotomy of pureblood and Muggle-born; whether magical India had been colonized by Britain as well; whether to use Tamil or Sanskrit words for the spells (maybe a Westernized elite, people like her, used JKR's Latin spells); whether to make her protagonist an orphan, like Harry. On that first day she got as far as a paragraph.

The city that the Muggles used to call Madras and now call Chennai is really two cities. The second city is present everywhere but visible nowhere; unless you know how to look. In other countries, witches and wizards seclude themselves, build villages far from Muggle eyes. In the Tamil country, there was never room for that, so they learned camouflage instead.

For two months Kannan, whose general pessimism rarely took concrete form, had been tormented by the prospect of Malathi's arrival. There were days, no, not entire *days*, but on most days there were periods, sometimes several consecutive hours, when he thought the afternoon in the park was an infallible prophecy of years of happiness. He hadn't got any better at knowing whether this was a story he told himself, or what he truly believed. Sometimes this vision flashed involuntarily across his mind, too fleeting to be an epiphany, or anything more than a spasm: it left behind no rapture, only more confusion. Most of the time, the other side looked to have the upper hand. In an afternoon he had condemned himself to open up his life to a girl he didn't know. And, what was surely worse, she seemed determined to love him. This way of thinking, too, could return spasmodically. Invariably, when he had got into the shower, convinced that, as far as arranged marriages went, he had been miraculously lucky, the first jet of water sent a malignant frisson rising up within his chest like the sudden onset of a fever: what have I done?

It was only outside the house, on his walks, and that too only fleetingly, that he was able to think of the question rationally, to allow thought to follow thought without feeling himself wrenched repeatedly from side to side. In these moments he reminded himself of how little he knew; of how little she had done to justify his dread. And that they had more to go on than a solitary suspension of disbelief in Cubbon Park. There was the night of their wedding; her understanding, her resolve. They had passed that easily enough. Hadn't he fallen asleep in her arms? And there were her emails. He could go back and reread them and learn again all that he seemed to have forgotten about her.

But then he would climb the stairs and enter his apartment and see before him a living room that bore the marks of a husband awaiting his wife. Kannan had bought a coffee table, and a vase that he'd filled with daffodils, and even a puja set, of all things, so that she might feel herself swiftly at home. His living room, *his* life, and every piece of it to be laid bare before her, either given to her or given up. He didn't need to reread her emails. He knew what was in them: her love and her commitment only highlighted the horrifying finality of it all. Another man might have deleted the emails. Kannan didn't need to. Not looking at them was a requirement of getting through each day.

In two months, not once had he come close to telling Grimmett. There was no urge to confession and there was the certainty that Grimmett could not help. The only person who could, Santhanam, he couldn't approach. Forget all the other obvious reasons why not: it was Santhanam who had placed him here, who had been proud to do so. Not confessing hadn't meant pulling away from Grimmett, but he was sure his friend had noticed that just as their friendship had grown to no longer require Harry Potter as a daily anchor, Kannan had begun to drive conversations back towards it. Fandom wasn't a distraction: it was authentically his, somehow separate from the question of Malathi, notwithstanding Harry Potter's role in their marriage.

In all this Rebecca, not Rebecca herself but the question of Rebecca, the question posed and left unanswered, a non-answer being as good as a no, loomed as one of many abandoned futures, as a means to think of all the universes in which he hadn't married Malathi. He only had to alter the chronology slightly to think of meeting Rebecca before, rather than immediately after, his trip home. As brief as that first ecstatic obsession was, it would have been sufficient to inure him against the possibility of accepting Malathi. Then there was the idea of Rebecca, of a real-life version of the kind of romance that he had spent the past two years reading about and investigating. And a thought that had arrived as soon as he returned home from the walk, and that he allowed himself to revisit from time to time: a romance with Rebecca would mock everything Santhanam or his parents had ever made or expected of him, but it would do more than that, it would be living beyond anything Santhanam could ever dream of for himself.

He set these thoughts against, first, a sense, born not out of pessimism but simple realism, that he was never likely to have gone very far with Rebecca, and second, the fact that when presented an opportunity, he hadn't even bothered to see where things might go. But the question of Rebecca, and of other potential Rebeccas, remained unsettled.

And it wasn't just that he had turned Rebecca down. He hadn't had the chance either way. The first time he met Rebecca he was engaged; by the night of the walk he was married and his wife was less than three months away from joining him.

Twice he set out to email Rebecca, proposing a walk of his own curation—one that would end in the South End. He never got any further than the salutation. 'Dear Rebecca'; no, 'Hi Rebecca'; 'Hello Rebecca', was that more British? 'Hey Rebecca'? She would hate that. He tried 'Dear' and 'Hello' once more each, and then trashed the draft. What would be the point? She would say yes, and then there were four possible scenarios. This second walk might kill off any possibility of interest on either side. Or she might be interested, and he uninterested—okay, this was hardly likely, but there was no need to rule it out; hadn't she been the one to initiate the first walk? In this case he would just have another person to disappoint. Or he might find himself under enchantment again, but publicly this time, and have humiliation follow. Or, or, something might lead from it. The first two possibilities were harmless. Even the third he could risk. But the fourth: with Malathi about to arrive? He'd never had the chance, and never would.

But the Deathmarch panel was approaching, and he surprised even Grimmett with the intensity of his preparation. He went back to the first thread of the online Deathmarch and reread them all, not skimming over a single post, making notes on every single argument that had ever been made by the Ron/Hermione side and its possible refutations, looking out for any Pumpkin Pie argument that the other side didn't seem able to counter. If he'd worked like this at computer science, he'd have outdone Santhanam, ended up at MIT, not Northeastern. But in that life he'd have been like Santhanam, which would have meant never knowing Harry Potter at all.

13

Having seen how Kannan reacted to his gift of the Deathmarch panel, Grimmett grew greedy. He wanted to give Kannan another gift: to surprise him. He wanted to fly Perdita in from Chicago as keynote speaker. She was Kannan's favourite author; they had corresponded; and through this, she might become his friend.

Rebecca was tasked with getting Perdita to agree. Grimmett would cover all her expenses. He seemed to be paying for all of this himself; there was no talk of a sponsor, no public appeal for donations. Was Grimmett wealthy? The wages of a weekly public radio host didn't stretch to hiring ballrooms at the Park Plaza.

All she had to go on, really, were Kannan's fandom posts, but Rebecca had concluded that where Kannan's commitment was to Harry Potter, Grimmett, although he did genuinely love the books, was doing all this for Kannan. Getting to know Grimmett had meant measuring the amplitude of his feelings for Kannan without being able to make sense of them. Were they friendly, or paternal—there certainly seemed to be an aspect of protectiveness—or sexual? And what of Kannan's? In the fog of it all she saw devotion of a rare degree, at least on one side. There must be something to Kannan that justified it.

Perdita's reply was strangely curt. *Thanks, I'll get back to you soon.* That's all? She had written three effusive paragraphs, fragrant with dishonesty. How lovely the fans of Boston were, how much they loved *Time Regained*, what a lovely evening it would be. Connor aside, she'd gone entire years without using the word love this many times.

And then Perdita disappeared.

She posted every day on HP4BK, so even three days' absence was noteworthy. Three days became a week, then two weeks. The two most recent chapters of *Time Regained* that Rebecca had Britpicked remained un-uploaded. She wrote a follow-up. No response.

IRL was how fandom referred to everything else: in real life. Which emphasized fandom's idea of itself as escape. An unexplained absence like Perdita's must have some non-fandom cause: an illness, a family crisis. Maybe it was something as mundane as exams, but in that case, why not say? Rebecca was worried not as a fan but as a friend.

Perdita had been gone three weeks when, for the first time since the walk, Rebecca heard from Kannan. *Hey, any idea what's going on with Perdita? No posts in 22 days and she's never gone this long between chapters.*

Three more brief emails were exchanged. He even offered, unsolicited, a pair of fanfic recommendations while they waited on Perdita. It was as if he was saying: we can have an acquaintance, as long as all we do is talk Harry Potter. Kannan must be one of those people for whom fandom *was* real life; everything else was the distraction. He was agitated about Perdita, but only as a reader. Surely he and Grimmett must talk about other things. But to Rebecca, this seemed to be all he was offering. To get back in touch in this way allowed for no other interpretation.

IvyEdge had a record-breaking year. Connie's decision to expand had been more than justified by results. The associates' bonuses were calculated based on the admissions achieved by their assigned students.

Each student who got into HYPSM—Harvard, Yale, Princeton, Stanford and MIT—meant an additional $1,000 for the associate. These were five of the six colleges that Connie rated 'elite'. The sixth, Caltech, didn't discriminate against Asians; applicants there were less in need of an edge. Despite the firm's name, Connie had little regard for the Ivy League. 'A club that includes *Brown* and *Dartmouth* is elite? Give me a break.'

Each HYPSM admit was asked to submit a testimonial for IvyEdge's website. And they received additional free services. Connie asked Rebecca to hold one-on-one seminars with the seven kids who had got into Harvard. How to write essays at Harvard, how to navigate campus socially, how to take care of your mental and physical health, how to choose classes and concentrations depending on your career goals.

Midway through the first of these, Rebecca thought: if only all of the job was like this. Back when she was an applicant, the girl before her had been distant, as if to emphasize the professional nature of their acquaintance. Now the girl looked at Rebecca with acquisitive curiosity. Now they were both Harvard women, and Rebecca represented a possible future. And Rebecca looked more closely at her, too: sizing her up, working out how she would do. At Harvard, said the poet, you find yourself or founder. This girl was too self-possessed and firm to founder. She was rapidly outgrowing her physical awkwardness; in a year or so she'd have plenty of male attention, if she wanted it. But you couldn't find yourself unless you were looking. If you entered Harvard this confident, you wouldn't find yourself, you'd find others like you.

When she called her mother to tell her about these seminars, they chuckled at the lame banality of her account: the nostalgia for being an undergrad and choosing each semester's classes, the sadness provoked by the knowledge that these wide-eyed seventeen-year-olds, with their blueprints for development work in Africa or biomedical research, were more likely to end up at investment banks.

'Some of them looked at me almost reverently,' she said. 'Because they're so eager to start college, they want to take everything in. But I think some of the others, the more worldly and knowing ones, were thinking, and *this* is what you end up doing after Harvard? This satisfied your aspirations?'

She could hear, on the line, Liz's wordless approval. Ever since she started this job, she knew, her parents had been waiting for her to quit.

One thought, even more pitiful than the others, she didn't share. If she had enjoyed these meetings so much, and had felt herself to be good at what she was doing, then surely she ought to keep working with kids this age? Not in admissions consulting, of course, and here the insight turned into the horrific phantasm of Rebecca, aged forty, a professor like her father. This was a vision that was going to recur: she knew it, and she knew that she had to suppress it each time with all she could throw at it. We aren't doomed to turn into our parents. We can fight it. We must.

A week before the Deathmarch, Perdita posted a message to HP4BK, and to the GCR board dedicated to discussion of *Time Regained.*

Dear friends, shipmates and readers:

Many of you will know that the two most important entities in my life are Harry Potter and my church, not necessarily in that order. In recent months, I've had a series of meetings with my pastor and other leaders in my church about Harry Potter and about fandom. There is a wicked and inaccurate stereotype about Christianity and Harry Potter, and I want to emphasize that many in my church, including my pastor, have read the books and appreciate their moral, spiritual and literary qualities. But these conversations have forced me to interrogate my own role in fandom and, in particular, the fanfics I have read and the fanfic I have written. It has become increasingly clear that my activities are inconsistent with the doctrine and expectations of my church, and with my own expectations of myself. In the next two weeks I will be taking *Time Regained* down from every site where it is currently hosted. I have been beyond moved by the response to the fic. All I ever wanted to do was write and in these past months you, dear readers, have made me feel a writer. I can't thank you enough for that. I'm leaving the chapters up for a few days in case any of you want to download and keep them. I'm so sorry to have to disappoint you by not finishing the fic, but this is as far as I can stretch my conscience.

Yours forever, Michelle.

Rebecca's correspondence with Michelle, during its brief flourishing, had moved far beyond Harry Potter. She thought she had made a friend. She had been aware, in some abstract way, about the importance of the church in Michelle's life, but how could you ever know something like that in a way that wasn't abstract?

What could possibly be objectionable about *Time Regained,* a story so tender and optimistic, uplifting in every sense, to this pastor who apparently loved Harry Potter? Only the sex. On the ratings system that GCR borrowed from the Motion Picture Association of America, *Time Regained* was rated R. No Christian film ever had such a rating.

The Harry Potter books themselves were about children who barely showed signs of puberty, let alone sexuality—at fourteen, they had none of them had a first kiss. Her own job on *Time Regained* had been Britpicking, but she couldn't help underline the sex scenes, if only to tell Michelle how much she enjoyed them, how well she wrote sex. What she didn't say was: what makes these scenes so good is how lived they feel. These aren't fantasies, they're written by a woman who knows exactly what good sex is like.

And Rebecca saw the real nature of what was being lost, and she felt it as she had never felt anything that was not hers. Not their friendship: the fact that Michelle had told her nothing, that she had learned of her retirement in this public way, showed how little that was worth. What was being lost, given up, was everything of Michelle that had gone into *Time Regained*: the joy and heat and love of visceral pleasure, in this world and in the imagination. Whatever Michelle thought she was gaining in exchange, Rebecca couldn't see how it could ever be worth it.

Michelle did write to Rebecca to apologize. But their correspondence ended there. And with it the fraying thread that connected Rebecca to online fandom looked ready to snap, and she had no interest in stopping it. Of course she would continue to love Harry Potter, and to think about it. But these thoughts could be private, or for Annabel.

That didn't mean there weren't things she could be grateful for, or keep in a life after fandom. In a year, hopefully sooner, she and Annabel would stand in line together for their copies of Book Five. If she ever had children she'd count down the days until they were ready for *Sorcerer's Stone*—they wouldn't have to wait until twenty-three, as she had—and then, when they were old enough, she'd give them a bound version of *Time Regained*. And there was Grimmett and, who knows, maybe Kannan. Giving up fandom didn't mean giving them up. If she missed it, she could live vicariously through them.

From the street, the triangular Park Plaza looked less like a hotel than a grand ocean liner in port, its windows a constellation of portholes. Not that Kannan knew what a hotel should look like. In India he had never been to a five star. The world 'hotel', in Bangalore, more commonly referred to a restaurant. The Park Plaza, he had read, was 'iconic', and quintessentially American. He felt himself about to enter another era, more glamorous than his own. But once inside the lobby he found that time travel was overrated. This could not be a proper five star. He could hear Santhanam beside him, calling it dingy, musty, outmoded. Time to tear it down and build something fit for 2001. In the ballroom, with its absence of windows and its too-bright lighting, he thought, this place has nothing to do with Harry Potter. He stood in the front as Grimmett went up to open the evening.

Grimmett announced that he had only one thing to say, which would surprise anyone who knew him, although that one thing would be familiar to those who listened to his show. Harry Potter, he said, was a wonder of the world, but also, for America, an opportunity: to open ourselves culturally, and more specifically, to transform our relationship to Britain, the country that was most important to the American past and, hopefully, to its future.

Kannan had heard Grimmett described as an Anglophile, without quite knowing what that meant, especially as his friend spoke so rarely about Britain, even about his years there. Now he learned that the basis of their friendship was not, in the truest sense, a shared love: Grimmett had come to Harry Potter from an angle Kannan could not comprehend. But if they both loved Harry Potter, what did it matter why? The manner of the love's expression had scarcely been different at all. And before he started to judge other fans on the sources of their love, he ought to reflect on the fact that Grimmett knew, had investigated and had found the source of his own.

Why did Kannan love Harry Potter? He didn't think he had ever wondered. It wasn't that he hadn't phrased the question to himself in that way; but he always dismissed it as a question not worth asking.

The person Grimmett introduced as the next speaker was someone that Kannan had always suspected of not loving Harry Potter at all. Ezra Miller had built potterworld.com on Sorting Hat and 'What Animal Would Your Patronus Be?' personality quizzes. He had arrived today in a black hoodie that bore the slogan: IT'S COOL TO BE A RAVENCLAW. Had Grimmett been compelled to choose him for his celebrity? Potterworld had a hundred, maybe a thousand, users for every one on GCR.

Ezra spoke as if pitching Potterworld to a group of potential investors. Maybe that was the only way he knew.

The growth of fandom up until now, he said, was just the beginning. The next stage, fandom 2.0, would be worldwide, accessing markets that up until now had been left out of every global cultural conversation. He had partnered with a local company to translate Potterworld into Mandarin. Hindi was next. You can't just ignore two billion people.

'With that,' said Grimmett, 'it's time for us all to have a drink or two. And then we'll have what you're really here for: the Deathmarch.'

'Could I just say something really quickly, Curtis?' said Ezra. 'On that subject, one final point.'

'Of course, the floor is—'

Ezra didn't wait for Grimmett to finish. 'I just think that for fandom to really grow and to achieve its potential, we have to move beyond this ridiculous ship debate. Guys, it's like debating the future of operating systems: Windows vs Macintosh. It's over. Windows won. Yeah, there'll always be a few people who, while they're totally tech illiterate, use Macintosh, and try to preach the gospel to the rest of us, because they're think they're smarter. And more importantly, because they think they're *cooler*. Just like there will always be a few people out there who ship Harry/Hermione. They don't just think they're better than the rest of us. They think they know better than J.K. Rowling. When they're really the ones who are deluded. It's like they have an eyesight disorder that allows them to read the books really closely while missing out all the obvious places where she shows that Ron and Hermione are going to get together. It's like, even if they openly declare their love and get engaged in Book Five, these people will say, you don't understand symbolism and classical references, Harry and Hermione are destined to be together. And when that doesn't end up happening, they'll say if only JKR knew what she was doing, Harry and Hermione would have been together. Or my favourite, yes, Ron and Hermione might end up together in the books but later on, Harry and Hermione will be with each other, in real life. *In real life!* This stuff isn't like sports. You can't just pick a shitty team in the hope that they sign some free agents and win next year. Windows won. Ron/Hermione won. And the sooner we all accept that, the better. Especially if we want JKR to take us seriously as fans. Given the level of interest, I don't blame you guys for scheduling a Deathmarch to build your community. But this should be the last time. When I got to meet JKR last August and talk fandom, she didn't mention shipping once. I hear from people in the know that she thinks it's a real joke. I mean, Harry/Hermione, guys? Seriously?'

The worst thing about this attempt to undermine their very reason for assembling was that anyone familiar with Ezra's work could have expected it. Potterworld was dominated by the kind of Ron/Hermione fan who found the ship debate itself offensive. But it soon became clear why Grimmett had invited such a person. Potterworld had arranged the food and drink. That kind of thing was beyond Grimmett. Ezra might be fourteen and well-pimpled, but he had a handful of adult associates, and it was one of these that thrust a 'Butterbeer' at Kannan.

Whatever it contained, it was frothy and brown and tasted like the urine of a diabetic. He put the cup aside. Some things, he believed, should be left to magic. Some things we are better off not knowing, like the taste of Butterbeer, and what it feels like to play Quidditch.

Doing the rounds with Grimmett, meeting dozens of people that he knew online, finding that everyone knew his posts well and admired his erudition, being asked more than once why he didn't write fanfic, Kannan thought of his wedding, barely two months ago. There too, he was taken around, introduced to dozens, no, hundreds of people. There he had been an object of curiosity, subject to evaluation; here he met warmth, and an unfamiliar familiarity. What curiosity he encountered was uncorrupted by judgement. But here, as at his wedding, he couldn't make himself fully present. He couldn't return the warmth and interest. He longed to be back at his desk, talking to the same people, but online, with time to craft each post.

After an hour or so, Grimmett said he wanted to talk briefly to the other Deathmarch panellists. Kannan said go ahead, I won't join you. Without moving, he looked instead for Rebecca.

He spotted her, not at one of the stalls or in the too-narrow corridors between them, but by an exit. She was talking to a man, and as Kannan's angle of view was diagonal, he could see the man's back with only a sliver of profile, not enough to know for sure who he was. A white checked shirt and hair cut as closely as a new Marine's. Whoever he was, he was doing most of the talking, with what looked like earnestness, and although Rebecca's expression could be seen, Kannan could tell nothing of what she made of what she was being told. He was at a distance, but he thought the man wouldn't be able to tell either. She held a blue plastic cup, disfigured by the Potterworld logo, and she was leaning slightly against the door, which suggested they had been talking for some time. If she leaned any further it would push open, an act guaranteed in red letters to raise an alarm and thus to be resorted to only in emergency, although Kannan had yet to find a door of this kind that actually worked that way.

Rebecca had taken him on a walk, and while he had been inclined not to overrate that gesture or to overload it with meaning and, most importantly, had denied it the follow-up that it asked for, if not deserved, Rebecca, not Rebecca herself but the question of Rebecca, had not gone away. It had been resolved formally, at the level of a shared romance, but it had not gone away. Rebecca had taken him on a walk, but she wasn't in love with him or anything like that. He was no judge of these things, he had neither abstract nor empirical knowledge, nor had he applied his mind in any focused way, but there was no reason to think that, right now, she wasn't being hit on. Maybe she would end up spending the night with the crew cut. It seemed as plausible as anything else.

Without knowing why he did it, or even really that he was doing it, he found himself walking towards Rebecca and the checked shirt. He was conscious of no jealousy, nor of any curiosity about him, of nothing more than the urge to interrupt them. Rebecca had evidently been keeping a discreet eye on the rest of the room: she saw Kannan approaching a dozen steps away and turned to face him.

'What are you drinking?' asked Kannan, with untraceable familiarity.

'I believe it's called a Bubble-Head Charm,' said Rebecca. 'More commonly known as a French 75. It might be in a blue solo cup that advertises the worst site in fandom, but it's pretty delicious. Although sadly I don't think it actually equips me to breathe under water.'

The crew cut, who held no drink, regarded Kannan with mild puzzlement. He looked like a practical man, whose view of life was essentially simple. He wasn't rattled.

'Ned,' he said, the syllable accompanied by the American male handshake that Santhanam, in that otherwise-so-comprehensive letter, had failed to warn him about. After four years of these handshakes, Kannan had finally asked Grimmett: why do they want to yank your hand off? It shames me to say it, said Grimmett, about my fellow Americans, and forgive my crudeness, but the truth is that they fear that if they don't shake firmly enough the other guy will think they have a small penis, and in this country there could be no more debilitating failing.

This guy must have a monstrous dick.

'Nice to meet you.'

Kannan said nothing for so long that Rebecca had to say, 'This is Kannan.' She was impressively close to saying it right. 'He's also from Boston, he and Curtis Grimmett run the Gobstones Club.' From Boston, that was a new one. He liked it.

It took less than five minutes for the crew cut to see that Kannan had no intention of going back to wherever he had come from. In that time Rebecca had explained Ned's situation: he had just moved to Boston himself, to teach English at a prep school. He was a huge fan, but not yet active in fandom; he had come today in the hope that fandom might help him make friends in his new city. Presumably she said all this to make Ned feel involved in the conversation, and because he seemed to have no urge to say anything further to Kannan himself. Eventually he said that he had better go home, as this was a school night. He was sorry to miss the panel. But before leaving he had Rebecca's cellphone number and email, without either offering or being asked for his own. Hair cropped that short can hardly be said to have a colour, and it was only as he walked away that Kannan noticed that Ned's was red, or would be if he allowed it to live a little. Red, but only just on the other side of brown, not Rebecca's pomegranate peel-red. It definitely wasn't dyed.

Should he suggest that they go on a walk? No, he could just settle instead into Ned's place by the exit. Like the second in a series of candidates being interviewed. Or the second suitor in a swayamvar. Working thus far on instinct, he began now to think of what he might say.

'How did you like the fics I told you about?'

'They were okay,' said Rebecca. 'To be honest, there was only one fanfic writer I really cared about. Perdita. And I'm still processing her announcement. Actually, I'm trying to figure out *how* to process it.'

'Did you know she was so religious? I remember that she used to say a lot about herself on HP4BK, about her life, but I don't remember that.'

'I knew that she was brought up in a deeply Christian household, their lives built around their megachurch, and that it was an important part of her identity. I'm not religious, and I wasn't brought up that way, so I never really felt capable of understanding that side of her. I guess I thought, on some level, that like a lot of young people who are brought up in a Christian or other religious community but move out into the secular world, she must be figuring out the place Christianity could play in a life that was so different from her parents' without giving it up altogether. But now I just feel like I never knew her at all the whole time, not in any true way.'

He half-expected her to ask if he was religious, but she didn't. But how could he rationally expect anything at all? All he had to go by, really, was Grimmett. And she was nothing like Grimmett. Except that, as the conversation went on—later, he would estimate they spoke for over twenty minutes—with her doing most of the talking, and the topics changing, sometimes even leaving the plane of Harry Potter, he couldn't help be reminded of how things had begun with Grimmett last July, and to think that, later, there would be questions, many that Grimmett had asked, including whether he was religious, and new ones. And the thought gripped him, and he knew it wasn't a feverish fantasy like the one sparked by their first meeting, but a real thought, with depth and truth: there could be something here akin to what he had with Grimmett, different to the extent that Rebecca was different, but with as much ease and generosity.

And he said, 'I'm sorry I never said anything after our walk in March. I've been very busy with work. And I don't know you at all, but I really think we could be good friends. We agree on everything, or at least everything important.'

And she laughed, except that it wasn't a laugh but something that is called a laugh but isn't, a non-verbal sound of happiness like a birdcall.

'You're right,' she said. 'And I'd like that.'

'Now I have to go prepare. Wish me luck.'

The crowd had grown restless. The drinks were disgusting, and most people really were there to listen to a Deathmarch, rather than to make new friends. But Grimmett had gone missing, and even Ezra Miller didn't feel entitled to suggest they start without him.

When Grimmett returned he came straight up to Rebecca, with a face that combined sadness and agitation, as if he had suffered grave disappointment but held out hope of stopping his losses.

'I, I mean we, need a favour,' he said. 'It's a lot to ask. But I trust you with it.'

'What happened?'

'Kannan won't be taking part in the Deathmarch. I'm asking you to take his place.'

Rebecca knew that he didn't intend to say why Kannan had dropped out, even though Grimmett had told her, and she had wondered if this constituted a breach of trust for a friendship as close as his and Kannan's, how loaded this panel was for Kannan with moment and meaning. It would be little exaggeration, Grimmett had said, to say that he may think this the most important day of his life. That didn't mean she didn't have the right to ask anyway. But she allowed herself to feel some satisfaction in not asking; in respecting Grimmett's omission, and in his awareness of that respect, because he could not but be aware of it.

'Aren't there many better qualified people here? There are so many prominent Pumpkin Pie shippers.'

'Prominent, perhaps, but that doesn't mean they'd be more eloquent or convincing. And I suspect people like that wouldn't like being asked to do this at such short notice: some of them are probably pissed off they weren't asked in the first place. And, most importantly, I don't feel that I know them. I trust you. And remember: none of this matters that much. It's just a debate about hypothetical romantic pairings in a series of children's books.'

She wanted to say, what makes you say that *now*? You of all people? If he had guessed that both she and Annabel had decided that fandom wasn't for them after all, that in years to come she was sure she would consider it a *phase*, the kind of thing she thought you stopped having at eighteen or twenty-one, or some age that she thought she'd passed, and that this phase was ending, how could he have guessed that? But all she said was okay, of course I'll do it.

'Wonderful. You know all the arguments already. The format will be explained for the benefit of the crowd, but the first Ron/Hermione speaker will go first, followed by your partner, Clara. Then the second Ron/Hermione speaker, then you, then rebuttals, then audience questions, then a vote at the end. Ezra has flooded the place, so they'll win the vote, but that's irrelevant.'

Clara was, other than Athena Alice and Perdita—Michelle as she had come to think of her, but Perdita as she would now have to be, the self Michelle had shed like a snakeskin—probably the most popular Pumpkin Pie author out there. Rebecca didn't think much of her stuff, which was Mills & Boon with a shot of James Bond. But for box office appeal and, hopefully, charisma, she was a worthy ally to have. Grimmett walked up to the lectern to introduce the panel.

14

Malathi had heard all about how it used to be. Going to America was becoming almost commonplace. Once, it would have been enough to get your name and face in the newspaper. Now there was no delegation to see her off, just her father; but there had been a party at home, high tea rather than dinner as her flight to Frankfurt was at 3 a.m. Her sister had come all the way from Coimbatore, but she stayed only long enough to be the last guest to leave, spending the night instead at her in-laws'.

Her father asked her to go over the things in her suitcases one last time, to check them against her list. 'Before you close the luggage I have one thing to give you, whenever you're ready.' She came downstairs to find her father holding what looked like a long wallet. She was sure of what was in it: foreign exchange. It was something that she knew she needed, but had trusted her father to take care of. She had never asked him about it.

'These are some dollars for you. Here, count them.'

'No need to count, I'll just take a little out, however much you recommend, and store the rest safely.'

'You should always know exactly how much money you have. Count it now in front of me.'

She opened the wallet-like thing. It was made of a synthetic fabric rather than leather and felt somehow more new and expensive for it. She counted with deliberate slowness. Twenty notes, all of them $100. She recognized the face from an old social studies textbook: Benjamin Franklin. He had discovered electricity by flying a kite. Something like that. It was over eighty thousand rupees: not a lot, she knew, compared to how much Kannan earned—however much that was—but, to any normal person, a huge sum.

'Appa, this is much too much. I don't need this much money.'

'Don't be silly. I don't want you to worry in an emergency. And it is not so much. Besides, when you arrive, it will be nice to have a little something of your own. Who knows how much Kannan will give you to run the house?'

Her father's driver did most of the talking on the way to the airport. She should thank her father who had arranged such a wonderful match for her. It was life beyond dreams. She must have done something in her past life to deserve it (the driver, a convert to Catholicism, liked to hedge his bets). All through, her father hardly looked at her, which gave her plenty of chances to look at him. What was he thinking? Surely he had to be more sad than happy. Happy that he had done all he could for her, happy that she could expect happiness, but that was the kind of happiness you felt in the abstract, or came to feel in the long run, but could not summon at a moment like this. At least not a man like him. Sometimes he looked to be silently praying. At other times she saw a fugitive smile arrive and disappear, a desperate smile. He *was* sad, and his thoughts must be directed towards consoling himself with abstract happiness. You couldn't expect conversation of him at a time like this. And looking at her would make it all unbearable.

For international flights, passengers were not permitted to take guests inside the terminal. This meant saying goodbye on the pavement, the driver waiting in the car. And now her father looked at her at last, with his face of effortful stoicism, and she could not stop herself, even if she wanted nothing more than to be able to, she had directed her conscious will only to the purpose of not saying what she was about to say, but she was not strong enough. The most she could do was moderate her tone.

'Appa, I am a little worried. Kannan has not replied to me in two weeks. I even placed an international call but he didn't answer. I sent him my flight details but he never confirmed he would pick me up.'

Later she would think that her father had replied so quickly that he couldn't really have processed what she said. It was almost as if he was determined not to.

'It will all be fine. Don't worry. Of course he will be there! Some people are funny. They don't reply and confirm things properly. But that doesn't mean there's anything to worry about.'

'But what if this is a sign of other things? I am going to a new place, a strange country, and I only know him. I am dependent upon him.'

'Haven't you told me so many times how loving and enthusiastic Kannan has been in his mails and calls to you? He is your husband and he loves you.'

There were goodbyes, more than one, and an embrace so long and tight that it held the illusion of eternity, and the requests that she have a safe flight and call him from Boston, things that even she, who was doing this for the first time, knew to be formalities, except that they seemed to fulfil deep primal needs. But all through she could see only her father's face as he had said Kannan loved her, a face of wild humour, like a dying man clinging to the idea of a miracle cure. On the flight, as she saw this face, his moustache seemed to dissipate, as if it symbolized his confidence in the truth of what he was saying. She had never seen her father without it, not even in photographs, except those of him as a child, but now the clean-shaven vision implanted itself like one of those viruses that having entered the body cannot be expelled. All she could do was try to forget about it, but as the attempt to forget only provokes the opposite, the unwanted image only advanced further, until

she thought that the only thing that could dislodge it was the sight of
Kannan, waiting for her at the airport, out of love and not duty.

Malathi was not a superstitious person. It was one of the few things
she knew for certain about herself. There was so much of it around her
that you had to know one way or another where you stood. There was
the scientific superstition of jathagams. But for those who believed
in astrology without practising it, there was what she thought of as
omenology, a view of life as a system governed by luck, luck that
could reveal its future movements to the observant through signs:
not portentous visions, but signs embedded in the everyday. The
Immigration and Naturalization Service queue at Logan Airport for
those who were neither US citizens nor Permanent Residents moved so
quickly that she didn't have much time for thinking. But she thought:
I am so nervous about what I'll find beyond that I'm not nervous at all
about this interview. And: if I were an omenologist, I would look at the
interview, at the face of the INS agent and his demeanour, for signs of
whether things will be good beyond. But I know better than that.

She found herself face to face with a man who looked like he might
be the brother of her interviewer at the consulate in Madras. Did this
kind of job run in families? Or maybe it was the same man, sent home
after his stint in India. Latha perima had said: he will ask whether
you and your husband intend to settle down permanently in the US.
Obviously the true answer is yes, but at all costs you must say no. But he
didn't ask her anything, he just looked at her passport, said everything
was in order, and then, 'Welcome to the United States. Welcome to
Boston.' As she walked through, she wasn't sure if she had actually
heard him say that or if it had been the video message that played on
loop while you waited in the queue. She turned to look back at him and
saw a bald man, middle-aged and stout, at his desk.

She emerged through customs unprepared for the smallness of it,
the arrivals area. They couldn't miss each other here. And it took only
a few seconds to be sure. He hadn't come. But then she looked at her
watch, which she had set to Boston time on her first flight. He must

have budgeted more time for customs and immigration; no one could know it would go so quickly. But Kannan must know this airport well. It must take longer usually: this was an aberration. She couldn't just stand here: she knew how she must look, like a girl stood up by a date, only worse, so much worse.

She found three seats opposite a Hudson News, enough space for her bags and a clear view of every person entering the terminal. Soon she saw that she needn't have bothered: not only did no one bother you here, but no one really looked at you either, except, presumably, if they thought you might be who they were waiting for. No one had to worry about humiliation. Nor was her predicament unique: what else were these chairs for? There were other seats, and other people waiting, other late husbands. The terminal, she could tell, wasn't really America. It was as clean as everyone said, but it smelled of warmed-up stale bread and some kind of disinfectant, like a hospital with a bakery. The other travellers were so unhurried as to seem not wholly alive, as if they were in a waiting room for the next life, but with absolute confidence about their destination. She hadn't really been paying attention to the people coming in. She was sitting in a place where Kannan could easily miss her. No, he hadn't come yet. She sat down again and now she focused only on the doors.

Forty-five minutes since she had checked her watch. She laughed a little, a grim laugh, but she couldn't deny herself that, you could even call her proud of herself, for preparing so thoroughly for something while praying, with more force than anyone should have to summon, for the opposite, for what she should have the right to expect. In her handbag was a sheet of paper with Kannan's address, plus, if that should prove insufficient, directions that she hadn't asked him for—not that he would have replied—but had compiled from maps of Boston she'd found online, and one hundred-dollar note. That would cover the taxi. In their first emails she had asked Kannan to describe Boston. I'm not any good at this kind of thing, he had written, but you will be amazed by how small it is, how compact. Most days you can get from my apartment in the South End to the airport in less than twenty minutes.

Kannan lived in a third-floor apartment on Columbus Square, which turned out to be not a square but a kind of meander off Columbus Avenue, with a park in between like a small oxbow lake. This was not any America she had seen on screen or in her imagination: it was far too picturesque. Every morning she would wake up and jump out of bed and run straight to the window—if their bedroom faced the park— to look out on all this. This was a place to make a life, a place worth crossing the earth for, a place that redeemed her uncertainty. Columbus Square was a single block; it looked like one house, except that some of the facades had departed slightly over the years from the original design. Maybe it had been built for a family—maybe Americans too had once lived in joint families—and been sold off bit by bit.

There was only one problem. Kannan had said, more than once, that he lived on the third floor. She hadn't printed the emails out but she couldn't have mistaken that. And this building didn't have a third floor: there was a ground floor, first floor and second floor, but nothing beyond that, not even an attic, whatever an attic looked like.

Kannan had said the third floor, said it in those first emails that were like bottled selections of his spirit. It wasn't love that had made her trust him. She didn't love him or think that she ought to try to: she wanted only to get to know him, and into those first half-dozen emails he had put so much of himself that she wanted to say to someone, do you know how much intimacy someone can put into an email? You don't, but I do. All those aunts and uncles liked to talk about the 'lost art of letter-writing'. They had spent their lives composing those letters, enough paper to fill a warehouse, and that wasn't even counting the rough drafts, because you couldn't send a letter with misspellings and words crossed through; but those letters had nothing on these emails, indeed they probably lost, in the meticulous pedantry of their construction, any intimacy that might have crept in by mistake. But she couldn't now think of those emails and fence them off from all the emails that had come after, the life and detail and vigour declining in geometric progression, or the two weeks' silence, or his failure to turn up today. She had to be open to the idea that everything in them, or if not everything than anything, was faked, and that over time he had lost the energy required to keep up the deception.

She couldn't trust even those emails. Trust, a substance of such fragile purity that a single drop of some contaminant means throwing away your entire supply. What was it her father said about trust? It's like virginity: you lose it once, and no god can give it back to you in this life. She was standing with her suitcases on a pavement outside someone's house. Who knew if Kannan lived on the non-existent third floor, or on this street, or in Boston?

The door of 6 Columbus Square opened, and Kannan stepped out. 'Hi,' he said. 'You can come in.'

Her flight was scheduled to land at 4 p.m., which meant 3.40 earliest, which meant she might even be through immigration at 4.10—Sunday afternoons were quiet—and into the arrivals area by 4.15. All this could take hours longer, of course, but he had to factor the earliest possible times. What was the minimum amount of time it would take her to give up on the prospect of his showing up? She could call him from a phone booth—she wouldn't have any coins, but could easily figure out how to get some. Let's say she examined his absence in the light of two weeks' silence and concluded that he wasn't late, and waited no more than fifteen minutes. What were her options then? She could call her cousins in Atlanta, but he didn't think that likely. She could call her father, but that wouldn't be much help. What if she concluded that there had been a mix-up, that he had got the wrong day? That would be like her, she might have the capacity for that much charity. But if she thought that way she would wait much longer, and/or call him. So assume she didn't. Five minutes to get to a taxi, twenty minutes in the taxi. She would have written down his address—it was a basic precaution, even if she had total confidence in his being at the airport—and every taxi driver would know the place. At 4.55 he stood by the window—he was still standing there when he saw a taxi pull up at 6.15 and his wife get out.

He had asked Grimmett if they could meet in the morning instead, although he knew his friend to be a late riser, or whatever it was you called someone who gets out of bed late even if he wakes up early. Grimmett said he spent his mornings in contemplation, because the one thing all the ancient philosophers agreed on, whatever their philosophical system, was that this was the highest, indeed the only proper moral life, and as he possessed the two necessary preconditions, money and solitude, he had no excuse. Kannan knew he would make an exception this time, and knew too that the price of this exception would be that they talk about his disappearance at the Deathmarch. Grimmett thought, he was sure, that Kannan was suffering from post-traumatic stress disorder, although Grimmett probably reproached himself for using that phrase even in his thoughts. Either he could confess to something like this, and avoid any further suspicion; or he could now tell Grimmett about Malathi, which would archive, perhaps permanently, the question of the Deathmarch. It was only as they sat down at 1369 Coffeehouse that he decided on the former.

As he watched Malathi on the pavement he was aware, always, that he would have to let her in eventually. It was a question of how long he could push it. Today with Grimmett he had wavered, but only in his head, and in the end he had stuck to the course that he had realized he was on rather than chosen: he was going to work this out, if it could be worked out, by himself. One way of justifying this was to remind himself of his own role, to ask why he had gone to Bangalore resolved on refusing a marriage and weakened. To the extent that he was responsible he was accountable, and beyond that, there was no reason to think that people who had engineered his situation were worth turning to now for sympathy, much less assistance. You are being an idiot, Santhanam would say. You are throwing your life away when I have given you everything on a plate, and for what? That left

Grimmett. Perhaps he could be sure of Grimmett's sympathy; anything else would be unfair to their friendship. He could also misrepresent the background, say he had been forced into it—had he? He would go to Grimmett later, if he was desperate. It was some kind of comfort to have that option.

He tried, though, to construct what Grimmett might say. He couldn't think of any practical advice, but perhaps Grimmett might ask him what he owed Malathi. This was a new way of looking at things. Until now it had seemed axiomatic that being true to his own self meant defaulting on all his obligations to Malathi. He had no desire to be cruel, but what greater dereliction of duty was there than abandoning a wife? But Grimmett might say, even if you are committed to ending the marriage before it begins, let's find the way of doing it that is most fair to her.

What would an approach like this look like in practice? He would have to be honest, of course, recompense for his earlier reticence and deception, even if that had been as much self-deception as the other kind. But, just as importantly, he had to project only one idea: the marriage had been a mistake, and had to be reversed, abandoned, backspaced, no, CTRL-Z-ed, undone, as soon as possible. There had been no dowry; he could accept all the blame, refund her father's marriage expenses. He didn't know anything about the law, but he was sure, or had the sort of hope that depends upon calling itself certainty, that ending a marriage this quickly meant no D-word, a word that would brand Malathi for life, that would precede her everywhere. He could not allow her to think that some part of him was unsure, or willing to attempt a marriage. Partly because not giving false hope was something he owed her, but also because such an attempt would only mean a more wounding end later, and the D-word. Going to the airport would violate this resolution, complicate the message. But not letting her in now would be unfair, and it would be cruel. As he walked down he knew she was going to burst into tears and ask him why he hadn't come, and what could he say? Come up and let's talk about it. I'll carry your suitcases.

He told her she could come in. She looked at him as if this encounter were prearranged but they had never met before, as if to say, is this really Kannan? This must be deliberate, and it was well done.

'You told me you lived on the third floor,' she said. 'But this building doesn't have a third floor! Did you lie to me on purpose? I thought maybe you don't live here at all.'

'In America the floors are numbered differently. What's called the ground floor in India is the first floor here, and so on. I forgot to explain that; I have gotten used to the American system.'

She was standing several feet away from her luggage, which made it easier, more natural, for him to pick the suitcases up, one in each hand, without having to say anything. She had packed lightly; unlike the house she had grown up in, she was unencumbered by trifles. He guessed she had thought bringing too much would be an imposition on him, an excessive intrusion of the old life into the new. Seeing as she would be going home soon, it was just as well. He held the door open for her with his left foot and led the way up the stairs in the rapid stagger demanded by suitcases. He had spent weeks getting the apartment ready for this day: something she would never know.

'Will you have some tea? Or coffee? I make filter coffee here, degree coffee.'

'I'll have some coffee.' No tears, no accusations, no insistent questions: she was trying to shame him. He didn't deserve that, but he also knew he would never get her to see things that way. Three years prior, he had chosen this apartment for its separate kitchen, the only one he had seen on his search. In his distant period of pure optimism, in those hours spent planning his married life in Boston, he had commended himself for this instinct, one that would ease the adjustment, to him, to marriage, and to America, of a girl who had probably never seen an open-plan kitchen. When he returned from the kitchen she was sitting, leaning forward with her elbows on the table, her chin resting on clasped hands, and her gaze as if it had never left the kitchen door. He noticed now that she had been wearing a jacket earlier: it looked too big for her.

'Here,' he said, and he didn't sit down. 'You want to know why I wasn't at the airport. Why I haven't been replying to your emails. And I'm going to tell you everything.'

He paused out of some sense of obligation; what he had to say ought not to come out in an unimpeded flow; he would give her chances to speak, and to see that everything he said had been deeply thought through, that none of it was madness. Usually, when he visualized this scene, it was at this point that she asked him whether he had a woman in America, a lover, a girlfriend, even another wife. But she didn't, or at least not yet.

'Our marriage was a mistake. A terrible mistake. But not a fatal mistake. I should never have married you, but I don't want you, I don't want both of us, to suffer and ruin our lives for a mistake. We have our lives ahead of us … and our only chance is to end it now. That way, eventually, it will be as if it never happened.'

If she had understood him, he had successfully avoided having to say the D word. Still she said nothing, still she didn't break her gaze; and she looked blank, no, not blank, he thought she looked dead, as if her body still functioned but he had committed some solely mental form of murder. He had to look away. But that was what, more than anything, he had committed not to do while saying all this, and so he attempted to angle his face in her direction, without actually seeing anything, using the tricks he had developed ignoring faces on the street. If there was any life behind that face, she would see through this.

'I thought, and maybe this was all wrong, but I thought it sincerely, that if I stopped replying, if I didn't come to the airport, maybe you would start to sense how I felt.'

Something in this revived her. 'How you felt? How am I supposed to know how you feel? Or anything about you? When you have lied to me for months!'

'I never lied—'

'Either you're lying now, or you have always lied. Why are you acting like a victim? Why did you marry me? No one forced you. If they had, you wouldn't be trying to get out of it now in this shameless way. And then ...' And now the tears came, first loud and then silent, but interrupted by percussive coughs, and while he was prepared, for every visualization had featured her crying, he had concluded that the only fair policy was to offer no comfort whatsoever, whether verbal or physical; it would only confuse and mislead her. Even if there was some allowable degree of comfort, he told himself, it wasn't as though he would know how to give it. Nor could he really speak while she was crying. And her tears gave him the chance to look away, and until he was sure she was finished; for now, he looked at the wall.

'If you say you didn't lie, then why did you marry me? And say all those things in those emails?'

'When I said our marriage was a mistake, I meant, I made a mistake. I didn't want to get married. When I met you, I liked you, and for some reason, a reason I still can't understand, or maybe there was no reason, I agreed. And for a time, I believed ... no, I was under a delusion, a fantasy. I thought everything would be easy, that marrying you guaranteed a life of happiness. Isn't it understandable that someone could have a delusion like that? Should two people be condemned to unhappiness because of it? Or should we save ourselves while we can?'

'When did you come out of this "delusion", as you call it? Was it because I said I wasn't interested in those Harry Potter fan websites? Because that seems to be the real delusion in your life.' This he hadn't expected. What a farcical accusation. He was relieved—for her to say something so ludicrous allowed him to advance a little, morally; it showed how right he was about this marriage lacking all foundation.

'Of course I could never think any such thing. Until our marriage and shortly after, I was completely deluded. And then I realized that things weren't so simple and for some time I felt conflicted. Some days I was confident, although not like before; but most days I felt only dread. And eventually, in the last two weeks, I realized that we had to end it now, while there was still a chance, before it had begun.'

'What do you mean? Before it had begun? We have been married for three months. We got married in front of hundreds of people. You are talking as if you're telling me why you don't want to marry me. But we are married. I have come all the way to be with you.'

He was going to have to be explicit. Before he could do that, she started again.

'I think you have gone crazy. Maybe this is what happens when you live alone in a place like this. But I don't have any choice but to stay with you, so we will have to try to be happy. You say you were conflicted and then you realized the truth. But how can you just know something like that? Earlier you thought things would be wonderful, now you know we'll be unhappy? You don't know anything of the sort. You have convinced yourself of it. Why can't we try?'

She had given him an opening.

'What if we did try? What if I was right? I know myself. I am not what you think or thought I was. I don't need to know you to know that I'm not someone you would be happy with. And then what? Years, even months later, when it's clear that we are miserable and always will be?'

He would have to say it now.

'Do you know what happens then? We would have to get a divorce.' He said it the way his parents said it, with a long I. He had known divorce was common in America, as routine as pizza delivery, but he really understood this only when he heard the word used here in conversation. Saying it the American way took all the terror out: no wonder they could be so casual about it. Said the Tamil way—if there was a Tamil word for it, it wasn't ever used in normal conversation—the first syllable was the verb form of death, but it was a fate worse than death, at least for a woman. 'No other man would marry you then.'

'Now you're threatening me. What sort of a man are you? Do you have no humanity?'

'I'm not a man you want to be married to. Not a man you want to be stuck with.'

'You keep talking about yourself. What you want, what you know, how you feel. As if, having married me, you can just decide and inform me of your decision. Why didn't you say anything all these months? You could have told me you had doubts. Worst comes to worst, I could have postponed coming or something. You tell me nothing, you wait for me to come and then you say all this?'

'I'm not going to defend myself. Maybe the way I did it was wrong. I've already said that it was I who made the mistake. And now I've sprung all this on you. You need time to think about what I've said.'

'How kind of you to give me time. How generous.'

He turned away from her and walked to the window that looked out onto the park.

'I need to call my father to say I've reached. He'll have been waiting anxiously all this time. What do I say to him?'

'Just say you've reached. You don't have to say anything else right now.'

He had meant the offer of time kindly. She had thrown it in his face, but he knew that she knew she needed it and would take it. How long would she take? A week at the least. Probably more. Hopefully not too much more than that. Part of her, perhaps most of her, must still feel that time would show they could coexist, that these were understandable worries for a man about to lose his independence to marriage, and that, indeed, in time he was giving her a weapon, because she could prove that they could be happy. Who knew how long hope like that lasted? All that mattered was they not have sex. Then she would be damaged goods, and all his talk of getting out while they can would have been a viciously false promise. Both his aims, of extricating himself while not being cruel to her, would collapse in a single act of foolishness. Unlike the last such mistake, there would be no redeeming this one.

15

The first time that Kannan made an excuse, the evening of the day they had met in the morning—a Saturday; he said that he couldn't meet the next day—Grimmett had known this wasn't like past occasional absences. If Kannan made an excuse again the next day, it meant an extended separation. And how extended was out of Grimmett's hands. There was every chance that Kannan blamed Grimmett for his humiliation. And why shouldn't he? Grimmett didn't need to reprimand himself for reserving a position on the Deathmarch for Kannan. Kannan had been moved by it, and not because Grimmett wanted him to be. But he should have proposed it rather than announced it, and he could have helped Kannan prepare, even done rehearsals. He had been afraid of patronizing Kannan; his friend, after all, knew more about this subject than anyone else. Kannan was the person best qualified to represent the Harry/Hermione side in any debate, and if he needed Grimmett to place him there, that was only because fandom, like all systems in this country, by default denied these kinds of opportunities to people like Kannan, by never reaching out to them, by making them feel these things were inaccessible.

Then there was the possibility, and this seemed more true to Kannan and to their friendship, that it was not a question of blame or resentment but of embarrassment. Kannan must feel that he had let Grimmett down. This notion could be easily corrected, but to assume it would be condescension. Why did it have to be about him, anyway? It was simply a question of trauma, which might seem a term out of proportion, like describing something as a holocaust, but even if the circumstances were trivial, the experience was not, not when Kannan had invested so much self-worth.

'I'm still a bit shocked about last Sunday,' Kannan had said that morning. 'I can't quite explain what happened, and even if thinking about it more would help me understand it, I'm not sure I want to think about it.' Yet the sight of Grimmett would force him to, even if Grimmett kept the conversation securely distant from Harry Potter.

Kannan's email was followed within minutes by one from Rebecca. This was out of the blue, but would he like to get coffee or go for a walk tomorrow? 1369 Coffeehouse would be a betrayal, it would be as if he were substituting her for Kannan. I would love to, he replied, and let me set a challenge for myself. Let me see if I can take you somewhere on Harvard's campus you haven't been before.

They met outside the Harvard Book Store. 'The place I have in mind is only a few yards away,' he said. 'All we have to do is cross the street, more or less. I could, or at least could have when I was younger, throw a rock from where we stand and land it where we're going to go.'

'I don't see how this is some place I don't know, then.'

'We'll see.'

They walked through Dexter Gate. The words above the archway—ENTER TO GROW IN WISDOM—were Rebecca's only visual memory of her first day on campus as a freshman. This place isn't shy of pomposity, she had thought. But that's also something to measure your time here against, eventually. God, the pomposity is rubbing off on me already. Grimmett turned right.

'You aren't taking me to the Henry Moore outside Lamont Library, are you?' she said. 'Most students don't notice that, but I always used to stop there when I was giving tours for the Admissions Office.'

They were by the west door of Lamont, infuriatingly closed to students.

'Almost there,' said Grimmett. He turned right again and now they were walking through an open wrought-iron gate into a kind of wooded path. Seconds later they stepped into the sunlight, the rear of Lamont to the north and, incredibly, Mass Ave. to the south. She could see the Harvard Book Store. They were standing in a garden, a *secret garden*, in the English style of affected but still lovely wildness, with a low bench in one corner and, in the centre, looking out onto the world, a long curved seat that looked like two abstract reclining nudes that had been welded together.

'How did you know about this place? The Dudley Garden, is that what it said on the gate? How come *I* didn't know about it?'

'You must have seen this gate,' he said, pointing the one that led to Mass Ave. 'And wondered what lay behind it.'

'I saw it, of course, but I guess I never noticed it, or wondered. So this place has been hiding in plain sight all along. You know, if a guy wanted to impress me in college, bringing me here would have been a great way to do it.'

'Rest assured I had no such intention. But I'm glad I met the challenge I set myself. I brought coffee,' he said, pulling a flask out of his backpack.

He was wondering how long it would take her to ask about Kannan, and what she might say. All she said was: 'Is Kannan okay? After last weekend?' And he said he didn't know. He had looked for Kannan in all the adjoining corridors, had been up to the room they were sharing, and had been on the verge of going out into the street when he thought of the men's rooms. In the third one he checked, he found Kannan in a stall. Grimmett had recognized him by his shoes, through the gap between the door and the floor. She shouldn't underestimate how much this had required of him. He wasn't built to crouch down that low, not at his age. Kannan had said he couldn't do it, and in a way that emphasized the futility of further discussion. That's when he had come looking for her.

'I have an awful confession to make,' she said. 'Well, awful is putting it strongly, but what I mean is I hope you won't be upset. The Deathmarch helped me realize fandom isn't really for me. Don't get me wrong, I adore Harry Potter, but I don't think Annabel and I are going to stay too involved in fandom. But this, asking you to meet today, wasn't a way for me to say goodbye. I'd like to be able to stay in touch and see you even if I'm not coming to Gobstones.'

'I'm not upset,' he said. 'I'm touched. And I would like that very much. And to be honest, I've been having my doubts about all of this as well. You couldn't call the Deathmarch a success. And Gobstones went stale a while ago.'

After that they spoke no more of fandom. She chose to direct the conversation, by asking him questions: about what it was like to host a radio show, about his early life, his years in Britain. Everything except what you might call his personal life.

Until: 'I feel like I'm taking a liberty by asking this, but something tells me you won't mind. But I've been curious for a while about your friendship with Kannan. Not just because it's an unlikely friendship on the face of it, I mean with your ages and backgrounds. But because he seems sort of impenetrable to me. I said he was enigmatic once and Annabel said you don't know that: the fact that someone is hard to figure out doesn't mean there's anything worth figuring out or even *to* figure out. And you seem so close, as close as any friends I've seen. And I thought about how I don't know if I have any friendships like that. And how I don't have any older friends. Or friends you wouldn't expect me to have.'

'I don't know that I can say much to that that would really answer your questions. I don't ever say that I'm lost for words, it would be shamefully insincere, but I don't really understand these things in a way that lends itself to narrative or explanation. I mean that I don't necessarily find Kannan, or my friendship with him, any less mysterious than you do. The mechanics of friendship—why we form the friendships we do, why a friendship takes its particular form—these strike me as less susceptible to understanding than any other kind of human relationship.'

'But do you have other friendships like this one?'

'If you mean in the sense of other young immigrant friends, no. My friends have tended to be like yours: people it would be reasonable to expect me to be friends with. If you mean other friendships this close ... well, who am I to judge closeness anyway? It seems infantile to rank your friendships, and there's no standard for it. But it's true that I see Kannan most days, almost every day, actually.' And he paused again, without suggesting that he had finished, and Rebecca thought that he might be about to get to the point.

'This might answer your question to some extent, or at least it might interest you. I met Kannan after a period of several years where I had let the few relationships in my life wither, out of pure neglect. None of them was with the kind of person who is willing to keep things up, to do all the running when you do none. And I had a narrative. I believed that, just as our brain cells are condemned to slowly die after a certain point, and the connections in the brain too, and just as after a certain age blood sugar and body fat rise, slowly but inexorably, or not slowly, in my case, while muscle mass and flexibility decline, so too my capacity for sociability was declining, and there was no arresting it: it was an entirely natural phenomenon. I don't mean to romanticize my loneliness: I wasn't happy about it, just resigned to it. Age and disappointment, especially disappointment, these are the things fatalism feeds on. It wouldn't really be fair for me, now, to say that I have friends other than Kannan. And I don't think he would mind my saying that he didn't, and doesn't, have other friends either. That doesn't mean that on the day we met, almost a year ago—only a few hundred yards from here we waited in line for *Goblet of Fire*—that we were, in a sense, waiting for each other: that even given our natural dispositions we'd stretched our solitude to breaking point; anyone would do. Something like that wouldn't sustain a friendship through literally hundreds of encounters. Then you fall back upon the kind of explanation that imports the language of romantic cliché: we were made for each other, we connected in some unique but inevitable way. You see why I prefer to respect the mystery of it.'

She said nothing to this, she waited until she was sure he was done and then she said, 'Would you like to meet again next weekend? In return for today I can give you the tour you missed out on that night. We can start at the Harvard Book Store.'

As they walked out, she looked up out of habit at the other side of Dexter Gate. DEPART TO SERVE BETTER THY COUNTRY AND THY KIND. If she hadn't lived up to that exhortation, neither had most people who had walked through in the century that the gate had stood. And she could hear her father, imaginary words but not an unfair caricature: 'You are serving your kind: you're making sure the children of the highly educated and privileged retain their rightful hold on education and privilege. No one could accuse you of being a traitor to your class.' To which she could reply: 'thy kind' means you, not me: whoever chose those words was addressing his fellow white American men. My very presence here is an affront to those words. As is my helping Jewish and Asian kids achieve no more than their effort and focus deserve. Rhetorically, she thought, she had him beat.

The following Sunday, Grimmett was resolved not to bring up Kannan if she didn't. His friend had followed three daily excuses by saying that he was going to go off the grid for a little while, days, not weeks. There was no need to make this more than it was. But today's Rebecca wanted to talk about something else, the same thing he did: herself. She didn't quite neglect her duties as guide but nor did she give him the full tour: it was only at points of particular interest that she broke from the conversation's regular course. She talked about England, how through her adolescence it had taken up a role in her imagination in inverse proportion to her memories of the place. Spending a year there after graduation had been a plan, not an aspiration, and she had also been sure, she knew now, that that year would be the prelude to a life there. Connor had never needed convincing of anything if it was what she wanted.

She wondered if she was supposed to have some kind of reckoning with all this, if England's rejection of her was meant to signify that her attachment was fantastical, except nothing was *meant* to signify like that, but she wondered now if Harry Potter had been a way to delay that reckoning, to keep the fantasy going a little longer.

'Now we've come to *my* favourite place on campus, although I'm sure it's a place you know,' she said. 'The Center for European Studies. The building itself is named for Adolphus Busch, who founded the corporation that makes Budweiser and still bears his name. It used to be a museum of German art, a gift from the Kaiser when he was trying to sweeten America up in the lead-up to World War I. When German-Americans were the biggest ethnic group in the country, before they were forced to give up their language and country and identity. I was fascinated by that; I briefly wanted to do my senior thesis on the vanishing of German America. Speaking of vanishing: Adolphus, or Adolf. That's something else that had to disappear, those names. As if there was something in the name itself, as if Hitler's life was proof of nominative determinism. If I ever had a son I think I would name him Adolphus. This garden is only open April through October: I always thought that rather than a museum or a Center for European Studies, this building would make the most fabulous house, especially for garden parties. A few lucky professors have offices that look out onto the garden.' It was a courtyard as much as a garden: more Italian than German. They sat down on neighbouring benches.

The monologues didn't look to have come easily to her. He thought she was straining against her own nature to speak in a kind of stream-of-consciousness. Maybe she thought that was how he spoke, and wanted to make him feel at ease. Rather than interrupt her now with comments or questions that weren't even worth voicing, he decided to wait until she had quite finished.

'I've been thinking,' she said, 'now that I'm detaching myself from fandom, about why it is that I got so lost in it to begin with.' She looked at him so directly that he couldn't tell whether she wanted a response or whether, busy tracing the arc of the thought, she didn't even see him.

'Is that even something worth thinking about? The over-examined life isn't worth living, is a maxim I believe in, although I don't practise it assiduously enough.'

'Oh, I agree, and I don't mean to attach weight and meaning to everything in my life. I guess I'm attracted to the idea that this, fandom, might shed light on something larger. I know I sound like my own therapist here, and I always thought therapy was kind of a joke.'

'Go on.'

'Well, in a sense, the appeal of this kind of thinking is that one can never know. It's like trying to interpret some character's actions in a novel. It's all unfalsifiable speculation. So I tell myself, now, that these past few months, no, I guess it's almost a year, I've been on a quest to surprise myself. That I had a subconscious fear that I was on some boring, unoriginal, prearranged path, never making a choice that wasn't obvious. And that I'd felt that way for a long time: so, in college, I joined a final club because it was going totally against my socialist upbringing. And then, after graduation, I made my professional plans around my boyfriend's, because my parents brought me up to be a feminist, and I was bored of all that. If I was going to be a feminist, it wasn't going to be because I'd been put on that path. Not that this was ever consciously my thinking. But late last year—other people would say this is because Connor broke up with me, but I like to think it would have happened anyway—I realized, if you can use "realize" to describe the subconscious, that even those choices had been so conventional and typical for a person in my situation. I was still on the path, broadly defined. And then came Harry Potter, and discovering fandom. And burying myself in that *was* genuinely crazy. I felt like I was stepping outside myself. Which justified the amount of time I spent on it. And then I wanted to surprise myself on a grander scale, which led me to the idea of dating Kannan. But that didn't go very far: he clearly wasn't interested.'

'What makes you say that? Maybe he just needed drawing out a little.'

'Yes, maybe ... But I don't know if I know how to do that, or wanted to do it quite enough.'

She had tried, he thought, to find a phrasing that had not a whit of smugness.

'I don't think this narrative of yours is fanciful at all. But I wonder why you're presenting yourself as having been driven by mistaken impulses. On the contrary, I think your impulse was noble, indeed essential. Most people live entire lives without realizing the extent to which they were imprisoned by what was expected of them. You've realized at the start of your conscious life, more or less. And making decisions out of the desire to break away from those expectations: why, I don't see how that's any more foolish or ignoble than any other way that people make choices. Besides, if our motivations are to some degree unknowable, even to ourselves, all we're left with is how we justify our actions, and as a justification this strikes me as much better than most.'

'It's very kind of you to say all that ... no, I know you're not just being kind for the sake of it, I know you mean it all, but I don't think it's quite healthy for me to go on acting or thinking this way. Especially because other people can be the unwitting casualties. Anyway, when I was back home over Christmas, my parents kind of freaked out when I told them about Harry Potter. They thought I'd lost my mind, which thinking back, probably only made me more committed to fandom. It's so childish, I'm ashamed to admit it, but it's true. But my father recommended a couple of novels to me, books he said would serve as a corrective, an "antidote", that was the word he used. And I went out and bought them and read them both.'

'What were they?'

'*Disgrace* by J.M. Coetzee and *The Human Stain* by Philip Roth. Both came out in the last year or so. And I know they're both really famous writers but I hadn't read anything by them before.'

'I've read both books, but I want to hear what you thought first.'

'Well … I think it's me, not the books, and it's really making me worry about whether Harry Potter has messed me up. I mean, I think Harry Potter is brilliant, and I would defend it on literary merits to the death, but all this time reading children's books and then fan fiction has to have been unhealthy. I soldiered through both these novels, but they just didn't speak to me. It felt like they were supposed to be weighty and profound and provocative. But I thought: I don't want all this grand self-importance. And then all the politics was accompanied by sudden bursts of melodramatic plot. And just no lightness anywhere. Unremitting seriousness.'

'Did your father tell you why he wanted you to read these books?'

'I don't remember exactly what he said, but I think it was something to do with the weight and profundity and seriousness.'

'I can assure you, it isn't you, it's Roth and Coetzee. Perhaps if you'd never read Harry Potter you might not have been as turned off, sure. But I think these books—although really one could say they're the same book—they both say, look at me, I'm a commentary about the end of the world as we know it, and along the way I'm going to make you feel uneasy, you bien-pensant liberal, by showing that nothing about race and power is simple. And why is the world ending? Because the writer is ageing. Coetzee was supposed to be a champion of racial justice but he finds he can't live in a South Africa run by blacks. And Roth thinks PC culture is ruining America. Look at these young people who aren't comfortable with racially loaded language! In the good old days, when the American mind was open, anything could be thought and said. The spirit of the Enlightenment. You don't need to apologize for reading this and thinking that J.K. Rowling is the real great literature of our time. I'm betting your father hasn't read any Harry Potter.'

'You know, he definitely hadn't, but I wonder if he has now, out of curiosity, because of me. If he has, maybe his silence is proof that he couldn't resist it. He's not in the habit of saying he was wrong.'

Should she quit IvyEdge now, without any plans or direction, or should she stay until she figured out what she wanted to do next? Without fandom she had plenty of thinking time. She knew how unnecessary and self-indulgent it was to seek advice on something so trivial, but she did it anyway. There was some comfort in knowing that she'd changed. And when the advice came in, it was if she had scripted the whole thing.

'It's so obvious,' said Annabel. 'The *first rule* of switching jobs is you do it while at your existing job. Both because you're in a position of strength, as well as ... When you're moving, do you sell your current house *before* choosing a new one?'

But what if it wasn't simply a question of switching? What if you were selling your house to become a nomad? All she said to Annabel was that all of that made sense.

Her mother, of course, said the opposite. 'The ability to face the future without anxiety, to be comfortable with uncertainty, it's a luxury most people don't have, but you have it. I'd even say there's no point quitting *unless* you have no plans.' Go travelling, preferably in the Third World: that was the answer to everything. 'South East Asia would be great: that's a part of the world your father and I don't know at all. It's the big lacuna in this family.'

She did know one person who was professionally in the advice-giving business. But that would have to wait until after she had given her notice. She wondered what Connie would say. She must know that Rebecca had decided she wasn't going to make a career of this. Would that knowledge enable her to counsel a girl of whom she was evidently fond, or would she ask Rebecca to get the hell out and not bother her again?

She had to decide soon, because their lease was coming up for renewal, and while Annabel would have little difficulty finding a replacement roommate, another recent Harvard or MIT alum, she said that if Rebecca left she would move back in with her parents. It didn't make any sense to pay Cambridge rent when she was out four nights a week, and she could start saving for the down payment on a house. Rebecca promised to let her know by the end of the month. Living with Annabel hadn't redeemed the way in which she'd chosen to spend this year in Boston, but it meant that she didn't have to regret the consequences of the decision. It was the only thing she had left that she wasn't looking forward to giving up.

Curtis Grimmett said she should leave as soon as she could. Boston was no place for young people once they'd left college. This was interesting, she but didn't ask him to elaborate. She wasn't going to ask any more people for advice.

But if she was going to leave soon, there were people she should see. She e-mailed two professors, ones who had written her recommendations, for the first time since she'd graduated. And Kannan. There were many other acquaintances from her years in college. They didn't each need an individual goodbye. But she had one invitation, from her newest acquaintance, Ned Wilcox, the ex-Marine English teacher, that she had accepted, even though Annabel had said she was on no account to say yes. Ned had asked her to have dinner with him, at his apartment.

'It's as if he's never dated before,' Annabel said. 'Do these military guys not know how to behave in the real world? It's obscene for him to ask that on a first date and crazy for you to say yes.'

'What if it's not a date? And maybe it just shows a strange kind of self-confidence. One that might even be attractive.'

'Well I'm just glad that you're going to have to disappoint him. You better tell him that you're leaving town soon.'

'*If* it feels like a date, of course I'll tell him. Not to do so would be unfair.'

Ned lived in Somerville, a place she knew was favoured by graduate students, rent refugees Annabel called them, and he didn't live in the gentrified part, if there was one. She passed a liquor store on the way and, realizing she was empty-handed, bought a bottle of rosé. His street was two sad rows of 1950s two-storey houses with grey gambrel roofs, like residents in a retirement home who had been made to wear an unflattering uniform. With the summer solstice approaching, 7 p.m. ought to be early afternoon, but the street was curfew-quiet. This wasn't a place to escape the loneliness that, lazy cliché as it was, she couldn't help associating with the return of a Marine to civilian life. Ned lived on the second floor, and as she pressed the buzzer she heard the letterbox being opened on the other side of the door, and what sounded like a growl. She bent down to open the letterbox from her side and was eye to eye with a black cat when Ned opened the door.

'What was that about?' he asked.

'I'm, I'm sorry, I don't know what just happened.'

'This guy belongs to my landlord. When he hears someone outside he checks the mailbox, and when it's actually the mailman, he usually gets his teeth into whatever's in there. Good thing no one sends me mail. Would you like to come up?'

The apartment was well-sized for whatever he must be paying, although she thought it might look larger than it was because it was so empty, as if he was still moving in; but this might just be all he owned. There was a small revolving bookcase with framed photos of what must be his parents on top, and a TV in the corner with a PlayStation. No rug or carpet anywhere. The walls were bare. If he had a desktop it must be in his bedroom, and she was determined not to go there, not today; it would only legitimatize Annabel's complaint.

'I was worried it might seem a little weird of me, asking you to come home rather than go to a restaurant or something,' he said. 'Presumptuous, even. But I haven't really gotten to know the places around here, and I like cooking, so I suggested this without really thinking about it.'

'That's okay,' she said. 'I was kind of surprised, but not in a bad way.'

He had thanked her for the wine but didn't suggest opening it; instead, he offered her a beer, and directed to her the couch that faced the TV and console, while he pulled up one of the three chairs from the kitchen table.

The first time that she wondered when he might mention dinner, or if he would at all, she noticed that they had been talking for over an hour. He was no different than he had been at the Park Plaza; but while there she had thought him too earnest, too American, too military, now, as he leaned in slightly closer, which meant he thought it was going well, he hadn't misread her. Why was she enjoying herself now? He was bright, yes, but she hesitated to call him interesting; not that he wasn't, but because all except the very dull can seem interesting at first. It might be the lack of artifice or strategy, 'game', the stuff that is meant to project confidence but instead signifies nerves.

His time in the Marines had been quiet, by no measure was he a disturbed veteran, but, on Diego Garcia, the most obscure and isolated outpost of what was left of the British Empire, in the middle of the Indian Ocean, he had been as far removed from social life as it is possible for even a soldier to be. This was the obvious explanation for his straightforwardness, but she preferred the idea that this was simply how he was. He had made no attempt, either at the Deathmarch or here, to either conceal or exaggerate his interest in her, and she knew she wanted to see him again. She couldn't spring it on him over dinner.

'There's something I should say,' she was about to say. But then she thought no, nothing's happened yet, nothing's been said: why say anything about leaving Boston?

Dinner turned out to be beef lasagna with a side of sautéed spinach, unpretentious but satisfying—oh no, she was imagining some form of transubstantiation whereby the food took on Ned's personality. But it was far from bad: he was a better cook than she was. She had suggested drinking the rosé, but he had no corkscrew; he had opened the beers with his keychain. He didn't drink wine. None of the Wilcoxes, to his knowledge, ever had. She turned to look at their photographs. He thought she was looking at the books beneath.

'Those books are closer to my heart than anything in this world,' he said. 'You could say they are imprinted in me, that's how many times I've read some of them.'

'Were you able to access books when you were on Diego Garcia?'

'Oh, not a chance. They told us there would be a library, but it turned out to be a bunch of syrupy romance novels that men's grandmas had sent them. Thinking, I guess, that it might help ease their loneliness. They had been read, but not by me. I had taken a few books with me, all of which you see there. And my best friend there, my mentor, Lieutenant Farnsworth, Geoff—a Harvard man, like you—loved books as well. So we pooled our supply and read and reread. Ever since I've been back in normal life, reading new books has been a struggle. It's hard for them to match up to these. Except Harry Potter, of course.' She was thinking of what to say to this, but his mind had already moved on.

'I guess I should have asked you this before, and maybe I don't need to ask you now, but anyway, I never asked if you were seeing anybody, if you were single.' She didn't say: that's never a question anybody ever needs to ask anyone. If the answer is worth knowing, it'll soon be made implicit. Was it Kannan that he had in mind? No—someone like Ned could never conceive of someone like Rebecca being with someone like Kannan.

'No, I'm not seeing anyone. I mean yes, I'm single.' She thought about leaving it at that and, for no discernible reason, said, 'I was in a relationship, a fairly serious one, for two years, but we split up last November.' Ned listened to the story of Connor, which she told with the concision it deserved, and then he did something that she had always found infuriating, and asked her a series of questions whose answers her narrative had contained.

'You dated this guy for two years?'

'Yes, a little over two, actually.'

'And you chose your job so that you could be in Boston, where he would move after a year.'

'Yeah.'

'And he broke up with you. Via email.'

'Yup.'

He was out of his chair and selecting a book from the case—he could have probably found the right one blindfolded—and before she could see what the book was, he said, 'Now Geoff Farnsworth always said, never use literature to seduce a woman. That's not what it's for. That would be cheapening your relationship to literature and to the woman. So that's not what I'm trying to do. But listening to the story of your ex, I was overpowered by the need to read you this. When I first read it … actually, let me read it to you, and then I'll explain.' He showed her the cover: *The Sportswriter* by Richard Ford.

'I've heard of it, but I haven't read it.'

'Good. I'm glad. Okay, so here's the context. The narrator is in his late thirties, still in love with his ex-wife. He's sort of a failed novelist who writes for a sports magazine. He comes to the office to finish an article and meets a beautiful intern, down from Dartmouth. He's sure she has a boyfriend ("Dartmouth Dan", he calls him). And then:

> But the sight of her in my doorway, healthy as a kayaker, Boston brogue, "experienced" already in ways you can only dream about, is a sight for mean eyes. Maybe Dartmouth Dan is off chewing dad's 12-metre, or still up in Hanover cramming for his business boards. Maybe he doesn't even find this big suavely beautiful girl "interesting" anymore (a decision he'll regret), or finds her wrong for his career (which demands someone shorter or a little less bossy), or needing better family ties or French. These mistakes still happen. If they didn't, how could any of us face a new day?

'The first time I read that, it didn't do anything for me. I guess I couldn't relate to it. But I'd read the book enough times that I knew it, it was imprinted. And then, when I met you at the Harry Potter event, and I had no way of knowing what your situation was, I remember thinking, these mistakes still happen. These mistakes still happen. And now you tell me that not only do they happen, they happened here.'

As he had introduced the passage she had thought, this is the first time his instincts have led him astray. The whole preface about his friend's advice was the sort of half-assed hypocrisy she had thought him free of. And she agreed with his friend. Even when seduction wasn't the direct aim, using other people's words to make your point was an admission of your own inadequacy. And the passage itself reeked of the worst male sentimentalism. The narrator was in his late thirties, Ned had said; the girl was still in college. And the sight of her turned the narrator into a blithering teenager, romanticizing his fantasies. She didn't want to be associated with a passage like that. But she hadn't been turned off, exactly, as he read it. She had to tell him, now—that way, it wouldn't seem as if she were rejecting him.

'There's something I should say. I've been thinking about leaving Boston, actually I've been planning for a while to quit my job, and I'm going to be leaving, most probably at the end of the month.'

He didn't even look disappointed. And she saw that the whole exercise of reading that passage hadn't been aimed at moving her. He was satiated by his own pleasure.

'I was waiting for you to say that,' he said. 'When you were talking about your job, and then about why you're here in the first place, I knew you were about to leave. You can't have everything just fall into place, I guess. But leaving Boston doesn't mean you're walking out of my life.'

She would give him a chance, later, when he was calmer, when he had come down from this high. She wanted to be able to review the evening as a whole, to not be swayed too greatly by how it had ended.

'I've had a really good time,' she said, 'But I should go. And I hope we'll see each other again soon.'

Back home, with Annabel away on work, she thought of calling her mother, or even Lydia, who was sure to have a view on Marines. Let that wait until she knew what she thought herself. Kannan had replied to her email at last. He was very keen to see her. He needed her help with something. Saturday, she replied. Any time. And then she felt the impulse to get into bed with *Harry Potter and the Prisoner of Azkaban*, to read first just the Quidditch scenes, a narrative of ambition, despair and eventual triumph that spoke to some previously dormant sports fan within her. Ned was onto something with all his talk about the joys of rereading. She didn't fight it.

16

That first night he lay with his back to her, and while he daren't look, he hoped she did the same. He thought she lay as far away from him as she could without risking falling off the bed, but he couldn't be sure, because he couldn't risk an investigative movement towards her. For as long as he could remember, he had slept only on his back. But a vision came to him now, and he willed it to be a memory, of his training himself to sleep that way, to secure his share of the bed that was not quite big enough for two against Santhanam's incursions. This meant that the new position was his natural one. He was like a man, whose natural tendency had been beaten out of him as a child, learning to write left-handed as an adult. He needed to give himself time. He thought she had fallen asleep before him, which was as expected after two long flights. This meant she would be awake when he woke, and he couldn't do as he had hoped, and leave the house with her still asleep.

But he didn't set an alarm, in case he did wake up first, and in the morning he was glad of it. He left her a note saying that on Sundays he bought groceries and did other errands, and that he would be back soon. None of this was untrue. To take her along would have been ruinously counterproductive. Twelve hours after his telling her their marriage was untenable she would be a housewife pushing a shopping cart. When he came back she was still in bed, but awake, and reading *Goblet of Fire*. His copy.

'These American editions are so awful,' she said. 'Such childish drawings! And they've ruined the spellings and half the words.'

'Not half the words. That's an exaggeration. And it's just a different way of spelling, it doesn't affect the book in any way. I have the British editions also if you prefer.' Was the whole thing a ploy to sucker him into warm conversation? He checked himself, and indicated the shopping bags. 'I wanted to say that while you're here you don't have to cook. I'll do that.'

She managed to eat two meals that he'd prepared, bathe and change without further attempts at conversation. Most promising was the fact that she hadn't unpacked her suitcases. At the very least, she was giving everything he had said real consideration. As Rebecca might say, she was processing it. Process: it seemed too corporate a word for Rebecca. Brendan and Eric liked to make fun of sports executives who talked about 'the process'. When he wasn't in the kitchen, he only looked away from the computer when he was sure of not meeting Malathi's eyes.

In early drafts, his email to Grimmett had explanatory material about his attempts to process—useful word—his failure to speak at the Deathmarch, but the version he sent said only that he regretted that he couldn't meet tomorrow. He spent the rest of the day reading the forums. Whatever Grimmett might fear, he had no intention of leaving fandom, in disgrace or otherwise. Nor had he all that much to process. He had choked, and he knew as it was happening that it wasn't a one-off, and that it was for the best. If he had forced himself back into the room and up on stage he would have walked out either before or midway through his first speech. He saw now that his mistake had been to allow some ill-formed ambition of the status of a visible and esteemed Big Name Fan to call into question the self-satisfaction that had always characterized his involvement in fandom. It was only a blip, and if Grimmett had encouraged it, that was only because Grimmett would encourage anything that Kannan aspired to.

His choke had been useful, however, in pointing the way to his own future. They were approaching what he thought of as peak debate, especially ship debate: not soon, but eventually, there would be no new arguments to make in the absence of the new canon evidence they were all waiting for in Book Five. Already, positions were so fixed that the Deathmarch had become attritional trench warfare. He was going to write fanfic, and when Malathi had gone, he and Grimmett could plot it all together.

On Monday morning, before leaving for work, he gave Malathi his spare key. No matter how long or short her stay, she shouldn't spend it in a kind of house arrest.

'I'll be back late in the evening,' he said. 'I've left some money on the dining table.'

'I don't need it. I have money of my own.'

By Wednesday evening, as he walked home from work, he reflected on how quickly and easily the week was passing. Brendan and Eric had put the redesign off for now to negotiate with a potential buyer. It was the first time he could remember them both being out of town simultaneously. There had been no official indication of their whereabouts, but the most popular rumour had it that they were in Canada, of all places. Kannan thought this unlikely. He knew what they thought of Canada, at least when it came to sports. Brendan said the only reason the NBA and Major League Baseball had expanded to Canada was so that they could keep calling their winners 'world champions'. And any writer who wanted to stay on Eric's good side had better remember to refer to the Montreal Ex-pros and the Toronto Craptors. Kannan spent his time at work reading a new fic, *Time's Winged Chariot*, a love triangle set amidst a Triwizard Tournament in 1753. The title wasn't to his taste, but he was convinced that the author, Leonora, was a star in the making.

He never asked Malathi how she spent her days, although he wondered if she had ever left the apartment. The days must slowly be wearing down her faith, showing her the futility of pushing things much longer. He was coming to see that she had been right about one thing. He ought to have told her much sooner about his fears, early enough to prevent her coming at all. But, as with having married her in the first place, the knowledge of these mistakes only hardened his resolve to get things right now.

That night, for the first time since their first together, he found it difficult to fall asleep. His ability to sleep on his side appeared to be fading after a promising start, or perhaps it was just that he was over-conscious of his position. He didn't see what was so horrifying about potentially facing her anyway. Why had he thought having his back to her essential? He turned his body slower than he thought possible, but in one continuous movement, as if trying not to wake a baby, until he was on his back. She was on her back too. He closed his eyes again.

Later he would long for a Pensieve, something to allow him to construct a narrative of events that would settle definitively who had started it, whose movements were intentional and whose involuntary.

His version went like this: he had felt her foot touch his, in a way that felt intended, and she had turned over to face him, no two points on their bodies more than four inches apart. And they had kissed like animals with faulty instincts, the awkwardness of their wedding night replaced by a confused desperation that left them just as likely to bump noses. And she must have felt him harden under his pyjamas, for she seemed to slither away down the bed and then she was pulling down the pyjamas to a little above the knee. Later he would ask himself, why didn't I stop her then? She took his penis in her mouth, an act made more cumbersome by her evident unwillingness to touch it with her hands and, he sensed, by the fact that her eyes were closed. She disgusted him, her clumsy servility, her lack of dignity, no, her contempt for her own dignity when he had given her every chance to preserve it. But he was also curious, to see exactly what she was going to do, and what she thought she was doing, and what, if he could distinguish it sensually from everything else, it would feel like, physically. The interplay of disgust and curiosity, he decided later, had compelled him to let her go on. And it was when he was certain that there was nothing pleasant about the physical sensation that he forced himself away.

'No! Stop. What are you doing?'

'I don't know. You started kissing me!'

'No, you started it. And I shouldn't have responded.'

'How can you say that? How can you be so cruel?'

He got out of bed and turned on the bedside lamp so she could see him.

'Tell me, whatever this was, did you enjoy it? Are we a loving husband and wife? You know the answer, you don't have to say anything. I'm going to sleep on the sofa.' He turned off the lamp and said, 'I thought many times about excuses I could use, things I could say to convince you that we couldn't be married. I thought of telling you that I was impotent. But then I thought I had better just tell you the truth. Now I wonder if I should have just said that.'

He knew he wouldn't get any sleep on the sofa. He was about to turn on the computer and get back to *Time's Winged Chariot* when the phone started ringing. He should have left it off the hook. But that was something Santhanam had said he was never to do. It was their duty, as sons, to always be accessible in case something should happen in Bangalore. If, for some reason, their parents couldn't reach Santhanam, Kannan had to be prepared, which meant no phone off the hook. He answered it. It was Malathi's sister. When he opened the bedroom door Malathi was sitting up in bed.

'I heard the phone,' she said.

'It's for you. It's your sister.'

'At this time of night?'

There was no point keeping the short version of bad news from someone who was about to receive the long version.

'Your father died. She's waiting for you on the line.'

'Kannan, is everything okay? You look absolutely shattered.' Rebecca was late. He had asked that they meet not in a café but somewhere outside, with passers-by rather than neighbours. She had suggested the Commonwealth Avenue Mall, by the statue of William Lloyd Garrison. 'Sorry, that was a really silly way of putting it. Clearly things are far from okay. Why don't you tell me everything?'

Everything meant beginning with the email that had contained Malathi's biodata. He omitted only certain details of Malathi's time in Boston, such as his failure to go the airport, and the events that had preceded her sister's call. He was here for Rebecca's help, but sympathy was a necessary precondition to that.

'How, if you don't mind my asking, did her father die?'

'That's what makes it worse. He killed himself. That's an even bigger shock in India than it would be here. An intentional overdose on painkillers that his wife had been given during her battle with cancer. Apparently his business was in deep trouble. He couldn't pay off his debts.'

'And your wi—his daughters knew nothing?'

'He had kept it all from them. My brother says his aim was clearly to get his daughters married off before the situation reached breaking point.'

'Because then no one would marry them.'

'Exactly. And my brother is, I hate to say, probably right. In fact, he's always right.'

'I can't say how sorry I am for you, and for her. I know that's a stupid expression but I can't even begin to comprehend your situation. I'm going to have to go back and think about it before I can be of more help. But there are a couple of things I wanted to say. One, I don't know much about India or arranged marriage, but of course you shouldn't be forced to stay in a marriage for the rest of your life. Even what has happened doesn't change that. But, right now, surely the priority has to be her, and getting her through all this.'

'I've already bought her ticket to go back. But the question is, what next? The day this happened, I thought I was slowly convincing her that we couldn't be together. But now she says she has nowhere to go. That she'll have to come back here.'

'Well the other thing I wanted to say was, shouldn't you, now, talk to Curtis? I've been trying to figure out why you came to me. And maybe it's because you kept this from him for so long, that you think he'll be hurt if you tell him now. But I know he won't be. And of all the people you know, of all the people we know, he's best placed in every way to help.'

'I don't know that I can tell him, but I'll think about it.'

She had to go, but he wasn't yet ready to face Malathi again. He walked up and down the Mall, quickening his pace with every lap in a doomed battle with the statues that looked down at him, a demonic series of reminders of the impossibility of escape. And then it began to rain, in that lukecold summer patter that Grimmett said was the only way in which New England lived up to its name. He had no jacket and no umbrella, and rather than take shelter under an awning or in a Newbury Street store, he resigned himself to going home. He could do it in ten minutes if he ran. The rain intensified with every block.

The apartment was empty. After a week of staying in when he had given her a key, why would she choose to go out now, in the rain? She hadn't left a note, but she had made the bed with conspicuous care. He saw that the computer was on, his Chudley Cannons screensaver, the seven players flitting aimlessly. She hadn't signed out of her email—no, it was his inbox. But none of the new emails appeared to have been read. She hadn't sent anything either. He must have forgotten to sign out earlier. Someone was ringing the buzzer downstairs. She couldn't have gone far, must have turned back in the rain and left her key behind. He could walk down and welcome her in.

He opened the door to a delivery man with a parcel. Bangladeshi. The parcel for Harry Elkins, first floor, whom Kannan had never seen, whose existence was only corroborated by the parcels he received every few weeks. Kannan was forever letting these men in, but he refused to sign. The less scrupulous left the parcels in the hallway where someone, Kannan didn't know who, eventually picked them up.

The rain hadn't eased. He wasn't going to go looking for Malathi. She could have gone anywhere. He hadn't bought her a cell phone; if she was going back to India soon, what was the point? She must be waiting out the storm somewhere close by; she'd come back as soon it stopped.

Grimmett didn't know which had arrived first: Rebecca's call, or Malathi's email. For all he knew, the revelation of Kannan's wife and her situation made its way to him through Boston's phone lines by two separate channels simultaneously. When Rebecca called, he had been drafting an email of his own, to Professor Stuart Hall, a man he had never written to before and who, he was sure, would not remember him. But Grimmett had come to an inflection point in his moral and intellectual trajectory: or, rather, he suspected that he might be at such a point, and it was in this spirit of self-location that he had sought out the one living human most qualified to judge Harry Potter, both as a cultural phenomenon in itself and as a representation of Britain in the world. He couldn't be truly straightforward, he couldn't say, Professor Hall, I place my life in your hands, so he endeavoured to find other ways of engaging the professor's mind, of drawing out his insight.

No interruption of yours could ever be unwelcome, he said to Rebecca as she apologized for calling. She delivered her news with the calm briskness of an intelligence bulletin. He went back to his desk to find Malathi's email. Later, as he reread the email and tried to reconstruct the call, he wondered what he would have made of either in the other's absence. If Rebecca hadn't called, he might have dismissed Malathi as a crank, even a confidence trickster; her email a vile defamation of Kannan. But, if she hadn't emailed, he wouldn't have dismissed Rebecca's story, per se, but nor would he have been moved to any action. At the least, he would have waited until Kannan came to him.

Malathi had begun not by describing her predicament, but with the assertion that she had noticed that he emailed her husband many times a day, that they appeared to meet every day, and that she wanted to know the nature of their relationship. Then she told her story. He replied saying only that there was nothing of that kind between him and Kannan, and that she should come and see him as soon as she could. Five minutes later the reply came in: she would come tonight. No time was given. Tonight could mean anything. He had asked Rebecca to come as well. For twenty-five years Grimmett had never felt the want of preparation time. Time was something he had far too much of. It passed so slowly that sometimes he thought he had lived eighty years. Rebecca, he hoped, was more agile, more equipped for a day like this one.

The buzzer rang first at 7.30. He prayed it was Rebecca. But he had been left unprepared on his own. What was he supposed to say to this girl; he should think of her as a woman but she looked no older than fifteen, with her hair braided down to her waist, and her bright schoolgirl's face? Was the paternal the appropriate role or was it the height of condescension? And how was one to be paternal anyway? He began by offering her tea.

'Your email was a great shock to me,' he said. 'I don't want to suggest that I didn't believe you. But I know, or I thought I knew, your husband, if I can call him that, intimately. I regard him as my dearest friend, and he gave me every reason to think he considered me likewise.'

She laughed, except that it wasn't a laugh but something that is called a laugh but isn't, a non-verbal expression of the hollow derision that is the quest to turn mourning into humour.

'You say you knew your dearest friend. I thought I knew a husband. Neither of us knew any real human being.'

Until Rebecca arrived, he could fall back on what he knew and liked best to do. He asked her to begin at the beginning, not of her association with Kannan but *her* beginning. He wanted to know the story of her life. He said, in preface, one or two things about himself.

The buzzer. He hadn't told Malathi that they were expecting company. She didn't seem as if she would be thrown by Rebecca's arrival. He wasn't sure if there was anything she could be thrown by.

'Rebecca, I'm going to let you introduce yourself, and then I'm going to leave you two here while I retire to my room for a little while. I've learnt a great deal and I need to think about it all.'

Now Grimmett did something that, in four decades of living on his own, he had never allowed himself, despite frequent and intense longing. He got into bed with his shoes on. In his mind, this symbolized the languor of unmolested thought. For contemplation this pure to justify itself it needed a subject of sufficient gravity, and until today he didn't think he had found one; not one, at any rate, that might benefit from *his* contemplation.

He began by focusing intently on Kannan, and constructing a chronological memory-film of their association, mapping his own developing understanding of his friend. This was the first, and perhaps most fundamental question: whether he knew Kannan, whether Malathi's dismissal of Kannan's humanity, which was premised on his unknowability, could be sustained in the evidence of their friendship. But the closer his focus, the more details he assimilated, the less resolvable the question became. Everything that seemed true of Kannan, or of what he knew of Kannan, could simultaneously be untrue, and vice versa. And the grand deception—perhaps deception implied that more was owed to him than was reasonable; call it withholding— weighed down one side of the question like an hippopotamus set against ten thousand beetles. On the one hand he ought to set it aside, because it threatened to render negligible every other consideration. But on the other hand, perhaps that was exactly the point: what more proof was required that he didn't know Kannan at all?

Well, he knew some things. He had a rich supply of what you could call facts, always assuming, of course, that Kannan's withholding wasn't a symptom of some more pervasive mendacity. His own inability to lie didn't extend to a gift for knowing when he was being lied to; quite the opposite. But there was no reason to think that Kannan was a liar, and no need to invent one now. But—and here he felt the order and rigour of his thoughts being unsettled by a new notion, not an epiphany—this wasn't some suppressed truth escaping at a convenient moment, not a realization at all, but a differently coloured light that didn't alter his perception of any of the individual facts of Kannan's life, but radically altered what they summed to. He had always thought of Kannan as an immigrant, disempowered and excluded by a coastal America, supposedly 'liberal', whatever that meant, that coveted his kind as high-tech sweatshop labour, pliant and eager and numerate, but saw no need to invite him into culture or society. This had been Kannan as he had found him, and although it was not the basis for their friendship—he didn't see friendship as a form of charity, or guilt-repayment—he was aware of it always. To any neutral observer it must be the obvious descriptive fact about the friendship, and he had cherished too, he was not ashamed to admit it, the opportunity to, if not quite *integrate* Kannan—that made him sound like a parole officer—then at least to lessen his exclusion, both through the friendship itself as well as through fandom.

Now the facts of Kannan's life arranged themselves very differently. What did he know about Kannan? Kannan had been born and raised in Bangalore, his father an officer in a state-owned bank, his mother a housewife. The material circumstances of this life, as Kannan had described them, were, by Western standards, straitened. There was no hunger, or fundamental insecurity, but there was no disposable income either, no privacy or physical space, and a constant sense of deprivation, of the necessity of austerity. But what if he thought of all this in relative terms? 'Middle-class,' Kannan said, but Grimmett had read enough to know that, in India, this was a life of some privilege, his father's income sufficient to put him in the top five or three per cent of earners. Kannan and his brother, in financial terms, had made a frictionless move from the professional elite of a Third World country to a similar position in the US. Having an MS in engineering from Northeastern was a marker of success even in this country, let alone India. The self-image of deprivation oughtn't to be confused with the real thing.

Kannan was Hindu, and India now had a majoritarian Hindu nationalist government. And he was Brahmin. In his first researches on south Indian society, unable to resist the lure of analogy, Grimmett had thought of Tamil Brahmins as India's Jews: a community that had prospered around the world through native intellect, a gift for numbers, industry and a culture that prized intellectual achievement above all else. Now the comparison appalled him. How could he have equated a group marginalized through the millennia with a group that had installed itself on top of the most rigorously codified and enforced human food chain in all the world? Knowledge as a means of survival as opposed to the hoarding of knowledge as a means to power—he had been fatuously wrong to confuse the two. He didn't want to hold Kannan up as an exemplar, or as representative, but everything he had heard about his upbringing refuted the notion that Brahmins valued intellectual pursuit for its own sake. And Kannan was a man.

Grimmett thought himself feminist, in the way that he hoped he was always for justice and against injustice, but this feminism had stayed unformed, and it rarely troubled him. The professors and activists from whom he tried to acquire political knowledge warned against this, often, but he had been unable to avoid pitting forms of disempowerment against each other. There were so many axes of disempowerment, or discrimination: race, class, ethnicity, immigrant status, age, history of colonial exploitation, indigenous descent. It's not a contest, he had been told: different forms of disempowerment feed off each other like tag-teaming pathogens. You can't focus on one at the expense of the other. Don't fall into the trap of arbitrarily separating one axis out. Don't get suckered into thinking about whether a white woman is more disadvantaged than a black man. That kind of thinking is a means for those who hold power to divide those who don't. Grimmett wanted to follow this. But still he found himself needing to know exactly how disempowered someone was. Still, he spent mornings thinking about the white woman–black man question. Still, he believed that some axes were more potent, more disempowering than others, and that race was the trump card. What if he had been wrong? What if gender was the trump? Malathi was a Brahmin, well-educated, she spoke better English than any Indian he had met since leaving England, which was a powerful tool of professional advancement in India, perhaps equal to computer programming. And Kannan had married her and, for some reason never made plain to her or anyone else, by the time he was presented with the fact of marriage, he decided to discard her. More than anything it was a show of power.

He was almost ready to go back to the living room. Only this held him back. Kannan was his dearest friend, he had said to Malathi, and he didn't think he had been speaking or thinking in the past tense. And here he was assessing Kannan in sociopolitical terms, and wondering how well he knew him, and not what he might owe him as a friend. Did the situation require him to take sides? Helping Malathi would, in effect, mean helping Kannan, if he enabled a permanent separation. So there was no question of taking sides in the mutually exclusive sense. Having never addressed it in these terms before, he saw that the question of what he might owe Kannan was absurd. It lay totally outside the bonds of any theory of ethical conduct. Do we owe it to our friends to stand by them when they are guilty of the worst callousness? Loyalty of this kind is not a virtue, if the idea of a virtue is to retain any weight. There were other reasons to owe Kannan loyalty, selfish reasons to do with the sustaining power of their friendship, but he couldn't confuse that with moral obligation. And how was he to judge Kannan? How are we to judge any of our friends: by the manner in which they treat us, or by everything we know and see about them, by all the information we have? To do anything but the latter was to fail to even attempt moral seriousness. The only place where morality entered into friendship was when a shared sense of it attracted two people to each other: when they saw the prospect of discovering an ethical life together. Did all this mean that he must cut Kannan off? That wasn't quite moral either, not when you could reckon with your friend, shame or convince him into something better. This sounded too Christian for his tastes, but in any case he didn't see how it applied to Kannan, who disgusted him by not even living in relation to ethical imperatives, who had shut himself away to avoid moral questioning. In a life of disappointments, Kannan might be the greatest. He would have to try and put it down to his own declining judgement. In the long run, self-abasement was always the most palatable narrative.

He found the two women in a comfortable silence. He hoped it was only a break, inevitable in a long conversation between strangers.

'I'm sorry I took so long,' he said. 'I needed the time.'

'Oh no, that's okay,' said Rebecca. 'We've had a really great conversation.'

'I'm glad to hear it.' And now, making sure to address only Malathi, 'And what have you decided?'

'I don't know. I'll go back for a few weeks at least, until everything is settled. I might have to help my sister and her husband sort everything out. I think she isn't telling me everything about Appa's business affairs. And after that … I know I can't live with Kannan. Even if he decides he wants me, I can't take the risk. But I don't know what else to do. I don't want to inflict myself on my sister as some charity case. We are very close, but it would be unfair to her husband and her in-laws.'

This was what he had wanted to hear. 'I don't mean to exaggerate my own connections or influence, but I believe I can help you. I've seen enough this evening to know that you're a woman of great poise, intelligent and articulate, and really, there is no need for Kannan's actions, in practical terms, to be any more than a minor setback in your life. Go home for as long as you need to, but then come back, come back and study in the US. I know professors from every decent university in New England through my radio show. You're the kind of

PhD candidate any English department would only dream of. And you would be fully funded.'

For the first time since she'd showed up, he thought she looked weary.

'I don't know,' she said. 'I don't know if I could live here on my own. I think I would always associate it with all this. And with Kannan nearby ... I guess I'll just have to get a job in Madras. Stella Maris was keen to have me come back and teach.'

'Curtis, we don't need to save or protect Malathi,' said Rebecca. 'She seems more than capable of looking after herself. So much more than I am right now, let alone in a situation like this.'

But he wasn't going to give it up. How could he? In Madras the twin disasters inflicted upon her by husband and father would trail her through life.

'One of the great things about this country,' he said—he almost said, one of the things that makes this country great—'is that your past doesn't hang like an albatross round your neck. After your marriage is annulled, no one will know about it, no one will ask about it, and you can then shape your personal and professional life as you see fit. Your identity won't be as someone's wife or daughter, but as yourself.' He wondered if Rebecca knew the effort it took to produce such platitudes. They had been wasted on Malathi: they had only put her to sleep.

17

The airport closures didn't last as long as people feared. With the exception of Reagan National in DC, they had reopened for civilian traffic within a week of 11 September, although for most people it was many months before the act of buying an aeroplane ticket, let alone boarding a flight, let alone sitting on one, had its essential banality restored. Landing, that sad anticlimax of arrival—compare it with the first sight of land from a ship—became, for a time, almost sacred, as if touchdown signified that mortality had been put off a little while longer.

Flying had long since lost all glamour or moment. When Kannan first boarded a plane, in August 1996, any sense of the unfamiliar was counterbalanced by the certainty that this was part of the normal course of life. He knew exactly what to do without having to imitate his neighbours. Now, on 15 October 2001, he walked to his middle seat on this perfectly healthy 747 and, looking around him, thought, am I the only person here who is confident we're going to make it to Frankfurt? And then: after I get to Bangalore, who knows when I'll next have to take a flight?

He had been thinking about timing. Not so much about whether things with Malathi might have worked if they had started at some other point in his life. The thought had appeared, but he'd dismissed it easily enough. He didn't think that things like that were either meant or not meant, but that, in this case, there was no reason to think the timing was to blame. If anything, timing had had the opposite effect, leading him to say yes to her, because that day in Cubbon Park he had begun—and he realized this only now (or was this the only retrospective narrative he could construct that was satisfactorily explanatory?)—to wonder if aloneness had crossed over into loneliness, leading to a temporary suspension of the usual protections.

Nor, either, had he been thinking about tailgate.com, and the circumstances that had led to his being on this flight. Brendan and Eric had sold a controlling interest to an ambitious Canadian online media company that had seen in the site the beautiful truth that sports fans prefer their own opinions to the so-called experts' and thus a future of readers who generated their own content for free, and had made a counter-cyclical bargain. The new owners already ran dating sites, men's health support groups and a fan forum that ranged from Harry Potter to manga, and while Brendan and Eric had stayed on as editors, the back end could easily be managed from Waterloo. Kannan had always known his situation was untenable. It was a wonder he had pulled it off as long as he did.

Timing. Malathi had sent an email describing her experience at the consulate in detail. It was the first, indeed only time he had sensed an implicit reproach for his own failure to prepare her. He had never responded to that email, but he had read it and reread it. She had ended by reiterating her good fortune in the visa officer she'd been assigned to. What if it had been a woman, or an Indian? But no, the crucial factor wasn't the kind American man. It was the timing. What if she had applied for her visa in mid-September? Forget the matter of whether flights would be available. With all the facts pointing to their barely knowing each other, to this being an arranged marriage of shallow foundation, he was sure her application would have been rejected. She wouldn't have been able to join him at all. He could have put his foot down, forced a quick annulment. His parents and Santhanam would have been all for it. At any rate, they wouldn't have cut him off ('You are dead to me,' Santhanam had said. 'The one favour I ask of you is to not mention to anyone that you are my brother.') Of course, in this scenario, her father might have had to postpone his suicide, if he'd been able to hold off his creditors.

How unworthy a thought was this, anyway? It would have prevented much unhappiness on both sides, but especially hers. And surely the attacks of September 11 themselves had provoked many more unworthy thoughts, outside the mainstream of personal or patriotic grief. He wasn't thinking of those who cheered the whole thing on as revenge against a satanic empire. If he had still known Grimmett, he would have heard that his friend had, for the first time since the 1950s, felt a spasm of patriotism rising up within him, fighting against his Anglophilia like a new concubine who wants to displace the chief wife. Grimmett had been forced into the love of his country not by the attacks themselves— after all, as tragic as they were, other countries had worse tragedies—but by opening his *London Review of Books*, ready to view 9/11 from the most penetrating British and European eyes, to find that, according to the classicist Mary Beard, America 'had it coming'. Twenty-five years of lonely adoration for Britain and here he found that the Americans had been right all along.

But Kannan was thinking of survivors, not of the few that had survived the attacks, but of the families of those who hadn't. The assumption of universal grief was a delusion. Surely there were some people for whom the information that their spouses or parents had died, once the initial shock had subsided, was not all that debilitating. Was there anyone whose death in a plane crash would move him all the way to anything that was recognizably grief? He knew the answer just as you do.

But there must have been others still, not many, but surely a few, whose initial reaction was not even shock, in the way that it is normally understood. What of a man who had been about to make the uncomfortable confession of an affair to his wife? Who had been planning to leave her? What would have struck him first: guilt, or relief? Kannan thought it must be the latter. Not everyone who died on those planes was some sort of saint. If it had been him, how would Malathi have reacted to the news? All right, implicating Malathi was taking it too far. But no, if he was right, if Malathi reacted to news like that not with uncomplicated grief but with shock accompanied by a certain satisfaction, he wasn't sure he could think less of her for it.

Malathi had never said where she went the evening he met Rebecca, but he had known when, the day after she flew back to India, he received two emails, suspiciously coordinated. Grimmett said that Kannan's actions left him no choice but to irrevocably sever their friendship. Rebecca's was different. She stressed first that she was writing to let him know that she was leaving Boston. Only then did she say that, while she couldn't speak for anyone else, she thought he ought to go easy on himself. There had been no humane or truly virtuous way out of the situation he had been placed in. When he was back home, and settled, she'd love to hear from him again.

He was going home to a city in which his parents still lived in the flat he had grown up in and had now been told, in writing, that he was unwelcome in. This would pass. It would be months, not years, before his father called to ask him for help with something or the other. A son in Dallas was only so much use, no matter the rate of growth of his remittances. Vinay said that Kannan's savings would fetch a two-bedroom flat in Bangalore—in a newer suburb, not near the centre of town—with enough left over to keep him going at least a year. He had made no other plans, all plans seeming to him now as fragile and as unreliable as guides to decision-making, as his notions of falling in love. A return to India, on these terms and at this time, afforded only one interpretation: humiliating failure. At least Santhanam is doing well, his mother's relatives would say. But even he isn't married yet. I wonder why.

Kannan did have one plan; he had almost forgotten. He was going to write a fanfic, a trilogy like Athena Alice's. It would settle definitively the question he was asked so often in fandom: what is it like in India? Magically speaking, that is. He would spend this flight coming up with a plot and a new avatar, and on the other side, under that name, he would join GCR and HP4BK and write to Grimmett, who would be thrilled to help craft the first Indian wizarding epic. Hadn't JKR conceived of Harry Potter on a train?

Kannan had been randomly assigned the middle seat; it had been careless of him not to check. Now they announced that everyone had boarded, which meant the window to his left was empty. He moved over and thought, why not, it seems appropriate to have a window seat when you're leaving a place, a final lingering goodbye. But what would he look out for? And then he realized that as Logan was on an island, and they were flying east, he was unlikely to see anything at all except the skyline. As the flight took off he looked for the John Hancock Tower and the Prudential Center, which were all he could be sure of recognizing, looked back at Boston through the fast-arriving storm clouds, only to find them gone.